Don't Love

DONT LOVE ME,

JUDGE ME

"I write, therefor I am...

(a neurotic, OCD, self loathing, insecure, foolish, disgusting, schizophrenic, hyper-emotional, hopelessly romantic, addict idiot who kind of kicks ass)" nathan

FOREWORD

I've been apprehensive to call this an autobiography on account of several reasons. For openers, autobiographies are typically reserved for those who've at least invented, discovered, achieved and/or accomplished some thing or things that warrant the interest. Since I can't quite remember the last paradigm shifting manifesto I've written, humanity advancing technology I've invented or record breaking hit I've released, I really don't qualify. Additionally, the very term "autobiography" conjures up some sort of vanity, narcissism and/or self-adoration, all of which I lack thoroughly. I have however lived a bit of a surreal life. For one reason or another my identical twin brother Matthew and I have constantly found ourselves in situations and/or life circumstances that would be widely deemed extra ordinary. Since day we've handled each and every one of them with a humility and gratitude that has seemed to carry us right along to the next.

Throughout my life personally, I averted a kidnapping attempt at 9 years old, lost my mother in a car accident at 12, was pistol-whipped & car-jacked at 21, earned a scholarship to play NCAA Division 1 soccer at Butler University, moved to Florence, Italy for 9 months where I'd turn down an offer to play professionally in the Seria "C", taught myself guitar and signed 3 major label record deals as vocalist for Madina Lake. I've also won $50K on NBC's Twin Fear Factor, rose to relative International fame with Madina and I nearly lost my soul mate when he was beaten while intervening in a domestic dispute.

I'm technically an addict with depression and anxiety issues. The embattled voices in my head love and hate life simultaneously, but I don't believe them when they tell me we're schizophrenic. I'm a writer who despises words. I believe laughter is happiness, "God" is energy and peace of mind is the ultimate goal in life. I've had my heart ripped wide open only to find a new love inside that literally re-defined the word to me. My life has been blessed and cursed and since I believe in neither I spend the majority of it confused.

I've read a lot of autobiographies lately and I can tell you right now- I can't guarantee where mine will fall on the spectrum of quality. I'll repeat, I'll repeat, I'll contradict, miis-sphell, mis-punctuate, etc. but having said all that.. I'll tell the truth as best I recall it, I'll make you laugh, I'll make you cry. I'll make you wonder and I might make you sick. Most importantly, though, and I can guarantee this, I'll make you feel better about yourself. And maybe, just maybe, if I'm lucky, I might make you piss yourself.

DONT LOVE ME, JUDGE ME

Introduction

Since We're All born With 99% of the Exact Same Genetic Make-up, it's our Experiences That Make Us Who We Are

Fall, 1986, Palatine, Illinois -
My soccer team the Rolling Meadows Rowdies were tied with our arch nemesis The Hanover Harriers, 1 goal apiece and the clock was winding down. At 6 years old, the whole sport was brand new to me and I can hardly remember those earlier years but this one memory just won't seem to leave. Now don't get me wrong, it most certainly hasn't worn out it's welcome. We wound up with a penalty kick in those waning moments that could potentially win the game and our friend, teammate and neighbor Rudy Ellsmith was picked to take it. It was brisk out and most of us kids were wearing sweat pants under our jersey shorts, but not Rudy.. As a matter of fact he wasn't wearing anything under his over-sized white shorts.. which is curious in and of itself, in retrospect. None of us could really be clear as to when it happened along his approach but let's not look a gift-horse in the mouth here.. that's hardly relevant. The true star of this moment. The "gift" if you will, was the fact that Rudy, in his ultimate glory.. went ahead and shit himself. Now I gotta hand it to Rudy, ten times over in fact. He didn't skip a beat (or a stride as it were) when it happened. He must have known, these

things don't tend to be strangers once released. So there it was, with each wonderful step he took toward the ball, the shit was falling from the bottom of his shorts as his heels subsequently kicked it up into a mud-like fountain behind him (picture a human jet ski and the pooh being the water squirting out the back of it).

As if that weren't enough to get everybody on the field in stitches, it hit me so hard I went ahead and pissed myself. Thus began a life full of hilarity, laughter and awkward moments that have kept me pissing myself til this very day...

Hi, I'm Nathan and this is my story of glory, tragedy, persistence, depression, success, failure, integrity, shortcomings, love, addiction, stardom, devastation-turned-triumph and sheer ridiculousness. I'm in a band called Madina Lake and when I started this project we were just about to release our 2nd major record "Attics to Eden". Since then and throughout my writing of this book, we've toured the world several times, released an EP called Dresden Codex, another LP called "World War III" and also experienced some of the most extraordinary events imaginable. Lucky for you (or unlucky as it were), you're about to read about them in relative real time. Oh and by the way, I'm really only 1/2 of a person. I have an identical twin brother who's been with me every step of the way. Now remember, don't love me, judge me..

CHAPTER 1
What the Hell Are We Doing Here
Friday, June 15th 2008 Castle Donnington

I'm standing on the "artists platform" which is essentially a railed plank on hydraulics, raised slightly above the 10-foot makeshift wall separating "backstage" from G-pop and right next to the ginormous main stage. My twin brother Matthew and I are watching 80,000 kids go ape shit to a hardcore metal band called 36 Crazyfists. He's got his whole fist jammed up his ass as he battles an onslaught of IBS while I'm breathing into a paper lunch bag trying not to barf.

We exchange the looks that we'd exchanged our entire lives in moments like these. Looks designed to reassure one another while simultaneously crying out for help. He's always been the master of over-coming nerves and unfortunately for him he's also always been tasked the responsibility of overcoming mine as well.

We then stare into the endless abyss of people, knowing in a matter of minutes we're going to have to step out onto that goliath stage and play to all of them. It's every ounce of energy we have to feign excitement to each other over the sheer horror we're both dealing with inside. At any moment I could have a panic attack and/or an episode of depersonalization so we use each other to remind us everything is and will be ok. At this point, our "Meteoric Rise to Fame" as a recent Kerrang! feature put it was just beginning to show signs of resistance. See, we were never a metal band. We never considered ourselves an Emo band but once the major marketing and PR machines start rolling, you cannot stop them, slow them and most certainly can't control them. Our rock band was branded for us in the press. To be fair, our perceived "flare for hair" and "passion for fashion" weren't doing us any favors.

We'd been on the cover of the UKs juggernaut metal mag Kerrang!, much to the chagrin of a dying breed of metal head dinosaurs who cried foul. Kerrang! is the IT mag for England's counter culture and at this point they defined the musical trends. When entities like this last so long and grow so big they become pillars of pop culture instead of the counter culture and thus risk imploding on themselves.

The whole Emo scene began trending a few years' earlier and hair/make-up boy bands with battered heart, whoa-is-me sing alongs were everywhere. We were very aware and tried desperately to dodge the bullet but our lite-metal musical brand and natural look put us directly in the crosshairs. Regardless, we were still growing at an alarming rate and leaned on the notion that having haters only meant you were successful. Funny enough, "hating" was trending at the same time.

In the weeks leading up to Download we'd scoured the internet for YouTube videos from previous years festivals. We'd been warned by everybody from industry folk, random kids and other bands that had played this festival's main stage in the past that it could be brutal. It's a tough crowd. No, it's a fucking ruthless crowd and if they don't like you.. you don't get booed. You get glass bottles of piss heaved at you along with and among anything and everything in the vicinity..

A few years earlier My Chemical Romance got a blizzard of shit raining on them through their entire set (which was phenomenal, mind you). Last year the dude from Panic at the Disco got knocked out with a set of car keys. And this year, we were the new "it" band with gay haircuts, guy-liner and skinny jeans.. kryptonite to a metal head's peace of mind.

I couldn't believe how many people were there. I'd never seen anything like it in real life.. it was a never-ending ocean of heads, flags, banners and other euro-festival tradition as far as the eye could see. I don't think I can do this. Stevo comes swaggering over from the ramp off the main-stage. His walk is curious at best. Not quite DUI worthy but definitely would require a backward reading of the alphabet or more likely a straight breathalyzer.

His eyes had just a tint of yellow in them.. a surefire tells that alcohol was poisoning his blood in some way shape or form. Was he wasted at this moment? Hard to tell. Was he in at least solid enough shape to set up our stage and handle his technical responsibilities? Not even close.

He gets to the stairs leading up to the artist platform and yells up "okieee dudes, yoouuzz ready to dooz this!?" oh shit. nope. "You betchya Stevo!" we lie and off we go.

I vaguely remember walking up the ramp, which leads to the back of the main-stage. Once you get up there you, only a giant tarp banner and of course a million amps, drums and guitars from every other goliath band playing that day, separate you from the 80,000 kids in front of the stage. There were cameras and flashes going off from some media crew filming footage that was to be broadcast on the jumbo screens flanking the stage. There were sound dudes and guitar techs scampering everywhere like little worker bees tweaking and moving their respective bands gear around. Then there was my band. Matthew stayed by my side, constantly reassuring me that I'll not only live through this but I'm going to whip ass. This of course while he himself nervously runs in place, playing bass scales relentlessly to warm up. Jeezy seems relatively calm, stretching and tapping patterns with his drumsticks on a random road-case while his in-ear monitor headphones dangled around his shoulders. Mateo is loud. He tends to yell and scream a lot when he's nervous in an effort to convince those around him that he's not. To his credit, it beats barfing.

Stevo is running around absolutely frantic. Our fault really.. we'd blown up so fast that he was tasked to TM, guitar tech and bass tech because we were none the wiser and didn't know anybody else to hire over there any way. I knew something was wrong. I could hear the bass cutting in and out as he line checked it and when he suddenly put it down in the guitar boat and picked up Mateo's guitar I should have done something. But alas, I was too nervous to think about anything like that much less have to courage to ask somebody what was going on. He strummed the guitar for several minutes and we heard nothing. Suddenly the stage manager screams "2 minutes! You're starting in 2 minutes, ready or not!" This was probably the straw that broke Stevo's back because he simply put the guitar down, walked around the giant tarp curtain and said.. "I think we're good to go.. I mean, we're good to go".

The front of house music stops abruptly and the 80,000 kids roar from the crowd. Sheer terror grips each of our faces as Jeezy says "fuck it, let's kill it" and runs out and hops behind his drum kit. "Fucking kill it bucky" Matthew says as he squeezes my shoulder and runs out. "Oh well, here we fucking go!" Mateo says and disappears.. Fuck, my turn. I can feel the dark shadow of anxiety hover over me like an F9 Twister.

In my mind I'm completely frozen aside from that taunting little cunt of a voice that reminds me on repeat how far from reality I've gone and as usual threatens that *this time* I'll never come back.

Doctors call it depersonalization and most who suffer from it describe it as an out of body experience. Best I can describe it is as the most horrific, colossal, mortifying and unimaginable panic attack ever... on steroids.

I feel my legs start running underneath me and my autopilot kicks in. As I turn the corner and run out on stage, passed the drum riser toward a majestic sea of 80,000 screaming faces, flags, banners and smoke bombs as far as the eye can see, a quick thought darts through my head.. "This is insane, I should write a fucking book..." "Perhaps we could talk about it later?" the other voice in my head replies. I grab my microphone just as Jeezy taps out a 4 count signaling the start of "Adalia" .. "What's up Download, we're MADINA LAKE!" ....

I can count approximately 4 paradigm shifts in my life. Moments and/or events that have stopped the megalithic pendulum of destiny in its tracks and abruptly shifted its course. This was the 3rd one. As standard fair, this paradigm shift too begins and ends with a question I've asked myself regularly throughout my life.. How the hell did I end up here? well ... like this...

CHAPTER 2

Elementary My Dear Watson (345)

Winter, 1985, Palatine, IL

What a curious time these 3-6 months are. We finished the brutal Warped Tour, flew straight to England again to play Reading/Leeds, did a pile of dates back in the US to run down the clock and finally take some time off to write The Dresden Codex EP. My personal life just took the 3rd biggest twist of all time and I'm bathing in the glorious aftermath. More on that later, but for now I can't seem to stop thinking about boners. A curious lot they are..

Ahhh what a beautiful time in our lives when we finally sprout that first boner. So strange, so new. Scary, confusing yet exhilarating, and delightful. I remember watching TV with the entire family. Fortunately I was on the floor, lying on my stomach when suddenly a bit of a tripod began to develop. My ass magically lifted a few inches (I mean, more like 10 inches.. whats up).
I quickly adjusted it as a million thoughts/questions flowed through my relatively new and innocent mind. After several minutes of contemplating I snuck out of the room and into the bathroom.

When I dropped my drawers I couldn't believe my eyes. This lazy little thing that I'd used to piss with for my entire life was suddenly standing tall and staring romantically, into my eyes. I knew it wanted to be loved but had no clue how to be there for it. We'd been friends for like 10 years and I really wanted to help it out. Add to that a very unsettling feeling; I was starting to develop feelings for this lil fucker. Long story short; I tugged, rubbed, pet, punched and kicked this thing until it happened. My knees were week, face flushed, and my body felt like what I imagine heroin would feel like. Tragically, it was short lived; only about 4-6 seconds to be precise. The skin of my wenis was raw and scratched but alas, this new thirst was insatiable.... so I did it again. and again. Now, obviously from then to this very day there is simply no way to know how many times I've had a go at myself but there were a few notables that are worth mentioning. If you happen to be my dad or sisters, you might wanna skip to the next chapter (unless you party more than I thought.. in which case, more power to ya).

Anyhow, the first time I got concerned about my behavior was when the helmet of my wiener was so raw and scorched that I couldn't even walk. What did brilliant ole me do? I went to the one doctor I knew could help. I actually asked my dad to come into the bathroom and pulled out my rotten tomato of a wenis. Did you hear that? I showed my dad my self-mutilated penis. Of course I made up some story about how I was pissing on a thorn bush and then a beaver attacked it or something equally unrealistic. He gave me some magic creams and then concluded with his guiding words of wisdom... "hey buddy, when you're washing or whatever down there, go a little easy on it, k?". This was just one of the million amazing things my dad had witnessed, helped, experienced or otherwise got tangled up in parenting Matthew and myself. Much appreciated pal.

So the typical shower, bathroom, bedroom sessions had grown a bit.. shall we say boring? To quote the brilliant Axl Rose "I used to do a little but a little wouldn't do it so I used to do more and more" . Perhaps this was one of the early signs that I had a pension for creativity but more likely, I'm just a lost, sick, lonely/twisted banana boat that should be put away for the betterment of society.

I grabbed a sandwich baggie and some Vaseline. Headed into my bedroom and locked the door. I proceeded to fill the baggie with the Vaseline creating well, a poor mans vagina? Then I lifted the mattress and placed it in between the mattress and the box spring with the open side facing out. My bed and I shared a moment that even the most sexually satisfied couples would envy. Terrific, now I'm in love with my wenis AND using it to cheat on itself with my mistress the mattress.   It only got worse from there.

We had a gigantic stuffed soccer ball that we would kick around from time to time. It was huge, like up to my waist at the time. We kicked it so much that it tore a small hole.   I banged it. Ya know that toy that was a rubber-ish water bag that you couldn't hold cuz it kept slipping through your hands? Banged it. Brand new jar of peanut butter? Pregnant. I used to (still do) piss in the shower.. well the shower, the bathtub, the pool, the hot tub blah blah.. I mean shit, I even pissed on myself for a while... ya know, in those 'world is your oyster' days? don't knock it til you try it? leave no stone unturned? I'll try anything once?   You guys are disgusting.

 Well I don't know about y'all but I feel like I just got a huge load on your chest. I mean, off my chest.. I mean.. Jesus…   focus Nathan.

Ok now that we're all relaxed and opening up, let's start from the beginning with a quick background.. I'm a monozygotic twin and the youngest of 5 kids in my family with 3 older sisters whom you'll meet along the way. We grew up in a modest ranch house in Unincorporated Palatine, Illinois until about age 10 when we rather suddenly moved to an upscale neighborhood in suburban Chicago called Inverness, IL and I also love run-on sentences but, fortunately for you I'm also an expert punctuationist; as you'll see.

My father is a dermatologist who graduated High School at age 16, medical school at 22 and had his own practice at 30. His parents were straight off the boat from Piatracamela, Italy and had settled in Chicago because of its huge Italian community . Like most of his generation, they did so in pursuit of the American dream... for their kids.

His parents owned a dry-cleaning business on the first floor of their tiny Chicago apartment and pretty much sacrificed their entire lives to give my dad and his brother Malio a shot at everything the world could offer. That meant, however, raising him super strictly, giving little to no room for exploration.

They were militant about his studying and told him exactly what he would become. The celebrated events in their household were test days. When dad had an important test in school, his mother would bring home a live lamb, slaughter it in the shower and cook it up for breakfast because back then they figured that was a real brain jump starter.

Eventually he opened up his own medical practice and now has 2 hugely successful offices in the northwest suburbs of Illinois and is one of the top dermatologists in the country.

My mom was a rural farm girl from Pettibone, North Dakota. She was drop-dead gorgeous, incredibly artistic and an amazing mother who encouraged creativity and had a lust for life which was passed on to us.

Her father had all kinds of mental health issues and was a regular at the local shock therapy treatment facilities. My favorite story of his is how he used to go to the only pool hall in Pettibone and play hours and hours worth of pool by himself. When the pool hall demanded payment for the table, my grandpa would say "I won, get it from the other guy" and leave. *Regrettably, I have that same little invisible bastard in my head who constantly kicks my ass at everything.*

Mom, however was beautiful and brilliant and when she had had enough of the small town life she moved to Chicago to go to nursing school where she met my dad. They got married 3 years later and after a stint in the military and some medical residencies in California and Texas, my parents and their 3 daughters Allison, Jill and Paula finally settled in Palatine, IL. After 3 failed attempts to have a dude, they were done with kids. Much to the chagrin of my Italian grandmother who was so distraught over the lack of any males that I wouldn't doubt it if she poked holes in their condoms cuz 4 years later, mom got preggers again.

She was quite devastated from what I hear and I don't blame her. Kids are an arduous endeavor to say the least and the thought of carrying, birthing and raising another one gave her hives. I imagine those hives became warts when they found out that Matthew had split and they were having twins. It was a taxing pregnancy to say the least but by the time mom met us, all was right with the world. As far as I know anyway..

She was always frugal and insisted that regardless of dad's income, we would live very modestly so once Matthew and I were born, we all holed up in a small ranch house for the first 10 years of my life. Until age 10 we really had no idea that my dad had any money. Additionally we went to Willow Bend Elementary School in Rolling Meadows, which was home to mostly inner-city families that the government re-located through a new subsidized housing program. Accordingly, all of our friends growing up were a schmorgasborg of different colors, shapes and sizes. We wouldn't even know what racism is for years to come. We also never went to church which I'm eternally grateful for. To each his own but personally I've always felt that religion does more harm than good.

I've studied a wide array of religions from Christianity, Islam, and Hinduism to Wicca, Paganism and Scientology. Rest assured, I'm an expert in nothing but to me, most religions seem judgmental, hypocritical, oppressive and discriminatory. I should also take this opportunity to reiterate that I don't judge in any way shape or form lol. *and If you believe that I've got some land for sale in Wisconsin that grows cash for grass, diamond trees with little elves inside that give free HJs and has rivers of oil the size of the Nile. Not sure if you're into that sort of thing..*

But In all honesty I don't consciously judge anyone or anything unless and until I've been given reason to do so. Even then, I fully recognize subjectivism and appreciate differences. For better or worse, that is all a result of growing up as we did.

I was a hideous kid. Among my earliest memories is one of the reasons I was such. Around the age of 5 years old my mom took us grocery shopping with her. Naturally Matthew and I fought over who got to sit up in the high part of the cart because 1- fighting's just what we did and 2- it kicked ass up there. Well, contrary to standard outcome, this time I won. After perusing the aisles for a while I got a bit restless and decided I should probably get down and hunt for the delicious, cold, creamy, refreshing obsession of mine that is rainbow sherbet. Obviously that wasn't going to be a good idea cuz I couldn't climb yet and I was way the hell up on that seat.

Naive to consequence I dangled my legs over the cart and leapt.

I ended up face first on the floor. Somehow in my fall I tore a muscle behind one of my eyes? Hard to believe, I know, but it's true. From that moment on it was required that I wear not only a patch over one eye but glasses over the top of the patch. Of course I did have an almost exact version me that didn't have anything like that on his face so I became the hideous twin at that very moment.

This kept me shy and quiet for years to come, hiding in the shadow of my perfect twin brother. In retrospect, many memories from my childhood have erased themselves. I feel more like I was a spectator at a sporting event, watching life rather than being an actual participant. I'm sure nowadays some doctors could rip apart the reasons for all that but for what? who cares. I'm busy... ish.

I hardly said a word for the first 8 years of my life. I'd later find out my family was concerned at the time. I suppose I was too. It's pretty obvious that twins have no idea what it's like to not be a twin and vice versa. However, you don't have to be a twin to pick up on simple shit like people's reaction to you or how they treat you.

Often times people would meet Matthew, then get to me and gasp as if a 300 pound gibbon just queefed on their face. But alas, life is complicated and it always will be. Poor me. I want attention.

Aside from family core values, which are critical in my opinion, there are certain moments and/or events that shape who we are. As a kid I'd always been extremely competitive. Having a twin brother is like having a real life version of yourself to compete against and it can be a fabulous motivator. For better or worse. We both had an innate knack for sports and when we met soccer, everything was right with the world.

Spring, 1984
When Matthew and I were 9 years old, our life was like a real world version of the Brady Bunch. Even better on account of the fact that all 5 of us had the same 2 parents. I remember this year because it was the first time we began to suspect that Papa Boner (dad) was holding out on us, financially.

He came home from work one day in typical fashion.. put his brief case down and sat at the dinner table while we all gathered around to hear his incredibly entertaining tales of the day's patients. Don't get me wrong, he never broke legal protocol but would regale us with vague stories about a man with warts on his balls who actually sprouted wood during his examination or something like that.
Well on this particular evening he walked in with a giant roll of papers, which turned out, to be construction plans for a new house. Like I said we lived in a small ranch house and all shared bedrooms, which we didn't mind at all but this was suddenly exciting.
He went on to tell us that he'd found a lot in the newer, well-to-do section of Palatine called Inverness and wanted to build our family a

brand new house.   We were giddy when he went to describe a sprawling 3-floor, 5 bedroom mansion complete with indoor pool, hot-tub, dance floor, mini-soccer field and a virtual fantasy land downstairs. We couldn't fucking believe our ears.

Construction started shortly thereafter and for the months we'd go visit the construction site to witness the development of our new fantasyland, reality begun to set in. Dad was fucking rich. And our picturesque life was about to get exponentially better.. if that was even possible. To celebrate our forthcoming move we did what any spoiled family would and went on a Caribbean cruise.

Winter, 1985 The MS Starward
What Is It?

It was a gigantic ship. I'd never seen anything like it and we were about to eat sleep and live on it for 7 days while it traipsed us around the crystal blue Caribbean.   At this age, family vacations are won or lost almost solely on the demographic around you. We toured the massive ship for a minute and ended up on the Lido deck, which boasts a pool, hot tub, mini-waterslide and all the other brilliant clichés that adorn the cruising industry. You know, the Love Boat iconized shuffleboard games, bingo sessions and charming waiters centipeding around the dinner tables with flaming flan on their heads promoting a train to "Hot, Hot, Hot"? It was heaven.

Matthew and I met a couple of kids our age right off the bat and ran around the ship with them for just about the entire 7 days. One of the kids we kicked it with was from California and went by the name Don Jones. He was nucking futs. This was probably one of our first tastes of trouble and it remains one of the funniest memories to this day.

There was a revolving door that lead from the staircase out to the pool. He and a few of the other kids we would eventually befriend were running around the revolving door at an alarming rate. He jumped out when he saw us and introduced himself. It looked like fun until his sister came over. The other dudes were still running that door in circles, by now it was approaching F4 twister speeds and for no reason whatsoever Don grabbed his own sister and threw her into it. She broke her arm into a million pieces. This wasn't the funny part you evil bastards. *Although, unfortunately for me... I pissed myself a little. The full-stream piss party really came a few nights later just before dinner.*

The ship had one of these majestic staircases that spiraled up, leaving a clear and open view of the bottom floor from the top. The bottom floor was the entrance to one of the fancy dining rooms and the top floor was the entrance to an outside pool deck. This particular night was the "captains ball" and every passenger was required to dress formally.

Since there were 2 different seatings (one at 6pm and one at 8pm) and ours was the later, we weren't dressed up yet. There was however, a line of tuxedo and gown wearing early seaters that started all the way at the bottom of the steps and circled up a few flights. All in there were about 8 levels on the ship and we were on the top one watching the fancy people wait for dinner.

As our new friends and us peered over the railings, Matthew decided to take his gum out of his mouth and drop it down the middle of the spiraling staircase. Relatively harmless but nonetheless, got a decent reaction from our new friends and we all eagerly searched for other shit (no pun intended) to drop. Popcorn, Ice and a few other random items later and the laughter started to swell when we noticed Don had mysteriously disappeared.

3 minutes later he came back with human shit in his hands. He had run to the bathroom and shit into his own hands. This guy was getting cooler by the second. As all 4 of our heads peered over the railing, Don dropped the shit.

I immediately grabbed ahold of my wiener knowing it was only a matter of moments before piss would attempt to force it's way through. Don's shit wavered ever so gracefully passing each floor below us while maintaining its consistency and relative form. In fact, it remained intact for the duration of its flight, or at least until it hit the arm of a poor unsuspecting bastard on the bottom floor.

I'll never forget the sight. He had one arm on the staircase railing and the other around the waist of his fanciful wife when the shit impacted. It splattered immediately, sending shaticles over to several more innocent bystanders.

We dove for cover as soon as it hit and as you could imagine, a minor riot ensued below. When I say "almost" I mean to account for that millisecond gap of silence that often accompanies these types of things as a flash freeze frame for everyone around to comprehend what had just happened. In that millisecond, I hadn't pissed myself just yet. That is until I heard a woman's voice scream all the way from the bottom floor " HONEY!! WHAT IS IT!?". I didn't even fight the piss at that point and was forced to run down to our room and change.

For the remainder of that vacation, we continued to meet more and more kids and continued to terrorize that boat with nefarious shenanigans. Our eventual group included a handful of girls, which were suddenly intriguing. When it was over, we exchanged numbers and addresses and developed our first crushes.

No Rice Fo Me, Sank You!

Until that cruise, Matthew and I were 2 of the most straight-laced, morally sound well-behaved kids on the block.   Having pissed myself after seeing a dude drop a shit bomb onto fancy people coupled with new social exploits, I was left with a sparkle in my eye and the cruise became a coming of age experience. I think it's fair to say that innocence hath took its first wrong turn and was on route to becoming lost forever.

That summer we had to move out of our house because we sold it before the new one was finished. This was not anticipated so mom and dad had to scramble to find all 7 of us an apartment to live in for the summer.

Mom must have been in charge of this one because we ended up in a tiny 2 bedroom in a rather shady area of Rolling Meadows. With the 7 of us cooped up, it got a little crowded. Fortunately the complex had a pool. Mind you, I was still pretty shy and dependent at this point so my family was slightly surprised when one day I told them all to go to the pool without me and I'd meet them there in 5 minutes. Truth was I had to shit but it wasn't like me to voluntarily be alone. They took it as a good sign of independence and enthusiastically took off with towels and sandwiches in tow. I took my shit and was out the door maybe 4 minutes behind them. Memories are a bit spotty at this age but I'll never forget this series of events.

I stepped out of our apartment door, which was on the 2nd floor, walked around the corner and through the doors that lead to the stairs. With an extra little pep in my step courtesy of my forthcoming swim, I jumped down those red and blue swirled carpet stairs at a decent clip when I noticed an Asian fella holding the door for me at the bottom. He was a dad clearly (in my 9 year old mind), probably 40+ years old, shirt and tie and clean cut looking. His shirt was un-tucked but that didn't phase me and I skipped toward the door.

Then he asked me the strangest question; "have you eaten lunch yet?". As I suspect it would most, this caught me off guard. I thought long and hard about his question and soon PB&J sandwiches danced through my head, confirming to myself that I indeed knew the answer to this particular brain-buster. Replying "yes sir", he suddenly grabbed my arm and sternly declared "well, you going to eat again!" and proceeded to drag me through the door. What on Earth was happening?! Am I being.. kid-napped!? I remained rather limp and cooperative for all of about 20 seconds before deciding to catch him off guard with a sudden jerk, twist, run combo.

I was hauling ass toward the pool and for the first few seconds of my escape, he gave chase screaming some shit about rice and lunch.

Though I was too shy to yell myself, he gave up rather quickly and changed course.

As I ran though, a million thoughts raced through my head and regrettably only one reigned supreme. I might be considered cool because I almost just got kid-napped. I think I did anyway? Maybe he thought I was his Chinese son? Do I even look Chinese? Maybe he was blind? Nah Fuck it, I was just the victim of an aggressive kid-napping attempt and forced to bravely fight it off to exact my escape! Well that's my story and I'm sticking to it.. like white on rice?

Before I knew it, this guy was a Chinese National spying for the Russians and after me for some sort of clandestine value or information I had. Fortunately I didn't tell the cops that, just my friends. But yes, cops. It was a whole ordeal and for the next week police officers and detectives combed that apartment complex looking for my would be kidnapper-double-agent-shit-in-retrospect-maybe-he-was-going-to-sell-me-into-some-sort-of-sex-slave-operation-but-probably-neither-and-just-a-guy-who-accidentally-grabbed-the-wrong-kids-arm Chinese man. I mean Oriental. I mean Asian. I mean, sorry.

Our Humble Abode
3 months later we moved from 1620 S. California Ave. to 1492 Turkey Ct. Granted the address took a serious hit in the cool department,

31

our new house was ridiculous. It was on a 2-acre hill and in the back yard there was a peninsula with a giant tree that's branches and leaves canopied over a lake.

We'd always been slightly embarrassed by how amazing the house was. In the basement, aside from a big-screen TV, huge u-shaped couch, wet-bar, slot machines, pinball machines, fuss ball, Ping-Pong, air-hockey, a dance-floor with chasing lights, and an indoor pool/hot tub, there was also a custom-built mini indoor soccer field. I know..

About half the size of an official indoor arena, it had AstroTurf, built-in goals with nets, a scoreboard and Plexiglas on the viewing side (official? what does that even mean?.. reminds me of the word gourmet). There was also Plexiglas behind one of the goals that looked into the indoor pool/hot-tub room. You could access the pool from a door around the corner of that area and all of it looked out onto the backyard/lake. For the backyard we had an official sized soccer goal. In the garage we had 2 go-carts, a red one and a blue one. Yes kids .. Matthew and I were spoiled fucking rotten. Now, in our defense.. we were the furthest you could possibly be from actual spoiled brats. Our parents raised us to the extent that the year we moved into that house, we'd thought we won the lottery or died and went to heaven.. We never took any of it for granted and never presumed, expected, or felt entitled to any of it. We never thought we were better or cooler than anyone else because we weren't. We just 2 of the luckiest kids in the world and we lived a fairy tale life from age 10-12.

It didn't take long to make a pile of neighborhood friends. We did begin to see signs of the Frankenstein affect money could have, as some of them were pompous little cunts who's coddling parents actually bought into the idea that being rich meant you were better than everybody else. But the rest were badass and our neighborhood posse had the time of our lives.

After that first summer Matthew and I were headed to a brand new school for 6th grade. It was weird as fuck that every single kid in our classes was white but again, hardly phased us because we were too young to really notice stuff like that. 6th grade turned out to be pretty fun and after a relatively non-eventful school year, we buckled down for the summer that would change our lives forever.

CHAPTER 3
Coulda Done Without That (summer 1987)

I remember the day my mom died as clearly as it happened. It was summer and we were about to make the giant leap from elementary school to junior high. It was that summer you spend checking your balls daily, desperate to see a relatively thicker black pubis sprout out of at least one of them. We'd spent the summer flirting with the girls across the lake, riding around the neighborhood on our go-carts, getting chased by cops etc. and of course practicing soccer every single chance we got. So it was pretty much standard operating procedure when we asked mom to drop us off at the local HS soccer fields to kick around while she went to meet her best friend Arlene for lunch. On the way we'd picked up one of our best friends Bryan Chevy who's mom was actually supposed to drive but canceled last second. Regrettably, we'd find out 20 years later that Bryan harbored an agonizing and entirely misappropriated guilt about that to this very day.

Since the fields were only a mile and a half from our house we'd told mom not to worry about picking us up and that we'd walk home with Bryan to swim when we were done. I remember mom being extra affectionate in the few weeks leading up to that day so when she got out of the

car to ask for a hug when she dropped us of I
didn't think much of it.

She held on tight and teased me about how
getting embarrassed to hug your parents in
public at our age. I of course was not
embarrassed in the slightest and hugged her back
as hard as I could. She then reminded me to
work on my left foot and pulled away. Little did
I know that would be the last time I'd ever see
her.

We kicked around for about 2 hours and started
the 1.5 mile walk home with Bryan. We
laughed and teased each other and as most
conversations that summer, we ended up
inquiring about one another's pubic hairs. See,
Bryan had recently discovered some and
Matthew and I were pissed, riveted, confused
and green with envy.

When we got back to our house we went directly
downstairs and jumped in the pool. After a few
minutes of swimming we ended up in the hot tub
and of course continued our conversation about
boobs, pubes and chicks. We demanded to see
proof of his claim that 3 prickly black pubes had
recently sprouted from his stage left ball. After
several minutes of laughing about it, he finally
stood up and peeled his bathing suit down just
far enough to pull a ball out, squeeze it tight and
display the hairs. Sure as shit. Like 3 glorious
flowers in bloom lay Bryan Chevy's first 3
pubes.

At that exact moment I saw a figure approaching the pool door over Bryan's shoulder and my dad cracked it open. We all jumped and Ryan yanked his pants up quicker than you can say "faggots". When dad opened the door and asked if he could see Matthew and I alone for a second we thought we were in trouble for looking at Bryan's pubes. Ha I wish.

On the contrary, his eyes were deep red and he grabbed us both by a shoulder each and said the words that would echo in my mind for decades to come.. "Your mothers been in an accident and there's a good chance she's not gonna make it."

He put his arms around us both and held on for dear life as I for one struggled to get out. Matthew looked shell-shocked and I started screaming my face off. Dad held on and with tears pouring down his face said "I need you guys.. you've gotta be strong for me, for your mother and each other ok??". Per his instruction, we ran upstairs to get dressed and that's where I saw our sister Allison leaning weakly on the Kitchen table.. I'd never seen her cry before and I think she was trying her best to hide it from us. In retrospect, I'm convinced that some sort of existential factor was at play here because in that maelstrom of thoughts and emotions I remember specifically noticing a transition in her. She'd always been an omniscient genius and now she was already

subconsciously preparing for the role she'd
officially inherit in a matter of hours.

As the oldest sister of 5 kids, Allison would
have to double as surrogate mother. She would
be become the impetus and inspiration for just
about everything Matthew and I would love and
pursue in life. From soccer to music to
traveling, Allison imparted things upon us that
would become our greatest passions.

Anyhow, we piled into the car and drove 40
agonizing minutes to the hospital. The ride was
brutal but Allison was strong. I could hear a
muffled sob coming from her but otherwise she
consoled Matthew and I with every ounce of
energy she had. Shortly after we got to the
hospital we found out that my mom didn't make
it.

Of course there is a mountain of things we'd
hear or experience in the weeks and months to
come. I remember a relative telling me not to
worry because I'll forget about her in due time. I
remember a neighbor telling me to take it easy
when I tried to hug him after he offered his
condolences. I remember hearing that our best
friend and neighbor Ryan Aulenta said that
Matthew and I would probably go pschyo and
become shut ins forever after.

Well losing your mother at 12 years old is very
simply tragic.

Our family loved each other so much that from
that point on, we developed an unwritten law to

never discuss it. The individual intention behind this of course was not to have to remind each other, relive or remember the pain. We all wanted to be strong for each other and to do so was to pretend you were ok. So we swept it under the carpet.

I love my family more than anything in the world and I admire them beyond belief but it would be 23 years before we could even begin to understand that shockwave that hit us in the summer of 1988. Jeezuz you guys are depressing the shit out of me.. moving right along!

Since I can't stay serious for more than a moment or 2, a curse that would ultimately lead me to shit my pants and break my nose running through a screen door later in life, let's move on.

CHAPTER 4
Go Get Em Jr. (1988)

Well, off we went to Junior High. Fresh off of a tragedy, we hopped almost immediately onto the wonderfully horrific, exhilarating and baffling roller coaster ride that is puberty. Emotional changes hit first of course and new curiosities lead to explorations and new discoveries about the self, the world and it's possibilities. I've often asked myself what exactly led us down the more juvenile path we chose but at the end of the day, and despite my best efforts, I can only blame ourselves. Either way, here's how it started.

Pooh Toof
Fall, 1989 Palatine, IL.
In 8th grade we met a dude named Chris Connely. He lived about a mile away from us in a neighborhood called Whiteclyfe where a ton of our other friends lived. I remember we went bowling one night with his parents and afterwards he asked us if we wanted to sleep over. I fucking love sleepovers. Always have, always will.. We accepted.
He had a 2 story house with a furnished basement and all the video games a kid could ever dream of. The basement was perfect. It had pillows everywhere, scary little midget doors, an endless amount of his dad's curious

vintage items to probe, play with, and investigate, hiding places and creepy noises etc. We horsed around all night and finally passed out around 2am. About an hour later, I awoke to an ominous figure decked out in full camouflage, standing above me, nudging my stomach with his toe. I sat up and cleared the cobwebs from eyes just in time to see Chris throw a similar camouflage pantsuit into my lap. He had what looked like combat boots on, black paint under his eyes and a backpack. Long story short, this was the first night we snuck out to roam the neighborhood in the middle of night and see what kind of trouble we could get into.

I had never known the beauty of the middle of the night. The suburbs of Chicago are relatively quiet and at 3am there is a certain majestic quality in that silence. The neighborhoods were like labyrinths, the trees like bunkers and the air was so brisk and welcoming, it was absolute freedom.

We ended up breaking into a house that was under construction and climbed out onto its rooftop. From there, we could see forever and it truly felt like the world was our oyster. The 3 of us must have sat up there for hours soaking up the thrill, adrenaline and explorative nature of our adventure.

When he eventually opened up the backpack, we each armed ourselves with rolls of toilet paper and eggs before climbing back down to the street and adorning random houses with our decorative wares.

As the weeks went on, so did Chris' sleepovers. Our crew started to grow as did our ambitions and we went from egging and blowing up mailboxes to stealing cars, breaking windows, and sometimes doing completely gratuitous things such as turning someone's garden hose on and jamming it down their storm drain well and through the basement window in hopes of flooding em out. How's that for spoiled rich kids? Yes, we were and are and always will be ..white trash.

Obviously we were acting out in some adolescent, lost parent rage but why we all found it so funny and exhilarating is beyond me. For what it's worth, the guilt did haunt me for decades and we'd ultimately take several measures to balance the karmic debt. For the time being though, we were on a rampage. I could go on for hours about the things we did but one just stands out as awesome in every way.

We had this thing called a "winger". It was a 3-man slingshot meant for water balloons. Basically, 2 dudes would hold the ends of the rubber-banded contraption while the other pulled back a projectile chambered in a small nylon pouch, as far as the rubber would stretch. As soon as the gunner let go, the rubber bands would send said projectile hurtling toward the intended target. We started with golf balls, sending them through windows and garage doors but just as everything else, we had to push the envelope.

One of us had this idea that we would fill up little sandwich baggies with random concoctions and wing them through windows. It started with ketchup and mustard but quickly graduated to shit, piss, and every spice in the mcCormick spice rack. These little baggies were horrific. It was a perfect summer evening accept for one thing, the fog. It was so thick that night, you couldn't even see your hand if you held up it in front of your face. Invincible as we were, we determined the fog would serve as friendly cover and loaded up the little shit bombs in Chris' backpack.

We slipped out his parent's kitchen door around 3am, and began creeping down the smoky street at a turtle's pace. We had to stay close to each other or we'd get separated or lost. Our only sense of direction came from following the street curbs and since we really had no pre-determined destination, we just walked for what seemed like miles. The few streetlights only displayed vague images of houses in the distance so when we happened upon one giant image, it quickly became our target.

Again, it's difficult to explain the magnitude of this fog. At times you simply couldn't see a thing. At other times you could only make out vague shapes. This particular one being a giant square house a ways up a vast and open front lawn. All we could really see was the beginning of a driveway so we followed it up the front lawn toward the house. I remember I kept thinking, let's just launch this effin thing and get out of here but yet again our ambition got the best of us and we kept trying to get closer and closer.

Ultimately, we were so close that the looming image of the house disappeared into a cloudy darkness and we finally agreed to stop and set up the launch. The rest of what happened remains a bit foggy, no pun intended.

I can't remember who was holding each end but I loaded the shit bag into the nylon pouch and pulled that fucker back a good 10 feet which was extraordinary for the winger. When the tension became unbearable, under the muted giggles and with a heavy breath, I let go. It must have been a mili-second later that my world turned up side down.

Basically the house was about 5 feet in front of us and we hit a big bay window. I heard glass break just before being smothered in a torrential downpour of shit and piss. It exploded almost immediately after we released it and since we were so close to the house, it just annihilated us. All of us, bathed in an atomic whirlwind of our own shit, piss and spices. Fight or flight dictated that we run like motherfuckers. Only problem was, it was too foggy to even know where to go so in a mere moments we ended up piled on top of each other in some poor bastards front lawn.

It took about an hour to get ourselves home and we smelled like nothing you could imagine. What I saw when we finally got back to Chris' basement is something I'll never forget. Granted I had pooh in my hair and stuff, but Chris was smiling hard, reflecting on the event and his 2 front teeth were missing. I squirt a little piss in my pants before he wiped at his teeth and realized they weren't missing at all. They were just covered in pooh. I unleashed a full bladder of piss into my underwear and his cammo pants. Don't judge me, love me.

That summer became one of the best we'd ever live. Regrettably, our reign of vandalism only grew in both frequency and damage. But on a lighter note, we did find rock-n-roll.

Allison may have introduced us to music but one of our soccer coaches introduced us to Metallica. Tony Kees was super cool and we bonded over many a thing. When he saw that Metallica's "And Justice For All" tour was coming to town, he got 3 tickets and insisted that papa boner let us go.

We had lawn seats at an amphitheater called Alpine Valley. I'll never forget the feeling of waiting in the grass with thousands of other people absolutely elated to see their heroes. It smelled like beer, stale refer and fresh cut grass all at once. My ears were already ringing from the support bands. Above that muffled buzz were the distant sounds of the set-change music out of the PA and pockets of rowdy fans blanketing the amphitheater. When the kick drum finally started blasting for line-check the crowd went ballistic. Or so I thought. Moments later, the lights went out it was fucking pandemonium. Matthew and I both knew at that moment we'd discovered something that would be in our lives forever.

The show Metallica put on was still to date one of the best I'd ever seen. Classic late 80's stage props, pyrotechnics etc. it was fucking wonderful and it planted a small seed that would take years to find, cultivate and harvest but it was definitely planted.

They were the be all end all at the time but after some Guns N Roses, Pantera, Beastie Boys, Rage Against the Machine and Primus obsessions, we found Smashing Pumpkins. I won't bore you with the brilliance of this band and/or the extent of its impact on our lives but I will say that SP was our gateway into the entire dimension of music, which has been the lifeblood of our existence to this day.

We started going to shows regularly in high school. The whole grunge scene was defining a generation and we were at the very forefront of it as fans. Like most kids, we'd go see as many shows as we possibly could. Oddly we wouldn't think to actually try to learn an instrument for another 6 years.

CHAPTER 5
Social Politics
A Jungle, A Llama, A Boner & Me (1990)

Throughout this book you're going to hear a lot about us playing "Dares". Pretty damn straight forward, but in our case, the devil lies in the details. Our dares were absurd, humiliating, hilarious and disgusting. The first one I lost was in the summer of 1990, going into High School.

The contests ranged from simple knockout coin tosses or drawing cards for low card to some more elaborate, involved challenges. This one was rather simple. We all sat in our pal Niedermeyer's car on the side of Roselle Road with his bright lights on. Traffic was sporadic so we'd take turns guessing if approaching cars would flick their lights at us, honk or do nothing. If you said honk and they honked, you had immunity. Otherwise it was simply taking turns guessing yes or no and the last man to get one right loses. Not exactly exhilarating but efficient enough. So I lost and was tasked the joyous occasion of running the approximate 2 miles from Harper College to my house. In the nudes.

They stripped me of everything right down to taking my shoes. I hopped out of the car to haul ass and sure as shit they pulled around behind me and started yelling, honking, flashing their lights etc. which would continue throughout the entire first mile.

Now Harper is a big, well-lit complex with plenty of traffic so this already blows.   Once I get to Roselle Rd. my routing options dwindled to one, leaving me pretty much having to shoot straight down the street.

This stretch of Roselle of course was much heavier trafficked. This meant that I'd be exposed for the first 5-10 minutes, speed pending.   Since I didn't have any shoes and the only light to go off of was my asshole friends' strobing headlights blinking on and off my naked ass, I decided to stick to the lane.

It was a full sprint for probably the first .5 miles. As the rocks and sticks and various street debris stabbed the shit out of my feet, I began to slow down. As the wind left my lungs I slowed down even more until eventually, I was a mere shell of a man.

Devoid of energy, will and every ounce of dignity, my wang just swung softly, back and forth like a feathery pendulum in the wind. My increasingly moist asshole also swayed lazily as my thighs dragged each ass cheek to and fro. It was a liberating rhythm I tell ya.

Thanks to the ruckus my pals were causing in the car behind me, a minor traffic jam developed. Neidermeyer's jeep was stalking me the entire way, looking, sounding and feeling like a pinball machine stuck on multi-ball. You know, stressful, balls flying everywhere, lights flashing and horns going off while 4 clowns are in hysterics. I had to get off the road.

Since our house was relatively deep into a leafy subdivision I either had to stick to the main streets from there or roll the dice on an untested shortcut through what we called The Bush. The Bush was a massive section of mushy overgrown weeds, trees, grass, wheat or whatever the hell that separated our subdivision from Roselle Rd. and Harper College. We'd never gone into it for the simple facts that it was terrifying, unchartered and we'd surely get lost, attacked, eaten, fisted, or swallowed up by a pit of quicksand. I decided to roll the dice. Summoning my final burst of energy, I darted across Roselle in traffic to a symphony of car horns, cheers and jeers, headed down the slight ditch on the side of the road and straight into the abyss.

I remember the thorns first. They stabbed every part of my soul as I was tangled up almost immediately. It felt like I was walking through a giant wet toothy spider web, draped across a car wash. I was mortified. I'd been laughing so hard just moments early when the clown car was stalking my buck-naked ass on a major road but now things were different. I was alone. I was destroying myself climbing through the Bush and the worst part? I was totally and completely lost. I wouldn't doubt if I shed a tear or 2 at that moment but hey, no sense in furthering the emasculation of an already metro-sexual victim of circumstance. What? Whatever.

So I fucking trampled my way through it. Literally 3 hours later, I saw the outlines of a house just above the tall crap. With the moon as my only source of light, I headed straight for it. As it grew into sight I began to breathe a little easier.

I approached a wooden fence surrounding the houses backyard and was surprised that I didn't recognize the house. Our subdivision is really only about 3 big blocks and we knew every house in it. I hopped the fence and lost my footing in the wet grass behind it. After the torrential jungle I'd just traversed, a little slip on some dewy fluffy grass was a pleasure. The odd part, though, was when I stood up and was staring straight into the eyes of a goddamned llama.

The upside of course was that I now knew where I was. A couple on our street were notorious for the investment debacle they made in breeding llamas. To me llamas are just the poor man's camel and since camels are my second favorite animal (behind the gay sharks they call dolphins), I had no love for this llama.

At that ripe age of, I don't know 14, 15? No idea. At that ripe age I had no idea if llamas were chill like cows, aggressive like rhinos or poisonous like snakes. To be honest, at whatever ripe age I am now I still don't know. Obviously with age I've ruled out the

poisonous like snakes option but the 14 year old
me went ahead and assumed this thing was
going to chomp onto my wenis and tear it
off. So I crept ever so delicately passed the
grazing alpaca holding my boner in my right
hand. My what? You heard me. A boner.
I told you, these things have the darndest
timing. I don't know if it's because I'd been
traversing a suburban jungle in the nude, if it
was cuz I was scared, nervous, horny, into
animals.. shit I have no idea but now I had a
fucking boner to deal with. On my tiptoes, the
llama kept turning to face me each time I tried to
get behind it. I had to get to the other side of the
yard and over another fence to get back to my
street and home. I decided to forget about the
llama and just haul ass across the yard.
It was the early 90's and though this technology
has likely existed for decades, "motion detecting
lights" were just becoming a popular burglar
deterrent for the well to do. Sure as shit, just as
I reached the other side of the fence, the entire
yard lit up like a jailhouse in a midnight prison
break. I probably squirt a little piss in all the
excitement. After all, it's what I do. I definitely,
however, turned around just in time to see my
neighbor open up his screen door.
Fortunately these neighbors were relatively
reclusive and we'd never met before or since but
rest assured, he and I shared something in that
moment that neither of us will ever forget. I
sometimes wonder if the event traumatized him

at all. I often wonder what his vantage point must have been like. A strange, sweaty, nude 14-year-old kid standing on his wooden fence jerking off all over his fucking llama. He must have been in some sort of shock because he didn't even manage to say a word. As you can imagine, I ran and never looked back. Don't love me.

Sorry Coach
My high school soccer experience was brutal. Aside from the social politics, the darker sides of puberty minus the comfy confines of a mother's bosom etc., I had made an early but critical mistake that has haunted my life to this very day. Our entire existence centered on soccer. We'd had such a deeply rooted passion for the sport that anything else in life lacked substance entirely. In our minds, we'd enjoy a fruitful high school soccer career, parlay that into college scholarships and then explore professional opportunities in Europe. Sounded reasonable, right?
Well we did our part as kids and spent every waking second playing, training and developing our skills. They say it takes 10,000 hours to truly master a craft and Matthew and I had doubled that by the time we got to high school. Fremd HS was an affluent school with 2,600 students and a very competitive athletic program. Playing Varsity soccer as a freshman here was pretty well unheard of so we weren't

too concerned when we spent our entire first year scoring 5 goals/game each and leading the freshmen A. team to an undefeated season (high fives bros).

We'd later learn that the varsity coach, Mr. Pagnani was grooming this team to take State our senior year and thought the best way to do so was to keep us together for our collective Freshman/Sophomore year and then bring the star players up to Varsity toward the end of Sophomore and Junior year for experience. So when we ended up undefeated again sophomore year, coach Paganani asked Matthew, me and 2 other twins Marcus and Gavin Pope to suit up for Varsity for the rest of their season. Here's where I pissed myself.

See I had Mr. Paganani as my gym teacher sophomore year and since I couldn't behave myself, my fate was determined the instant I got assigned to his class. I remember the precise moment it happened. We'd become friends with the pile of cool kids a year older than us and one of them was a dude named Jimmy Smythos. Jimmy was super short and over the previous year had lost about 100 pounds giving him enough confidence to climb to the top of the HS popularity charts in a matter of months. He was a hilarious kid and aside from being a social terrorist, he was a good friend to have and when Jimmy and I got together in gym class, look out. Our school was gigantic and aside from the main basketball court, it had an entire back gym about the size of 3 basketball courts and divided by a mega tarp down the middle. This is where our classes were split between volleyball and pickle ball lessons. On this fateful day.. picke ball. Jimmy and I would take turns lobbing the hard plastic pickelball racquets way up and over the tarp into each other's courts. The near misses and subsequent shock of would-be victims who screamed and pissed themselves when a racquet came crashing down from the sky 2 feet next to them was kind of stimulating but it tired quickly.

So we decided to take turns kicking the volleyballs up at the lights. He went, then I went and vice versa for several minutes to no avail. The more we missed, the more we couldn't stop until one of us hit. I'll never forget the kick that virtually fucked my life up for many years to come.

I got one of the harder balls and from the side of the court. I spotted a giant row of hanging lights with their protective metal grates dangling directly over the center of the gymnasium and determined it was all mine.

With my back to the main door, from the gym to the locker room hallway, I fixed my sight on the center light. Once firmly in my crosshairs, I lobbed the ball about 6 inches up in front of me and blasted the living piss out of it.

It took maybe .2 seconds for that volleyball to B-line like a laser guided missile, directly into the sweet spot of the giant bulbs and explode.

The impact caused a torrential downpour of glass onto the whole classroom of kids below. It must have raining glass for a good 5 seconds straight. It just kept coming, showering these poor unwitting volleyball students with shards of glass.

I felt instantly white-hot inside. That rush of adrenaline, torn between elation, regret, pride and fear poured over my body like an icy waterfall over a picturesque Hawaiian mountainside. Jimmy squealed with excitement and disappeared before the glass even stopped falling. When I turned around to take off, I crashed directly into Mr. fucking Pagnani. He'd come through the doors behind me and watched the entire catastrophe. There goes my HS soccer career.

I was given 3 detentions and a Saturday School as punishment, from the very man that would determine my future in HS soccer. Don't get me wrong, this was all my fault but I had no idea how calculated, extensive and long-term my punishment would actually be. Mr. Pagnagni was ruthless. An egomaniac that'd been a bit of a local legend in the HS soccer circuit was hell bent on exacting a tormenting revenge that would play out not only over the next 2 HS seasons, but also have a physical and psychological affect on the rest of my life.

Author's Note: I'm like soo dramatic some times.. omg.

Summer 1991 Raleigh, North Carolina

That summer, 1991. Matthew and I always had this weird philosophy of back dooring our way into things we wanted. Knowing that the NCAA recruiting game was cut throat and actually getting the attention of top coaches was nearly impossible, we decided to pick a couple of schools and sign up for their programs summer training camp. It wasn't common knowledge at our age but we knew that in most cases, the University's Athletic Departments required a school sanctioned summer training camp to increase said University's cash flow. Protocol further dictated that their head coach had to run it. Often times, the bigger programs coaches would just act as figureheads, popping in once in a while to over see these camps and that was all we needed.

We sat down one afternoon and scoured the NCAA rankings. We then picked 3 schools we wanted to play for, narrow down the list according to research on their camp regiments and sign up for 2 of them. At the time North Carolina State was ranked #2 in the nation and since most of our club soccer had been tethered to the Midwest, we decided that's where we were going. So that summer, between our freshman and sophomore year, we spent 3 weeks up in Raleigh/Durham, NC attending their soccer camp.

After 7 years of travel league, a year of HS under our belts and of course playing together throughout, we were firing on all pistons. By the end of camp, legendary coach George Tarantino asked Matthew and I into his office. "How come I've never heard of you guys before?". "Well sir", we explained.. "we're only 16 and aren't really looking for schools yet". He went on to explain how that was good because he'll be able to snatch us up early and not have to compete with other schools etc. We were floored. I mean, we wanted to get on his radar but fuck, he was practically making us an offer and we still had 2 years of high school to play.

As the meeting ended, coach assured us that be inviting us back for an official recruiting trip. NC State would pick up the tab, wine and dine us for a weekend and try to get us to commit to playing there. With this phenomenal news under our hats, we headed back to Chicago to savor the remainder of that summer.

Spring 1991

Back in Chicago and finally 16 years old, it was time to get our driver's licenses. We'd been sneaking cars out and driving for a year already but I still managed to fail my test so Matthew defaulted to designated driver for the rest of the summer.

My dad bought us a brand new, black Nissan Pathfinder. This car was badass and though we always wrestled with the guilt of such luxuries, it quickly became a third twin. However, we nearly lost it the very first night.

Fresh out of the DMV, we picked up our best friend Tabucky and 2 lovely young ladies, Jenn and Ginger. Before we could leave Jenn's house, her dad gave Matthew a stern, 30 minute lecture on the dangers of the road and added a veiled threat about if anything happens to his daughter he's gonna fist Matthew or something. Grateful for the wisdom, we took off and in about 20 minutes, Matthew turned the wrong way down a one-way street and got pulled over. 2 tickets later, we embarked on one of the more unforgettable nights of our lives.

Though he was a little shaken by the cops, we were in stitches over Matthew's gaffe. I mean it was his first god damned night driving and with 2 chicks in the car he turns down a one way and gets 2 tickets. Awesome. But alas, it was just the beginning.

With nowhere in particular to go we just reveled in the glow of freedom. Driving aimlessly from neighborhood to neighborhood, we were loving the adventure. In the back of our minds I suppose, we all knew the Pathfinder had 4 wheel drive and that it was only a matter that we'd find the perfect spot to put it to use.

Things took a turn for the weird when we were driving down the infamous Cuba Road. It's a long, windy road with little to no light and a thick blanket of trees on either side. Stories of bizarre car accidents, murders and the like convinced locals that Cuba Road was haunted. The glorious imaginations of our youth only enhanced the majesty of this moment. Every half mile or so, one of us would surely spot an ax murderer just lounging about the thick forest off either side of the road or maimed animals hanging from nooses off the dark trees in the distance. All of which was bullshit of course but in the moment we wanted to believe it all and were scared shitless. Until that is, something real actually happened.

Out of absolutely nowhere, a car squealed out from behind us and began chase. Since there were no side roads from which it could have turned from, we determined it must have been laying in wait. We could see that it was a Jeep Cherokee and it was driving so recklessly after us that there was no question we were in for something. It was absolutely terrifying. Matthew handled it quite well in retrospect. He stayed focused and navigated the tight turns even as this maniac seemed to try to run us off the road. The girls were crying and we were fucking shitting ourselves for the good 15 minutes this went on. Everybody was screaming at Matthew of course "turn here!" "slow down!" "haul ass!", do this do that to elude our pursuer. As many an expert we had in the car, it didn't matter what Matthew did. This dude was after us and we weren't gonna shake him.

Making matters worse, the strangers erratic driving came complete with sounds you usually only hear in movies. Squealing tires, stressed metals as his car darted aggressively side to side and of course his bright ass headlights lighting up our entire car.

Eventually we turned off Cuba Road and onto a busier street that would take us toward our neighborhood. Despite the additional cars on the busier road and much to our chagrin, our stalker wouldn't relent. After 5 endless minutes on that road, Matthew decided to make a sharp turn into a labyrinth of a subdivision a few miles from our house. We weren't very familiar with it and after several more hairpin turns, sure as shit, we hit a dead end.

Matthew slammed on the brakes, skidding into an eventual stop. Short-lived as it was, only moments later, the Jeep rammed us.

We were all pretty stunned from the slight whiplash but there was no time to assess the damage. We still had to get out of there. Though a giant "DO NOT ENTER" sign stood tall directly in front of us, Matthew jammed the gear into 4-wheel drive and went for it. Nice balls.

Next thing we know, we're driving through a goddamned forest with branches and leaves smacking the hood, windshield and roof of our brand new car. As fucked up as this whole situation was and having just gotten worse, the psychopath followed us.

Now everyone was scared to another level. The adrenaline alone could have probably fueled a rocket as Matthew continued the bumpy sojourn through a damn forest. We were all bouncing uncontrollably, hitting our heads on the ceiling of the car when suddenly the path turned into a daunting mountain of gravel. Again, he went for it. Flooring it, all 4 wheels began to climb the steep mysterious gravel hill. We made it about 20 yards and lost momentum. The car began to slide backward, sideways. Just as it did so, the Jeep flew by our right side, over the gravel and onto somebody's back lawn.

We, however, continued our backward slide down the adjacent side of the hill for the entire 20 yards. Our primary fear had just pivoted from being raped and murdered by some psychopath in a Jeep to being mangled in a rolling snowball of metal, car parts and friends. Tabucky and I lunged to the front of the car in an effort to prevent it from tipping and rolling the rest of the way. Whether it worked or whether some guardian angel held it down, we managed to stay on all 4 wheels and the seeming free-fall finally stopped in a muddy pit. Moments later we began to sink.

The side rail of a 1991 Nissan Pathfinder stands a proud 24.6 inches off the ground *(I made that up. No idea how high it is. Tried googling it but got bored).* Basically we sank up to the doors in a quicksand like muddy swamp.

Comfortable that everyone was ok in the car, I climbed out the passenger window to assess the damage (*cuz I'm such a man*) when a shadowy image came running from the adjacent lawn and down the rocks. It was a creepy ass dude named Tony Bongo *(not his real name. But Bongo? That's the fake name I came up with?)*

He used to drive to our house after school and wait in our driveway. As many times as we'd try to dodge him, he always managed to worm his way in. A few months later, he allegedly stalked our neighbor Carrie Simoneit. Not the phone calls and locker type of stalking, more the standing outside her window in the middle of the night while chasing a mosquito from his pants kind. As much as I detest social status, hierarchy and the like, this guy was a creep and we wanted nothing to do with him.

Now here he was, laughing as if we were the best of friends just involved in an epic event together. He claimed that he thought we knew it was him.. but he did ram our car and almost kill everybody. (*there's that drama again*) Then the cops came and arrested us.

Our hero sister Paula to the rescue. She showed up at the police station with her boyfriend Mark and bailed us out. While we were being processed Mark went and had our car towed out of the swamp. Yet again, the spoiled little brats we were, got off scott free. Except for Matthew of course who moments later did in fact get fisted by Jenn's dad who took his own word quite seriously.

They say the youth is wasted on the young and by-and-large it is but that's only because people tend to let go of the exhilaration of moments. I get that youth brings with it infinite first experiences, feelings and emotions that dull with age but that's entirely the fault of the beholder. I know how lucky I've been in life and never spend a moment ungrateful. As ashamed as I am to seemingly justify all my good luck by pointing the equal magnitude of tragedy or hardship I've endured, life is certainly a balance. The trick for me is trying to find the positive in even the worst life can offer. Disappointment, blame or resentment are crutches people use to justify their own shortcomings. Well, logistically speaking, neither of those things will change your life circumstance. Blaming a God, a boss, a tragedy, a loss, a failure etc. does not correct, repay or replace anything. Nobody owes you anything ever and you're not entitled to anything. And THAT, is not a bad thing! It only means you have the gift of free will and can do with your life whatever it is you choose to do. So get out there and live it. Even if it occasionally leaves you sunk in a muddy swamp.

Kids Shouldn't Play (football) with Guns
Fall 1991 Palatine, IL

Around this same time, we had taken that adolescent leap from laser tag style games to paintball to straight up buying pellet guns and shooting each other point blank with them.

For some reason we decided to go to a high school football game. I'm not particularly fond of football and we certainly didn't have any school spirit to speak of but our team was in a play-off bid and if they won this particular game they'd advance. Still, couldn't care less but everyone was going and if everybody jumped off a cliff, well so the hell would I.

Fortunately, on this fateful night, a dude named Tommy Pondera joined us and brought with him his B-47 dual pump-action sawed off pellet rifle. Naturally. (ok yes I made up the name but I feel like my name more accurately describes the weapon).

As the game wound down to mere seconds left, our team found themselves in a pickle. We were winning by one point and the other team had a field goal attempt coming up. Pretty simple, they make it we lose. They miss, we win.

Tommy had a long black trench coat (no connection to the alleged trench coat mafia that didn't happen yet) hiding his pellet gun and when I looked over at him he was pumping the shit out of it. I knew something awesome was going to happen. This crazy bastard decided that if he could shoot the actual football, just as the other team's kicker was about to kick it.. surely he'd whiff it and we'd win. Naturally we supported the shit out of this idea.

Now you gotta think, we were up in the bleachers, maybe half way and below us was the track. In front of that was our team's bench all lined up against the sidelines. You know, the 20 dudes that blew but got dressed up in a jersey and a million pads each week just to tell chicks they play football. And of course, just beyond them was the actual field. Everyone in the stands was starting to get fired up as the players all got in a line and bent over with their noses up each others asses like football players do when they're about to start a play.

The kicker was all sorted, the dude that they hike the ball to so he can hold it in place was all sorted and Tommy had his aim all lined up and ready to go. In our heads it was perfect. Just before the kickers foot meets the ball, it would mysteriously fall over or pop or something and the kicker would probably kick himself in the face or something awesome and we would win.

The ball was hiked and the dude who catches it and places it for the kicker caught it and placed it for the kicker. The kicker, in all his glory took his 5 steps, wound up and in that precise moment of would be glory, an ear piercing shotgun blast goes off.

The kick went straight threw the uprights during the same moment that one of our benchwarmers dropped like a sack of potatoes. He was now on the field rolling around grabbing his helmet like he had a bowl of hot sauce poured into his ears. His name was Mike Nealy. Mike never played one minute of any high school football game. Week after week Mike dressed the part and stood on the sidelines in the freezing cold temperature to watch his team play, secretly desperate for his big shot.

This week, however, instead of watching the final play of the game, Mike got shot with a pellet gun through the ear hole of his helmet. The bullet went right through the damn ear hole and blasted his ear off. Naturally the entire crowd was baffled. Did this kid just have a seizure? Why is blood pouring out of his helmet?

Mike was rushed to the hospital, Tommy was expelled and me? well I effing pissed myself AGAIN.

Nothin Two Squirts of Piss Can't Fix
Summer 1992

It wasn't until the end of the year that we'd get the call from NC State. Coach Tarantino invited us to fly down to Raleigh Durham for an official NCAA, all expense paid recruiting visit. We were fucking ecstatic. Not only did it galvanize our prospects of playing Division 1 soccer for a Top 20 team but for me personally, it restored the confidence that Coach Pagnani had been demolishing. Once word got out that NC State was serious, we'd begin to get calls and letters from a million other schools following suit. The same bandwagon scenario that would play itself out in our music career years later.

Our visit was scheduled for the 4th of July weekend and Papa Boner decided to tag along. We'd fly out to Raleigh Durham and like the million times before, the 3 of us would explore a brand new place together.

When we landed, a car picked us up to take us to a fancy hotel on campus where we'd check in and get our weekend itinerary. The first day consisted of a campus tour, lunch at the fancy athlete-only cafeteria and then that night we'd be treated to a UNC/NC State basketball game. After that, the plan was to have 2 dudes from the team pick Matthew and I up for one of those beautifully cliché nights of college partying. Presuming we'd get that far, our meting with coach Tarantino was slated for the following morning.

We had a fantastic day and by the time we got to the basketball game, Papa Boner was fully decked out in NC State gear. An NC State scarf wrapped around an NC State hoodie over his NC State T-shirt. He even bought a little NC State flag just in case he needed some school pride in a pinch. It was white-picket fence awesome and we couldn't have loved it more.

Since I didn't even know the rules of basketball much less follow it, the game came and went without registering in my memory. Unfortunately for me, I wouldn't even remember that I didn't remember anything until the next morning. We finally dropped off Papa B at the hotel where Scotty and Dante picked us up. We'd met them at camp the previous summer and aside from being among the coolest people we'd ever met, they also happened to be 2 of the NCAAs best soccer players. They were our hosts for the evening and tasked with assuring we had a good enough time to verbally commit to NC State the following day.

The first party was at a house rented by a handful of players from the NC State men and women's soccer teams and from what I actually recall, it was a wonderful time. Everybody was super nice to everyone else, which was a dramatic difference form the social politicking of high school we were accustomed to. We hadn't really travelled much domestically at this point and though we definitely remembered the Southern Hospitality from attending camp here, these people were beyond amazing. Within 15 minutes of being there, we committed, at least to each other, to playing for NC State.

Apparently we'd spend a few hours at the first party and then head to another 2 parties before the night ran its course.   My lights, however, went out about 45 minutes into the first one.

I must have been having some kind of nightmare because I was suddenly cold and everything felt wet. As I wrestled to peel off the bits of reality from whatever dream state scenario my sub-

conscious painted for me, there was one
discernible reality I couldn't imagine
away. Someone was pushing and pulling
me. I'd be wrapped and suffocated in blankets
one second, then freezing and exposed the
next. As the eternity of the next 3-4 seconds
passed, things began to come into a very painful
focus.

It was light out and I saw my dad tugging on the
sheets, in his briefs. Our hotel had 2 double
beds and I must have come in and passed
out next to him on his. Much worse, it had now
begun to appear as if something awful
happened. Yes, definitely something
terrible. Dad's briefs looked half wet. They
were white but had a nonsensical darker line
halfway across them indicating half was wet and
the other dry. I felt my own panties. Yes, yes,
they were very wet. Not like dad's but wet all
over. Oh no, what have I done? "Does he look
mad?" I asked myself. "Yes, he does", I
answered. "Does he know I'd been
drinking?" "Yes, I believe he knows." "What
the hell is he doing with the sheets? and why are
my panties soaked and his semi soaked?" I
continued. That's when I began to do the
math. My bladder didn't feel particularly full
and on account of how much I'd had to drink last
night, it definitely should have been. The truth
was undeniable.

I pissed on my dad. I crawled into bed with my
god damned papa boner whose very

spermatozoa triumphantly conquered my mother's vaginal egg fort, miraculously bringing me into this world. Who raised and cared for me, provided for and nourished me through thick and thin. Who taught me right from wrong, good from bad, and who loved me unconditionally. I just pissed all over him. My only play was to man up and accept full responsibility for my actions. To reach deep within myself and face the awful truth with whatever dignity I had stored away in my ever-deteriorating soul and come clean with shameful apologies. So I mustered up every ounce of hangover energy I had and did what any man in my position would do. I pretended I was still asleep until he got into the shower.

Dad had a rich history of dealing with this sort of thing from us. I don't know if it was strategic, simply easiest for him or if he didn't see any other option but he did what I suppose I'd do in his position and climbed into the comforting bosom of denial. He must have tormented over his decision in the shower because it was at least an hour before he came out of that bathroom. Not sure if he was scrubbing himself down in a tearful rendition of the crying game or simply getting himself over it but by the time he got out, it was as if it never happened.

Fall 1992

Returning to high school 2-a-days that Fall, Coach Pignani began his reign of terror. He implemented a bizarre policy regarding twins. There were no fewer than 4 sets of twins on our team: Marcus and Gavin Pope, Jeff and Jim Bauer, Dyska and Yoska Inouye and Matthew and I. Since the Popes and us were the only capable players, coach Pignani decided it would only be fair to choose 1 of each set of twins to make a permanent fixture on the Varsity team Junior year, leaving Gavin and I to play JV and a handful of Varsity games if JV was off. Matthew and Marcus however were brought up to varsity permanently.

Now, Matthew and I had played together our whole lives. He is one of the best soccer players I've ever seen to this day. As impossible as it is for me to say one good word about myself, especially in light of this situation, I feel compelled to admit that I wasn't all that bad either. I mean shit we're both getting recruited to the #2 school in the country! *(god I'm awesome. Don't you think?)* Furthermore, Marcus and Gavin Pope were mediocre at best! *(I get that I sound like a vagina cleaning apparatus.. and I'm ok with it I think.).*

For both Matthew and I, it was a nightmare. At that age it was hard enough for me getting screwed over like this but probably even harder for him. That year he was top goal scorer and in the newspapers every day. As proud as he should have been, he was just as crushed as I was.

Anyhow, what did I do? Started throwing up after games. In retrospect it's pretty funny that we never connected the dots but from that very season I'd get violently ill after every single game and throw up for hours until I'd pass out. To verify the significance of my ailment, 3 years later my school would send me to the Mayo Clinic in Rochester, MN for a weeks worth of testing. I ate radioactive eggs, drank barium milkshakes, have a camera shoved up my ass and down my throat as they tried to diagnose the issue. I left with prescription toothpaste and crazy pills. Booya.

Passing Gas in Class
Senior year was everything and nothing all at once. On one side you're finishing your High School experience, transitioning to the next perhaps most significant, at least in my case, time of your life while on the other hand, aside from gay things like Prom, there's not a whole lot of action. Accordingly you end up with the easiest of electives you can find and get away with the least amount of class/effort you can possibly escape with. This very notion landed me in a class called "Notehand" which was learning a style of shorthand writing to help take quicker notes. Yep, as completely and utterly useless as the appendix. Add to that the teacher was, Mrs. Heywood (Giablomie) was notorious

for being easy, lenient, naive and "cool". Her other scholastic contribution, aka: reason enough to justify paying her, was coaching the Vikettes. These were the girls that couldn't stomach not being Cheerleaders or Poms and couldn't admit to the fact that they were biggens. I'm all for biggens but the ones that are in denial that wear clothes 10 sizes too small, throw their noses up to the clouds and think being a bitch is their god given right. They would tape up riffles or sticks and flip and twirl em to the march of a hip-hop beat.

Anyhow, it was supposed to be an easy A so everybody like me took it. Put a group like ours together and and it's gonna be trouble. I remember the classroom having computers at all the desks which b at the time was pretty progressive lol. We learned that by resting your books on the keyboard the computers would start beeping like mothercukers so naturally every day started with everyone laying their books on em. It would start in one corner of the room and just as Mrs. Heywoods eyes fired toward the beep, another one would fire off. Within in the first 3 minutes it sounded like a god damned circus in there. She simply couldn't stop it. This was mildly funny until she honed in on one of us and started screaming.. that's when inevitably someone would fart. It sounds so retarded and elementary but when the gas started over the beeping as

72

Mrs. Heywood was popping off on somebody I assumed the immediate threat of pissing myself. On one particular day this routine was playing out perfectly and somehow everybody managed to have gas. The beeping was right on cue.. "oh sorry Mrs. Heywood I accidentally put my books on the keyboard.." then the gas. kids were farting one after another as she raged on some aloof stoner. Thankfully I had so much gas that day that I was a major contributor to that aspect. They were big, bass-y and boisterous. I was firing em off every 30-45 seconds. The entire class was in hysterics and shock all at once as the whole situation began to climax. Mrs. Heywood finally slapped the chalkboard and screamed.. the next person to fart is going to the office and spending the rest of the years Saturdays in Saturday school. That's when my stomach swelled with a potent swirling gas that couldn't be reasoned with. I put my head down between my arms and pushed ever so slightly. The subsequent sonic boom was such that it literally startled her. It was a mere seconds after her threat and I swear she jumped 10 feet. The chick in front of me was so startled that her knees popped up involuntarily slamming them against the bottom of her desk. It was those little types of things that got my piss stirred up. The little details and/or side effects of an ordeal like that that I found the real humor in. The computers beeping, the timing, the moment, the other farts, the threat, the be all end all fart that ripped through the gaps of silence... all wonderful stuff.. but the real piece de resistance, the coup de gras, the true art of such an event is not any of those things but instead the slightly heavier chick that sat in front of me being so startled by such a loud and sudden noise that her knees rammed themselves up into the bottom of her desk. Her involuntary reaction. The reasoning behind which her brain sent a message to her body that it outta jerk up relentlessly in order to escape some sort of pending threat or current circumstance. It of course being a fart after all. It took a few seconds for everybody to process what had just happened and the hilarity of it all. When a teacher goes to the extent to slam the chalkboard and offer up a significant threat as consequence for students should they continue to fart, people pay attention. It's certainly not the moment you'd expect a colossal fart of a lifetime.. At any rate Mrs. Heywood screamed to get the hell out of her classroom and she'd deal with me in a minute. When a teacher says "hell" or "damn" that's another sobering moment. She write a hall pass sending me to the office to see the principal for "passing gas in class". I got 3 Saturday schools for it and proceeded to graduate without further incident.

CHAPTER 6
College

My dad had made Matthew and I a deal going into college. He'd been saving up for us to do so since we were little kids and decided that he'd give us the financial equivalent of whatever we'd earn in scholarships. We liked this idea very much and were quite lucky for it.

It all came down to 2 schools, NC State and Butler University. NC State was the better team by a mile. Still ranked in the NCAA Top 10, they were one of the schools that always had the chance to go all the way. We knew the level of competition there would be brutal and since I was throwing up after games, the added pressure didn't help. Butler, though no less competitive, had consistently remained in the middle of the table and it's 3.5 hour drive proximity to home made it a bit more appealing. At the end of the day however we got a much better offer from Butler so that Fall, we packed all of our shit into the Pathfinder and drove East for pre-season training.

Fall, 1993 Butler, Indianapolis
While most kids get to college with an army of family and friends to help them move in and get acquainted, Matthew and I rolled up with some garbage bags full of Metallica t-shirts and our soccer gear. Campus was pretty quiet since

most kids wouldn't be moving in for another 2 weeks. We'd arrived the evening before training camp started and "moved in" to our dorm room at Ross Hall.

Inadvertant Incest

Our dorm room was in the basement of a 4 story building. The first 3 were for dudes, top floor was reserved for freshman girls. I really should thank the genius who devised that plan. We were room-mates of course in a tiny room directly across the hall from one of the bathrooms/shower rooms. This meant that we could just strip to the nudes, grab a bar of soap and step across the hall when nobody was looking. A situation that lead to what would be the final physical confrontation Matthew and I ever had. and it happened on our 2nd day at college.

I can't remember what we were arguing about but it got heated and I decided to take the high-road. So I took all my clothes off, grabbed the soap and ran to the shower to diffuse the situation. Apparently Matthew was still stewing and decided to lock me out. I was none the wise and only realized he did it after my shower when I got stuck in the hall.

I suppose I could have just sat in the bathroom naked but that never would have gotten me back in now would it? The writing was on the proverbial wall so with one hand on my asshole and the other on my dick-n-balls, I set camp in front of our room and cursed him through the door. I was surprised how long he held out. For 30 minutes I crouched there ultimately meeting the entire floor.

They came by in droves. New students, their family and friends, RAs, maintenance folks, you name it, I met em. I was resigned of course to the sheepish "oh hey dude", or "ha oh hi, hey look sorry about this", or "hello, Nathan, Chicago .. pleasure to meet you.. um it's complicated" types of greetings as they paraded by in various degrees of offended silence. Eventually I heard the ever so delicate click of our doors bolt. Convinced I'd either had enough or that I was still hiding out in the shower, Matthew unlocked the door.

Before he could even take his fingers off the lock I kicked that fucking door down with the might of a mule, bull, donkey cross-breed ? *(I don't know, they're all relatively strong and seem to enjoy kicking shit)*. He flew to the back of the room and crashed pretty hard against the bunk beds.

What proceeded was a 15 minute brawl throughout which I was nude. We rolled around kicking and punching and swinging and rolling and falling and touching while my wenis and ball sac flopped, collided, smothered, slapped, squished and otherwise molested my twin brother.

As exciting as all that was, however, the real magic of those dorm days were still yet to come. and they would come in giant helpings of nudity, feces, urine, vandalism and hijinks that would help carve out the lovely gentlemen we are today.

It's Raining Shoes

A month or so later, we'd find ourselves with a day off at Ross Hall. A room-mate of a dude on our soccer team had to leave his dorm room for something and didn't have his key so he asked us to sit and watch his room for 20 minutes while he was gone and then let him back in. Of course dude, no worries.

We knew this hillbilly had a high powered pellet rifle under his bed and approximately 3 seconds after he left we loaded it up and headed for the window. His room was on the 3rd floor and the window looked directly over the front entrance of the building and the main street on campus. It must have been around noon or 1pm because pedestrian traffic was heavy. Since we'd never fired this particular rifle we decided a little target practice was in order to at least get a feel for how powerful it was going to be. So we picked a parked car about half a block away and aimed for the back window.

My friend Larsen took the first shot and almost immediately the back window spider webbed and crumbled. We were like WOW! it was half a block away!! We took a few other practice shots to make sure we knew just how many pumps were required to light up a person but certainly not hurt them in any way. I mean come on, we're not bad people. ? . Anyhow, we finally found the perfect target. Poor lady, I feel horrible.

Our victim was about 60 years old and very pleasantly plump. She was carrying approximately 8 to 10 shoe boxes across the street. You might have thought there were dinosaur eggs in them based on the care and delicacy in which she traveled. Slow as a turtle and extra conscious not to drop any. I'm not going to name the shooter but this person gave the rifle a few pumps and took aim on her ass. Now remember, the pumps were meant to startle her a tiny little bit.. like a spitball maybe.. which I think was ultimately the result. However, you wouldn't have guessed it watching this go down.

That little pellet smacked her ass just as she was about to cross the street and she jumped about 15 feet into the air. It was raining shoe boxes all over her as she wailed and moaned .. "I've been shot I've been shot!!" .

To her credit, she had been shot but come on lady .. a little dramatic?! Anyway, a million people surrounded her and yet again flyers were posted all over the dorms looking for the culprits. Our victim? well she hardly had a mark but she did have to pick up about 10 boxes and twice as many shoes. I'm a horrific person. A totally and completely horrific, urine soaked person.

That's Not What the Fire Department Thinks Stan

The crown jewel of our dorm days though was a bit that ended up on the local news, saw firemen pulling girls out of their 4th floor dorm windows and a University issued $5,000. bounty on Matthew's and my head.

On one of our previous soccer trips we stopped at a fireworks store and loaded up on bottle rockets, roman candles, black cats and an assortment of random shaped explosives that promised "reports". The stash was in Matthew's and my room where a small army of us devised a plan for them.

Since Ross Hall required that only dudes live on floors 1,2 and 3 and only girls on the 4th, we had to recruit a friend to rig the door so we could access it after hours. The fireworks promised to be grand but I didn't feel completely satisfied without a fire extinguisher to go along with them so I stole one from the dorms across the street. We figured we would creep up to the 4th floor, station ourselves on each of the 4 corners that made up the square building and synchronize our attack. I grabbed a Roman Candle and stuffed it in my pants in order to work the crown jewel of our arsenal which was my new fire extinguisher. We crept up the stairs and through the door before all splitting off to take our positions. We could each see 2 other friends from our respective corners and hand signaled the launch. It started with the roman candles. As this was one of our earlier ideas, the planning ended there. I just remember that it looked and felt like war.

Roman candles shot blasts down every hall and filled them with missile like reports and smoke. Then came the black cats, cracking like AK47s underneath the misses. It was going so well and I got over excited so I started with the extinguisher. These things are amazing. I shot it as I ran down the hallway back toward the exit stairway. It filled the hall with a thick, choking powder that eclipsed all vision. I couldn't see anything so I just kept running and shooting. The site of roman candle blasts through the fog was something to behold and it got my "juices" flowing. I could tell it wouldn't be long before a little peepee came out. It was a war zone on that floor and I couldn't believe what I was witnessing/creating. It took all of about 20 seconds for the fire alarm to get wind of our activities and it blasted a wailing scream that woke up the whole neighborhood.

The terror on my friends' and my faces was palpable as we thought for sure we were pinched but hauled ass down the stairs anyway. By the time we got from the 4th to the 2nd floor, the RAs were already evacuating people. You see, the thick powder from the fire extinguisher ironically looks like smoke. The smell of actual smoke from the fireworks didn't help either and as far as everyone else in the dorm was concerned, we had a real fire on our hands. We kept running all the way down to the basement where the halls were already empty and snuck into our room. I guess you could call it poetic injustice but while the rest of the kids were stranded outside in the freezing cold, we were holed up in our room, snug as bugs. The reality of what was happening was beyond our comprehension. See, the girls on the 4th floor thought this was the end. Many of them began throwing their valuables out the windows in effort to preserve them and I'm sure some were close to jumping out themselves as the powder poured into their rooms from under the door. 4 fire trucks, a news crew, and the hundreds of kids that lived in the dorm were all outside while we slept. We're bad people I suppose but it goes without saying that I needed a fresh pair of underwear.

That's Not a Bar Stool!

As I write this, we're on our way home from Florida radio show with Staind and Chevelle .. Indiana is not like a lot of places. It's in the Midwest, the middle of the Midwest, buried and landlocked by cornfields and hillbillies. It makes for the perfect college campus. We were only 19 but couldn't wait the agonizing 2 years to get into bars so we got to work on getting fake IDs. Well, real fake IDs.

In Indiana, all we had to do was grab a copy of a birth certificate, put a tiny piece of paper with a new birthdate on it over the birth date section and photocopy. Then a friend of a friend stole her mom's notary stamp (which they handed out like candy), stamp it and go to the DMV.

At the DMV I gave her all of my "info" and as she typed it into the computer she would occasionally turn the computer around to have me look it over and make sure it was all "correct". I could have told her I was black and still would have gotten this ID. Anyhow, an hour later we had real fake IDs that said we were 23.

We took these all over town to become regulars at several bars across Indianapolis and Broadripple. One of these mainstays was a bar called the Patio. On Wednesday nights the Patio had a .50 Cent you-call-it club night which featured the latest and greatest in Rave and techno DJs and an odd cast of characters from the gutters of Indy and it's suburbs. We loved it. Several wonderful moments came out of the Patio Wednesday nights but one still makes me piss myself if I think about it too much.

We brought this dude named Scott Lawler out with us. He was one of the assistant coaches on the soccer team and always a hilarious guy. He had a frat-boy vibe to him which usually I despise but his was more in his sense of humor and adventure. But like all frat boys, take him out of his comfort zone and he falls apart. Naturally we took him to this club full of weirdo's and misfits. We were already pretty drunk when he got there and brought him to the bar to get his first of the night. He was visually nervous to be in that place. He fidgeted and giggled and looked around trying to take in the whole "scene".

Now. there were many regulars at this joint that we saw each and every Wednesday night. There was the super hot little raver with a tiny backpack, high gauge earrings, and tattoos everywhere, there was the cross-dressing just-came-out-of-the-closet giant dude that recently discovered the freedom of college and started wearing lip stick, and then there was the black midget chick. She was there every Wednesday and she was awesome.

As the Patio tried to create as rave-ish an environment as possible, they kept the place dark, foggy (with a smoke machine that we would later buy) and strobed out. We made our way from the bar to a tall table just off the dance floor area and each raced to grab one of the only 3 chairs. I got the first one, grabbed it, slide on to the top and scooted in. Matthew and Dan followed suit with the only 2 remaining stools but Scott didn't seem too concerned. As we were all running to assure that we'd get a stool, he casually strolled up to the table unconcerned about the prospect of standing. So we thought. When he got about 3 feet from the table, he grabbed the black midget and pulled her over while he hopped up and tried to mount her. He and the black midget went down like a ton of bricks. The shock, dismay and genuine what-the-hell-just happened feeling quickly dissipated when hordes of regulars surrounded us. After some pushing and yelling, Scott was forced to explain himself. He looked terrified and humiliated. He thought the midget was a 4th bar-stool and he tried to sit on her head. Don't love him, judge him.

Post Season Wrap Up

That soccer season was pretty amazing. We got to fly out to California and play Stanford, San Diego State and Fresno State in an Addidas Metlife tournament. We got to play #1 ranked Indiana University at our home stadium in front of 10,000 people. NCAA Division 1 soccer was fucking awesome. Unfortunately for me, it was also killing me. My barfing after games was getting horrific. I'd play my face off and as soon as the final whistle blew i'd have my head in a toilet. I'd throw up for about 2 hours after the game until I fell asleep which was the only cure. At least 2 hours of sleep would re-set me but otherwise it was hell. I'd seen a number of doctors and specialists and had tried about 2,3392309230 prescriptions but nothing helped. By the end of our Freshman year I was on prescription toothpaste because the vomit was destroying the enamel on my teeth.

We ended the season around .500 and some how got into the NCAA tournament. Our first game was against Notre Dame. We'd beaten them 4-1 earlier in the season but this was to see who advances to the final 32 which was a big deal. We'd given up a 1 goal lead in the 2nd half and went down 2-1 with about 10 minutes left. In that 10 minutes we absolutely peppered them. Hitting the post, crossbar, goalie and everything between, we failed to hit the net and were knocked out. The seniors were devastated but admittedly, we were excited. The season was brutal and we couldn't wait to get into the fluffy white clouded, harpsichord toned Heaven that was college.

As we walked off the field, Notre Dame's coach pulled me aside and asked if I'd consider playing there next year. I only mention this because having gone through the torment of high school soccer, this to me was a proud and liberating moment. *Jeez do I rule.. high fives.*
Back at Butler, our coach called Matthew and I into his office for a meeting to discuss the following year. He was rambling on about how much he's counting on us to be the heart of the team blah blah while Matthew had picked a golf club off his wall and handed it to me. Coach's dog was sitting next to the desk in between us and I decided to start rubbing its dick with the golf club. Matthew and I were in stitches. The dog was howling at the moon in doggy Heaven

as coach droned on about the commitment it takes to be a Division 1 athlete. The dog's moans were getting louder and louder and we were laughing harder and harder when finally coach stood up and screamed "what the hell is so damn funny!!??". In that moment, and just as I pulled the gold club away so coach didn't bust me, the dog exploded all over his golf club.

Summer, Chicago 1994

Going away to school for the first time is pretty much the most life-defining event in many kids lives. For most it truly begins the transition from kid to adult. For me, however, it just reiterated that I would spend the rest of my life trapped in the beautiful, if somewhat tortured soul of a perpetual child.

So this supposed transition for a white suburban kid like myself is relatively soft and easy, as we spent every summer coming back to the safety and comfort of dad's house and worked lame summer jobs to pacify his insecurities about our being spoiled rotten. The first summer back from school was pretty much the best summer of my life so far. As we spent the last year and a half in high school, we spent that summer mostly alone in my dad's amazing house with our girlfriends and best friends Bart and Tabucky. Inevitably though we'd have to whip ourselves back into shape and head back to pre-season training.

CHAPTER 7
Animal House
BUTLER, Indianapolis 1995

They Say Pigs Are Smarter Than Dogs

Sophomore year of college was chock full of action and hilarity. We lived with 6 other dudes from our soccer team at the time in a duplex house off campus in the ghetto. Matter of fact the day we were moving our furniture in, our neighbor had a gun to a dude's head in the front yard. He proceeded to steal the poor bastards bicycle right out from under his ass while we carried mattresses and shit through the front door. They managed to get our bikes 2 days later and despite sitting on them right in front of our faces, they'd claim they knew nothing about it. Awesome.

The units were connected in the basement via an ax- induced hole in the wall. Matthew and I lived down there on one side and our best friend Stan Golcheck lived on the other side.

The day we were moving in we found a newspaper left among the trash from previous renters. In the classified section was an ad for a Vietnamese Pot-bellied pig. It was $100. and the buyer had to drive out to some farm to pick him up. It was a no brainer and Albert came home 2 hours later.

When my room-mate brought him in he was squealing like a .. well like a pig I suppose. A very loud, obnoxious and anxiety ridden pig. He didn't stop for the next 6 months and though he'd also piss on everything, eat anything and otherwise destroy the entire household, Al provided some wonderfully good times in that house.

To potty train we were supposed to keep him in a box with half of it covered in newspapers to sleep on and the other half his litter box. Al however slept in his litter box and shit on all the newspapers for a week until we decided to let him roam free. He spent the rest of his time shitting everywhere and eating everything. He would eat socks, toilet paper, cigarette butts, beer cans, paper plates, books, shoes, remote controls, CDs, tennis balls, jackets, bicycle tires, and impressively, Al would even eat his own shit.

We used to bring him out to the front porch and pour buckets of beer into his giant bowl until he got belligerent. I know it's an awfully frat-boy type of thing to do but we were young and it truly was hysterical. He would stumble around the porch squealing, drooling and shitting himself. We would dangle pieces of bread in front of his nose and lead him down the steps in an attempt to teach him to climb stairs. After some regrettably hilarious tumbles, he finally mastered it. That's when things got super awesome.

Al would find an unsuspecting room-mate asleep in their room, make love to their head and then shit on their pillow before eating a wallet and peacing out. He had a weird cork-screw shaped penis that he would drag along the carpet all day long leaving his love stains all over the place.

One of our hillbilly room-mates Martin had a special connection to Al, likely on account of them both growing up on a farm. Their relationship became curious when Martin started letting Al fuck his leg while we were all watching TV in the family room. Of course Al would repay the favor by eating Martin's panties.

After a few weeks of getting settled in, we were set to kick off our 2nd season in the NCAA.

My barfing had only gotten worse Sophomore year so Butler decided to send me to Mayo Clinic in Rochester, MN for a week's worth of tests. It's pretty much the medical capital of the world and once I got there I was given an itinerary of tests. For the next 6 days I had cameras and tubes shoved down my throat and up my ass. I had to drink a barium milkshake while be observed through an x-ray machine. I had to eat a plate full of radio active scrambled eggs and on and on.

After the 6 days, my main doctor sat me down to go over the results. In a nutshell, I'm crazy. With absolutely nothing to medically contribute to my barfing, they could only deduce that I had a psychological issue. I had tried every prescription under the sun during my first season at Butler and by the time I left Mayo, I had a script for anti-anxiety meds. I conceded to the fact that I'd have to endure yet another season of torture and hell just to play the sport I loved which is exactly what I did.

We started that season well. Undefeated in our conference before heading out to California for an NCAA Adidas/MetLife tournament with the big guns like SanDiego State, Fresno and Stanford. They were all ranked in the top 20 and though we lost to all three by only one goal each, we proved we had a team worthy of giving it a solid go.

I was beginning to find a rekindled adoration and gratitude for the sport and my place in it. Unfortunately that was short lived when I shattered my shin against in a conference game at Wisconsin.

One of their dudes and I swung for the same 50/50 ball and when his boot hit my shin it exploded to the size of a grapefruit. That knocked me out of most of the season. In my final game at Butler, we lost a heart breaking 1-0 to Indiana University in front of 10,000 people at our home Kuntz Stadium in Indianapolis. Indiana went all the way to the final before losing to Virginia so we didn't feel

too bad but regrettably that would be the last
NCAA game we'd play.

"Fire in the Hole"
Fall 1994/1995
With the season over we focused our attention
on the amazing times we were about to
have. One of our room-mates had this super
white trash cousin named Nick. This guy had it
all; the mullet, the stone washed jeans, and even
a cool tick that made his neck twitch ever few
seconds. Nick used to come over about once a
week (except for the time we had the nitrous
tank, more on that later).
We never knew what he actually did for a living
but every time he came over he had some
different random pick up truck and lots of
drugs. He had this transformer bowl that we
would always smoke out of and each time it
made a complete lap around the table he would
casually change the shape of it. Something
about that made me piss myself every
time. Anyhow, on this particular night, we had
accidentally eaten some bad mushrooms that we
later found out our room-mate picked fresh off
some cow shit. This was the 2nd time I'd made
that darned mistake and I knew that they could
be a wonderful time but also that they had the
potential to send you into a psychotic paranoia
from hell itself.
We never knew when Nick was coming over, he
just showed up and this time when he did, we

were all out of our minds. Laughing hysterically at nothing and everything and talking a mile a minute. It didn't take long for the rotten mushrooms to amplify every one of Nick's amazing personality quirks. Needless to say, his surprise visit made us very happy. He sat down and we showered him with appreciation and laughter and after about 2 minutes he says "y'all wanna make a bomb?".

It got quiet for a minute as we pondered the validity of the question and weighed out a few pros and cons.. In that moment, not one of us could think of one possible "con" to the proposition. A bomb sounded like the single greatest idea ever.

So Nick traipses off into the kitchen bragging about the fact that he can make a massive bomb capable of destroying a small car with common, every day household products. He climbs under the sink and starts digging, throwing stuff around, mumbling to himself and twitching a little. We pretty much forgot about him until he came back into the room 20 minutes later with an empty 2-liter plastic Coke bottle, some aluminum foil and 3 or 4 bottles of cleaner, tarnish, varnish or whatever the hell else.

We were in no shape to even go outside (much less play with a bomb) so we decided to go into the basement. Aside from Matthew's, Stan's and my rooms down there was an ominous 4th room. It was dark and run down and nobody ever went in there except apparently my sisters dog who we dogsat for a few months. We couldn't get over how good the dog was and how he never had to shit.. well now we knew why. He was shitting in here.

It was a small, square dungeon and among the random crap strewn about, it also had a home made "bar", a broken ping-pong table, and a ton of dog/pig shit. On accidentally eaten rotten mushrooms, it seemed like the perfect place to set off a bomb.

There's only one door into this room and on the left of the door was the ghetto bar, directly in front of it was the ping-pong table and to the right was piles of dog shit. So we all put on ski goggles, shin guards, knee pads, lamp shades, etc. you get the drift and huddled behind the bar. Nick asks us if we're ready and upon our confirmation starts pouring all this different shit into the 2-liter. Remember, by the way, he's sober.

He puts the cap on the bottle and starts shaking the shit out of it. The anticipation was peaking and the mushrooms weren't helping any of us. Half hysterical laughter, half sheer terror, and another 100% enthusiastic anticipation. After a rigorous, 30 second shake, he throws it into the dog-shit corner and hauls ass toward us, diving over the bar. For the next couple of minutes we all screamed, laughed, braced for the end of the world and shit our pants.

We could hear the 2-liter expanding and contracting in the corner but none of us had the balls to peak over the bar and look at it. After all, at any moment now this fucker was gonna blow.

A few more minutes go by and now it starts gargling and hissing with the sounds of Armageddon but no explosion. The enthusiasm gave way to anxiety as we all exchanged worrisome looks.

Nick's crouched, peaking over the bar with a shit eating grin and says, very nonchalantly.. "oh by the way, this could take up to 30 minutes to detonate".

30 minutes!? Are you insane!? Not only are we freaking the fuck out on mushrooms, wearing ski goggles and lampshades, but the bomb was laying in a pile of dog shit directly in front of the ONLY door out of that room.

It sent us into a total panic and we insisted that, regardless of the potential danger, Nick had to either expedite the detonation or diffuse it. Admitting there was no way to diffuse now he finally agreed to hasten the process.

He creeps out from behind the safety of the bar and approaches the bomb which at this point was fucking whistling Dixie and just dying to explode. In a brave naivety, he grabs the bottle, gives it 3 rigorous shakes and just as he drops it... a blinding flash triggered a deafening sonic blast that filled the room with a heavy acidity as shrapnel smothers every one of us.

It was so smoky and the air was absolutely choking us but we managed to crawl out of the room. It took a minute to get our wits about us but once we did it didn't take long to figure out that the shrapnel was 100% dog shit. We all got hit by it but Nick was especially covered. I'll never forget seeing his hand mangled and the rest of him covered in dog shit, smiling and twitching.

Arther's Disclaimer- For the record, I'd like to add that though it seems as if we'd done a lot of drugs, we didn't. despite our very occasional, safe and regrettable indulgences once in a shameful while – we're not drug people and you shouldn't be neither!

Anywho, while we were all trapped behind the bar, Al decided to get crafty and eat through the screen door. We had no idea until our landlord called and told us that our pig was spotted running south on 38th street.

See, Al is a bit of an illegal alien as pigs are outlawed in the city of Indianapolis so we had to act fast. It didn't take long to spot him. You could hear his squealing a mile away. Not to mention he had holed up in a bush outside a gangster house.

It was quite a sight. There were 30 gangsters surrounding Al completely stunned by the fact that there was a pig in their bush. *Not sure if there's a pun there somewhere.* I don't think any of them had ever seen a pig, much less in their front bushes. They were losing their minds, yelling and screaming, which of course only set Al off. I'm tellin ya, ya aint heard nothing like it.

We squeezed our way through the crowd apologetically, grabbed Al and ran home. He screamed his balls off the whole way. Outside our front door, our landlord had had enough of the pig and finally used a city ordinance to have him evicted. It just didn't seem right but the law's the law and he had to go. There was no hiding him of course - he was loud, obnoxious, adventurous, smelled like shit and had a proclivity for annoying the piss out of anyone in his path. After much debate we decided to gift him to a well deserving sorority house on campus. Only problem was the sorority itself surely wouldn't see the beauty of having a pet pig until they spent some time with him which they would never agree to. Solution - break in to the sorority, plant Al in one of the less trafficked rooms and force them to deal with it.

Parker, Mills, Matthew and I were recruited to transport Al so we dressed up in all black (I think we even painted our eyes black for the added spirit of the mission) and headed over to Greek row. There was an alley behind all the frat/sorority houses that, by this time we knew like the back of our hands.

Parker had a real piece of shit car that we piled into and made our way down there at around 2 or 3am. Parking just outside the back door of Kappa Kappa Gamma or something with the lights off we devised a plan. We didn't really devise a plan, we just housed a bunch of beers and said our goodbyes to Al.

So, silly sorority houses always leave at least 1 window open and it's usually just a matter of looking around for it but this one was too perfect. The window to their kitchen off the back alley was wide open and it was pitch black inside. We were parked about 15 feet from it and decided to do some recon first. Leaving Al in the car, we ass-pushed each other up and through the window which was a good 8 to 10 feet off the ground. Stumbling in one after another, piling up on top of each other in the pitch black already had me in stitches.

In approximately 30 seconds time, Parker found the pantry. For those who aren't familiar, the pantry in a sorority house is something to behold. They are giant and they stock enough food to feed a small country. In the back of this particular pantry was a giant walk in freezer where a whole new pile of frozen goods are kept. I headed in, welcoming the all too familiar rush of adrenaline and threat of piss.

  Again it was pitch black and as I felt my way around the freezer, I got hit in the head with a frozen steak from God knows where. I adopted the duck and cover, and on my knees crawling through the freezer when I miraculously happened upon the stash of eggs. millions of eggs. as far as the eye could see there were eggs.

These things seem to happen so fast and soon we had an all out war going on in this kitchen. Oblivious, of course, to the fact that it was 3am and there were probably a hundred sorority chicks sleeping upstairs. Mustard, eggs, chicken, bagels, ranch dressing, olives, peanut butter, chicken wings, cans of soup, you name it - it was everywhere. The piss started trickling. In all the madness, Parker had been loading up on shit and he headed for the door. As soon as he opened it the alarm went off. He continued a casual walk to the car to drop off his payload and turned right back around for more.

We slammed the door shut from the inside assuming that would shut the alarm off but it didn't. It was loud as hell and now we could hear girls shuffling around upstairs. Matthew, Mills and I headed for the window again and started climbing out. I was the last one out and as I plummeted to the ground outside I heard 2 girls in front me. "fucking Leones, what the hell are you doing!?". I said oh hey! and ran to the car just in time to see Parker grab Al, run him to the window and ass-push him through it. (Al was not harmed in this story).

We all jumped in the car and drove from the alley, right across their front lawn and into a telephone poll. No diaper could have possibly handled the rapids flowing from wiener. Parker had this incredible stoicism when high and driving which somehow made him even more hilarious.

He put the car in reverse and casually put his right arm up over the passenger seat as people do when they back out of a parking spot.. backed up, shifted into drive and then .. mind you, we're on their front lawn.. put his right turn signal on and turned off the grass, onto the road and headed back to our house off campus.

We're not sure when/how/if they discovered their new room-mate in all the mayhem but I knew a girl in the house and asked her the next day. She had no idea what I was talking about. 2 days later the house mom was digging for some dry goods in the way back of a walk-in pantry and just about had a heart attack. There he was, cool as a cucumber, finishing off a bag of nachos and some laundry detergent.

*Arthur Notes- *Now don't get me wrong, we're definitely animal lovers and knew Al would be in good hands regardless of who found him and upon getting him back (the whole campus knew he was ours) .. we donated him to our room-mates uncle's farm and (this has to be the worst phrase ever) I-shit-you-not 4 years later he turned up on the front cover of a farming magazine.*

Summer Job

It was the summer of 1995 and Matthew and I were back at my dad's house. Working as delivery boys for Everfresh Juice Co., we'd spend our days driving this mini truck around Chicago stocking random Thornton's gas stations with our delicious fruit beverages. The job sucked but a couple weeks in I did something awesome.

Let me elaborate a bit on the truck. It was like a short bus of trucks. It had a separate cab but the actual cargo section was pretty small. Don't be fooled as I was, it was small but it was tall. Tall in the sense that things suddenly apply to you that otherwise didn't. For example, when you approach a bridge, sometimes you'll notice a sign of sorts indication how tall it is in the interest of "clearance". Well, I'd never in my life considered that just maybe a vehicle I was driving might not "clear" a bridge. That was something for the movies.

I'd woken up with a migraine which happened from time to time. I'm sure I tried to call in to work but definitely didn't end up staying home. So I raced downtown, got my orders for the day and hopped into the cab of my truck. The day sucked immediately. Lost orders, customers bitching, chapped lips from standing in the cooler too long stocking its shelves. It was around 11am and I was miserably ready for lunch.

That days route had me wondering around the south side aimlessly. Always lost and always late to wherever I had to be. My migraine was not cooperating and since I was starving, I pulled into the first McDonalds I saw. I was in the hood. It was crazy ghetto but I didn't care. I was too hungry and miserable to anything but eat so I parked and walked in. To reiterate, I'm not in the slightest bit racist so it's only in the interest of the story when I say that the second I walked in, a 13 ish year old black girl says to me "aw look at the white boy!". Was I afraid of her? Yes I was. Were the additionally a million of her friends and/or family equally as intimidating? Yes there were.

Well I didn't think twice about turning around and heading to the drive thru. They all laughed at me as I walked out where I hopped in my truck, backed it up and got in the drive-thru line. When it was my turn to order, things went off without a hitch. "I'll have 2 of your delicious limited time only McRib sandwiches please". "That'll be 5 foddy 9, pull round.". No problemo.

As I began my acceleration around the sharp turn I suddenly heard an obnoxiously loud bang and subsequent screeching noise. Naturally I slammed on my breaks and pissed myself a squirt or two. After that I took a look out the window to see if I'd hit the side of the building or something. As you may or not know, you're supposed to make wide turns in those effing things. Well, I didn't.

After a few more useless inspections, I'd cleared myself of any wrong doing and assumed it was somebody or something else.

Shifting back into drive, I coasted to the first window which was only feet away. The hideous screeching continued as I did so but I couldn't for the life of me figure out what the hell was causing it. Checking my side mirrors again as I paid, yet again, I hadn't hit anything. Nothing I could see anyways. In moments like these my face tends to get real hot and my heart kind of feels funny. I suppose in those few moments specifically, I'd assumed something was probably wrong with the truck but I could deal with that later.

As the attendant at the first window handed me my change, she had a look of horror on her face. In retrospect she must have been in some sort of shock cuz she didn't say a word. She just stared up toward the roof of my truck. I thanked her and continued on my way to the 2nd window. The screeching noise was deafening at this point. I stuck my head back out the window and looked up. Ehhhh bitch tits.

I'd fucking hit the roof off the drive thru and was now carrying it as I went. So I did the only thing I could think to do. Turned the wheel to the right and floored it. Didn't get my food, didn't stop to assess the damage, just hopped the curb and peaced.

That's when the scope of this thing revealed itself. As I pulled out of the side of the drive-thru, the entire roof/awning of it came crashing down behind my truck. I knocked the whole damn drive-thru over. As piles of people came running out of the restaurant to see what happened, I did what any young man in my circumstance would've done. Took the f*&cK off and never looked back!

So there you have it, life was beginning to add up. Seemed like no matter what we did, something ridiculous would happen. By the time summer was winding down we faced the now daunting prospect of returning to Butler for training. Haunted by memories of last season's injuries and barfing, I almost couldn't stomach the thought of going through it again. I'd get nauseas just thinking about it.

Matthew was having problems with his shins. Shin splints, as it were. Both of us had been getting them so badly that our trainers had us on 20 potassium pills before each game. But even with the potassium, it was still like playing cement blocks on your feet. After much consideration we decided we'd had enough and quit the team.

It was difficult and emotional but we didn't have a choice. It also, of course, left us with the looming question of what the hell were we going to do with our lives now? We decided to spend the semester abroad.. in Florence, Italy

CHAPTER 8
Ahh FIRENZE
Fall 1996

I remember being quite reluctant to go on this trip. After the difficult decision to quit the sport we'd built our lives around, we were a bit lost. Regardless, there are a handful of moments throughout life that become monumental in either causing massive personal paradigm shifts and/or moments that change you personally in some way, and this was one of them. It was also one of the best decisions we'd ever make.

Yet again, our sister Allison insisted that we study abroad and that we do so in Florence, Italy. She'd done it years earlier while at University of Illinois and like everything else she'd introduced into our life, she knew it was a necessity for us. With the blind faith that accompanied all of Allison's advice, we went for it.

The program we signed up for was via Florida State University, which had a tiny campus in downtown Florence, Italy. There were about 80 students total from all over the world on this particular semesters roll-call and we signed up for a pile of classes set to commence in September.

We flew to London about a month early so we could backpack around for a bit before school started. Truth was, we'd found out that Smashing Pumpkins were slated to headline that year's Reading Festival so we built our entire trip around that.

Now, since we could remember we'd been mail ordering magazine's and import CDs from the UK and each was ripe with festival news, stories, features, pics etc. Our obsession with all things Europe/UK started with soccer of course when we were kids but when we made our foray into music, our souls belonged to England. Everything about the people and culture connected with us on a very visceral level and by the time we got there, it felt like home and paradise at all at once. There were 2 things we wouldn't leave Europe without experiencing. First was attending a Premiership match and 2nd was attending a British Rock Festival.

Reading Festival took place on Aug 25th, 26th and 27th, 1995 and featured the all mighty Pumpkins as well as Hole, Greenday, SoundGarden, Beck and Tricky to name a few. In the states, the closest we had to something like this was Lollapalooza, which was great but perhaps 1/3 of the size of this roster. This was epic and a dream come true. We ordered our tickets months in advance and booked a flight from Chicago to London on the 23rd.

Our sister in crime Paula had recently gone through a series of bitch slappings in the typical forms life tends to fight with. Heart break, career pitfalls etc, so she decided to join us for 3 weeks worth of backpacking around Europe before dropping us off in Florence.

We were all massive music fans and particularly obsessed with the mighty Pumpkins so when the time came we grabbed our book bags and flew to England. As standard protocol dictated, Matthew and I shipped 2 suitcases worth of clothes ahead to our hotel in Italy and stuffed a pair of jeans and some t-shirts in our backpacks. This would turn out to be a significant issue on account of our luggage taking 3 months to get to Florence. At the time however it seemed par for the course and we were quite content wearing the same clothes for 3 months.

We landed at Heathrow, checked into the cheapest hostel we could find and headed out to Berkshire. I could go on for ages about the magic of every moment of that day but instead I'll just mention that seeing the Pumpkins with Matthew and Paula at Reading Festival in England in 1995 was among the greatest experiences of my life. In addition to filling my mind and soul with inspiration, hope and energy, it watered a seed that had been planted in the back of my mind a few years before. I would commit everything I had to writing, recording and performing music for the rest of my life.

From England we took ferries and trains to cities all over Europe and were loving every second of it. In France, we figured the best way to really steep deeply into their rich culture was to piss away a whole day visiting the tragically American, criminally touristy "Euro-Disney". I'm not really sure why we decided to do this. We had no real interest in the American version at the time and travelling 3,000 miles just to experience something we'd already experienced in Florida as kids doesn't make much sense but at the end of the day, I'm glad we did.

The train ride out there was at least a few hours and we sat in the caboose for it. There were a handful of other passengers but they started clearing out within the first hour. The further out we got, the emptier our train became until it was just the 3 of us and 2 Middle Eastern looking folk. This of course was pre 9/11 but it was in fact during a series of train bombings in and around.. of all places.. France. We, however, never thought twice about it. Until of course, the darndest thing happened.

They finally got off and now we were the only passengers left. As the train slowly accelerated away from the station, we heard a strange, moving, thumping noise behind us. It kind of sounded like a flat tire but actually a lot more like translucent canister with wires and duct tape wrapped around it rolling underneath the seats. We couldn't fucking believe it. A bomb. In the past week there had been some serious bombings, a couple of questionable looking dudes just got off and now there was a god damned bomb rolling around our feet. We all jumped up and started running as far away from it as possible. Unfortunately for us the door from our car to the next was closed and locked so we were trapped.

As the train adjusted its speed and wound about it's tracks, this thing was flopping and rolling all over the place. The 3 of us were dancing around like Mexican jumping beans trying to avoid it. I don't know if there's even such a thing as a Mexican jumping bean but it sounds right (at least I capitalized the M?).

The general tone of our trip was hilarious and none of us took anything seriously so as absolutely terrified as we were, it was fucking hysterical.

Having no idea how long it would take to get to the next stop was torture. I managed to get a closer look at the thing when it bowled over my foot. It looked like one of those Pizza Hut salt-shakers. You know the giant, jar like ones with the little metal flap on top? It had silver Duct Tape wrapped around both ends with green and red wires sticking out of one of them.

Each time it started rolling we each shit an onion brisket. In our heads it could go off at any moment but even sooner should it smash into a wall or seat leg. This thing chased us around for a good 45 minutes before the train finally stopped. Piled up against the door, we took off as soon as it cracked open.

Regrettably, we didn't even pause to mention it to anybody. We just hauled ass for a good 20 minutes straight before even thinking about it. Now I realize this makes us among the worst 3 people on the planet but in our defense. we had spent the previous 45 minutes shitting and pissing ourselves. We didn't speak the language and definitely didn't feel like being questioned, detained or even... tortured? Right. Good news is no trains ended up blown to smithereens that day. No thanks to us of course.

Pensione Pendini:

3 incredible week later, we finally made our way over the Pensione Pendini in Florence. It was a beautiful old hotel in the Piazza dela Republica with tiny rooms where we would now live for the next 8 months. After the 3 minutes it took to unpack a pair of jeans from our backpacks, we headed down the street to start classes.

I was one of the kids that despised public speaking. I was absolutely terrified of it. So scared in fact that by the time I got to college, I dropped 6 classes on the first day because the professors requested we go around the room stating your name, where you're from and my favorite .. "a little something about yourself". Honestly, I'd hear a professor start this bit and stand up immediately, sprint to the door and never look back.

Well, my life changing moment came in an Italian Politics class where every one of my worst fears joined forces and delivered a knock out blow.

There were only 4 kids in the class and on the first day we were assigned a 30-minute presentation of which we'd have to the following week.

As a lame strategy to comfort my nerves, I'd write the first handful of words on my hands and arms. Ya know, to get me started. Much like I'd do later in life when I had to perform live on the radio. Songs I'd sung a million times would be written all over my body in case I froze up and lost my place. All stemming from this particular Italian Politics speech.

I got the first sentence off without a hitch. My torturous inner voice quickly alerted my conscious mind to the already obvious fact that I was standing up in front of 4 other kids and a teacher. It was somehow enough to immobilize me. I absolutely froze.

It was an eternity of silence and with each moment that passed, my body would grace me with another visible symptom. First the sweat. Then the shakes. Then the tomato burst face. Eventually my teacher grabbed my arm and said softly "it's ok, just take a breath and gather your thoughts". WTF? You mean you're not going to excuse me? You mean that despite the inner voice pissing itself with laughter and calling me names I can't repeat anywhere while insisting I'll never find my train of thought again, you're going to make me finish?!

Well, by nature of being human I was presented with old fight or flight quandary and the animal in me decided it best if we just run. So I ran. Thus I was plagued with a stage fright I'd second to none. Ironic, as my career path would ultimately be based on my ability to perform on some of the biggest stages in the world, to crowds of 80,000 plus. And that would ultimately riddle me with a ferocious, ever present anxiety.

We finally started to settle in Florence and it became home. We spent most of our week-ends on trains to random European cities. It was quite amazing actually, we'd pick a place and anyone from the school we were taking classes at who felt like joining us for the week-end would. Needless to say we ended up with a bunch of random ass groups of people who hardly knew each other embarking on one adventure after another.

The Poor Man's Fiorentina

About a month in, Matthew and I had become chummy with the concierge at our hotel. So chummy in fact, that I forgot his name. Let's call him .. Salvatore? Anyhow, we'd see him 10 times a day and it didn't take long to find out he shared our passion for soccer. We told him how we played for our college team back home and we're dying to find a group there to kick around with. He was skeptical of course. At the time, Americans were better known for their ignorance of the world's sport and he could safely assume we wouldn't know the first thing about actually playing it. Regardless, he finally invited us to kick around with him and his friends that forthcoming Sunday.

We were thrilled of course. He was stressed. You don't wanna be the douche that brings 2 shitty American kids to an authentic Italian kick-around. Plus, it was starting to sound like his dudes knew how to play. That Sunday we put on the same damned pants and t-shirts we wore to Europe, on account of our bags never arriving, and headed over to a nearby field. Story of our lives. Since I can remember, at least one of us was always missing a sock, lost a jacket, wore sweats to a slacks function etc. Well, here we were again with some corduroys, hoodies and All-Stars, ready to impress our new friends.
There were probably 15 dudes all in and when Salvatore introduced us, he gave a quick disclaimer in Italian, they largely rolled their eyes and scoffed. We were told to wait on the

sidelines where we stood 45 minutes til they finally called us in.

You should already know by now that I think very little of myself but I must say, on this occasion, we whipped some ass. I'll spare us all the play by play but Matthew and were on fire. Teaming up as we've done forever, it didn't take long to amass a handful of goals each and earn some respect. The most rewarding was probably the pride Salvatore took in us. He was impressed to say the least and since he vouched for us to his skeptical friends, he gloated in our performance.

After the session, we all chilled on the grass and chatted briefly. One of the dudes invited us to play with him in another game that Wednesday on a real field under the lights. The whole invite and explanation of said event was confusing on account of the language barrier but the more this dude talked, the more Salvatore's eyes lit up. "Che? Che!?" we asked repeatedly but unfortunately Spanish is not the preferred language in Italy so our inquiries went ignored. When we got back to the hotel he was finally able to explain the situation. The dude that invited us to Wednesday's game was a scout for a 3rd Division Seria "C" pro team and he wanted us to play as a bit of a try-out. We were fucking floored.

By the time we'd gotten to college, the sport had beaten us up pretty good. Playing daily since 5 years old definitely takes its toll but the affect college soccer had on us was weird. We'd both broken some feet, toes, ankles from time to time but at Butler, my puking and Matthew's shin splints were debilitating. I'd thrown up after every game since high school but by sophomore year that crept into halftime.

When we'd played Indiana in that last game, 10,000 people had to wait for me to finish throwing up in the locker room to start the 2nd half.

So when we decided to move to Italy instead of continuing our 3rd year at Butler we'd kind of thought that was the end of soccer. Well here it is again but this time in the form of an unimaginable dream. Since we were kids we'd dreamed of playing professionally in Europe and just when we give it up, we get a shot. Deciding not to over think it, we just enjoyed the good news and prepped for Wednesday.

This time we played a bunch of real footballers under the lights of a small stadium. It was dramatically different this time as these dudes were professional. We managed to hold our own despite getting knocked all over the place and even spit on and shit.

After the game, our concierge and his friend introduced us to some of the coaching staff of a Seria "C" Club. They asked us immediately if we'd consider playing for them. It was difficult to fully comprehend what was happening. Not only was the language barrier riddling communication but the sheer magnitude of what they offering us was simply unbelievable.

The next day they met us at our hotel and we sat down to discuss it. The offer was for 30,000. US dollars/year. With one small catch. Italian governmental policy dictated that we'd have to live there for at least one year to establish residency before applying for work visas. So the club's offer included jobs on an archeological dig in the Chianti region that paid cash under the table. We'd live, train and work there for a year and then sign professional contracts. With the heaviest of hearts, we declined.
Since we'd already mourned the loss of NCAA soccer in our lives, it wasn't too devastating. Add to that the fact that we'd heard the Seria C was brutal and would especially be to a pair of 5"6, 130 pound American twins.

The physical aspect of the game had already taken its toll on both of us but the truth of the matter was that our new passion never really left us a choice. It was hard to admit it to ourselves because we knew the odds of having a successful career in music weren't exactly in our favor. There was also that other tiny little detail.. we hadn't the first clue how to play an instrument.
To justify the decision, we made a deal with each other and ourselves. If we were truly going to turn down the dream we spent 15 years

attaining, we'd better get to work on the new one immediately. We promised ourselves that by the time we moved back home to Chicago, we'd have taught ourselves to play guitar and have a plan of attack. Fortunately there was nobody else there to tell us how unrealistic, unreasonable and/or impossible that would be and so we were on our way.

Buying a guitar in Florence wasn't going to work for several reasons. We couldn't really afford it (except that we could) and we wouldn't be able to fly home with it (except that we could have) so instead we waltzed down to the ole Fiorentine library and rented a perfectly shitty acoustic guitar. There were strings missing but we were nonthewiser. The tuning pegs were all shanked but we didn't know what they were or how to use them anyway. The how-to-play guitar lesson book we also got from the library was in Italian but we didn't really speak it but hey, we'd now officially begun a new career.

AFRICA

After an amazing 6-7 months overseas, our dalliance with Florence was just about over. At this point we'd already had the good fortune to visit almost every major city in Europe. From Barcelona to Prague, Amsterdam to Monte Carlo, Berlin to Interlocken.. and we had loved every second of it.

By the time we got to our final week-end

abroad, we wanted to go somewhere ridiculous. Unfortunately we were on our last dime so options weren't exactly plentiful. Having about $300.00 each , and a pension for stupidity, we headed to the local travel agency and told them, as many probably do, that we wanted to ride camels.

It was just recently that Matthew and I developed a rather bizarre obsession with the ole camelus dromedaries (your standard 2 hump camel, to the laymen). I have no justification, inspiration or explanation for the obsession but I can tell you it was quite real and at this point we were hell bent on riding one or two of em.

The travel agent took it all in with an appreciated compassion and began plugging away at her computer. A few curious moments later she lifted her head, this time with a professional apprehension, and said "well, there are 3 seats left on a flight to Africa for $270. Each?"

We never even asked where in Africa, just handed over the money and took the tickets. Our pal Micheale decided to join us and though he had been on our last nerve for months, we figured his attention to detail and responsible nature would serve our better interests.

On the plane, Micheale wasted no time pulling out his "Let's Go Africa!" tourist guide book. Matthew and I didn't even care to know where the hell we were going, we most certainly weren't interested in reading a book about it. He pouted for a brief moment but eventually put the book down without having read a single word. A decision that I would soon come to regret with every fiber of my being, literally.

A whopping hour and 7 minutes later, we landed in Tunis, Tunisia, Africa. As we collected our bags and shuffled through customs, we were psychologically deafened by the sounds of proverbial jaws dropping. I reckon they hadn't seen much white folk in their day.. And touché, this was unique for us as well. We walked out of the airport without incident and convened for a moment to formulate a plan. In the process, we put our bags down and the instant we did so, a wily African dude ran over, snatched em up and headed for his car. Admittedly, I panicked. slightly.. but sure enough we'd inadvertently strayed into a taxi stand. Shame on me.
Our driver popped the trunk while we shuffled into his backseat and waited. Oddly, we just sat there exchanging WTF looks for several minutes until we realized there was no sign of dude. I peaked my head out the window to find him and another driver rolling around on the street beating the living piss out of one another. I panicked a little more.
In a spirited effort to save the day, I jumped over the seat and began pushing buttons, twisting knobs, pulling levers and/or turning on, off, activating, releasing and/or engaging every function in the effing car until the trunk finally

popped open. When it did, of course, so did the hood, gas tank, hazards blinking, car-alarm blaring, windshield wipers wailing on the windshield etc. It was going off like a god damned pinball machine. We hopped out and headed for our bags. Yet again, before we even reached the trunk, another wily African fella already had em and was now heading to a second car. We followed, got in and were off. Our new guy recognized the awkward nature of what had just happened with a shrug and gave us the old "where to!?" gesture. "The train station please!" I replied with an audacious presumption that everybody in the world should speak English. With Arabic as our only other option, Michaele decided to draw a picture of a train and what do ya know, it worked.

At the train station, a small army of militia looking turbonators (all respect) with M-16s, engaged us in a staring contest. Unable to restrain my smile, I broke first, and thus handing victory to them. Their expressions never did change but they also never pulled us over so we continued on our way to a ticket window. The agent there said something in Swahili (oops, Arabic.. all respect) to which I responded "pick a destination, any destination!". Long story short, we boarded an overnight bus to a small town called Tozuer.

The bus came complete with chickens, tiny little African kids smoking cigarettes and otherwise, people just wrapped up in so much shit they tripped over and/or bumped into anything and everything in their path (all respect). Awesome. 8 hours later, the driver stops the bus, walks back to our seats and with a poke says "Tozuer! Tozeur!". It was 5 am. Without any other options, we stepped out into a sandy abyss. Terrified at what the hell we'd just gotten ourselves into, we noticed a pile of small buildings off in the distance. After watching the bus shrink into the horizon, we made our way toward them. I was convinced the buildings were a mirage. I kept picturing those movie scenes of starved, dehydrated and sunburnt cowboy face-planted into a sand dune with a scorpion heading for his asshole. This town was in fact real and weird as hell- like a ghost town of shanti clay shacks with camels and donkeys meanereding about aimlessly. A cruel blend of heaven and hell for yours truly.

The first building we happened upon turned out to be the town post office. It was a small square hut of sorts, about the size of 4 phone booths. There were shoebox-sized boxes stacked up with hieroglyphs on them and flyers pinned up on the wall. Ok, they weren't hieroglyphs, that was my ignorant sense of humor. They were in fact numbered and each had a stack of envelopes inside. We scanned the room for some sort of information or universal guidance when we finally, saw it. There, on the left wall, amidst a sea of random bills, posters and ads, like a piece de resistance (I don't know what that is) .. a poster of an African holding a leash who's opposite end graced the neck of a giant, golden, camelus cunnilingus. The flood of feelings and emotions at this point, I can only liken to Harry and Kumar finally seeing the White Castle sign. We exchanged some emotional high fives and spent a moment thanking each other for our respective roles in the accomplishment, as if we'd just won some kind of academy award, when an African fella suddenly approached. You know how sometimes suburban dogs bark at black people cuz well they just don't see them that often? Well this dude didn't bark but the look on his face implied that he was just as befuddled as that racially deprived dog. Being the young, moronic, camel-loving idiots that we were, we jumped up and down enthusiastically pointing at the poster of the camel and yelling "Gemelli! Gemelli!". What on Earth made us think Italian would be a better language of choice than say… anything, much less that this would be a sufficient enough greeting for our new friend is beyond me.

I pointed to the poster and took it upon myself to then grab an imaginary leash, board an imaginary camel and gallop across an imaginary desert. Oddly enough, in what is still one of the most baffling seconds of my life, the dude then mounts his very own imaginary camel and starts riding the shit of it like a horse, singing "Jamaal! Jamaal! Qui!!".

Now mind you, none of us understood an ounce

much less a word of each other's native culture or language. However, in this mystical and incomprehensible series of moments and through a mutual passion for a water-hoarding desert loving animal, we managed to set up a date for the following day to ride camels.

See, "Jamaal" is the Arabic term for beauty, based in its root jml, which means camel. "Qui" is the Universally understood French word for "yes". So literally, within a 45 second span, we pieced together some Italian, a bit of French Matthew and I retained from 7th grade French class and set forth what would prove to be one of the most incredible experiences of our lives. He pulled out a pencil and drew a rugged looking clock with the big hand on the 12 and the little hand on the 2 (12:05 bitchess), the following days date and the word "Jamaal". We thanked him profusely and continued our blissfully ignorant walk down the main sandy road through town.

It was lined with small huts that sold everything from hookah pipes to bongo drums to Persian rugs. We stopped in every one of em where the owners would immediately invite us to the back to have tea and talk. It was extraordinary. They had such little, if any, interaction with Westerners and were so gracious, polite and generous. After an endless amount of tea, it was only a few hours later that I would seal myself a dismal fate.

We stopped at a table to sit for a minute and take

in the atmosphere. A woman draped in traditional Muslim garb approached and set down 3 plates of what looked like brown mini-rice and assorted vegetables. We of course didn't realize we'd sat at a restaurant of sorts but we were hungry so we plowed through it in no time, paid our bill and headed off to find a place to stay.

There was a rather bigger building at the end of the road, which turned out to be a hotel. We got a room and things were starting to come together. The following morning we woke up and set about looking for some coffee. Low and behold, right in front of the hotel stood 5 majestic gemelli and 2 beaming proud Africans. No idea how they knew how to find us but in retrospect, it didn't exactly require an inspector gadget type. So nevertheless, we were thrilled and one by one mounted our very own fucking camelus cunnilingus.

The 2 dudes boarded theirs and we followed them back to a village. This was nuts. It was very 3rd world, something we'd only ever seen on TV but the whole village had a charm and sophistication second to none. As if despite the poverty and struggle, they held a key to legitimate happiness that'd been lost on the materialism of the West. The whole village seemed to come out to prep and see us off. Women took turns approaching each camellingus and tying or strapping supplies to them. Mine had a few sticks wrapped in canvas and bags full of vegetables tied to it. The rest were outfitted with camping gear, food and other supplies and in no time we were off.

The kids in the village ran after us as our fleet shuffled out. It was awkward though on account of the fact that camelingi tend to top out at about 3 mph so the pack of kids ran circles around us for about 20 minutes. You can only giggle and wave so many times before you feel like a jackass. Finally, we approached the Sahara. I'm pretty sure we were in it the whole time but now we were in the actual vast expanse of about ten million square feet of imminent death. Where there is literally nothing but sand as far as the eye can see.

As sure as I was that these Africans likely played out in this desert as kids, I couldn't for the life of me understand how on Earth they tended to navigate this abyss. There were no signs, landmarks, no compasses or anything. But alas, we rode. For about 9 hours, we rode those fuckers into the middle of nowhere.

My camel was grouchy. He grunted and bitched and spit on me relentlessly. See, they collect saliva in the corners of their mouths and when it builds up enough they habitually thrust their heads to the side, showering their backs. If you're riding it, the spit ends up spattering across your face in some sort of kinky zoophilic manor. Fortunately, I was able to compose my boner. Eventually they signaled us, asking if it was a sufficient enough spot to stop and set camp. I took one last hard look at the sand and determined there were no Holidomes to hold out for and agreed.

When debarking a camelitus, its rider must first coax it to its knees. A nudge a command and a grunt later, it does so and you casually step off. Unless of course you're like me and just rode it for the first time, for 9 hours and can't move your legs. I felt like I just got ass probed by a horny rhinocauerous. Accordingly, I debarked like a stuck tripod and tipped over. Stretching it out and walking it off, we were ready to set camp.

The 4 sticks and canvas were to be a tent but since it didn't exactly come with instructions, we didn't know how to set it up. The language barrier prevented us from asking clearly how we could help but eventually one of the Africans got it. He reached down under my camels ass and picked up a piece of his shit. I was intrigued… and perhaps a little smitten. The guy loves shit, just like me. He then pointed to a small hole in the sand he'd just dug and the assignment became clear. We were tasked with collecting cameltoe shit. I was convinced they were fucking around with us but I didn't hesitate to show them just how far this little American was willing to go with shit. I collected mountains of it.. piles of it.. wet shit, dry shit, lumpy shit, green shit and dark spotted shit.

Eager to get to the bottom of the prank and impress/disgust my bosses with my pension for the stuff, I pointed to my pile. The African beamed with pride and began scooping it into the hole and eventually lit in on fire. The methane in camelitus shit is a perfect slow burning fuel and just like that, our campfire was blazing.. We continued to unpack and set up the tent which was surprisingly efficient. Granted it had about enough room for 2 medium sized dogs, it was solid shelter. This would only get awkward later when 5 of us perfect strangers would ultimately spoon one another to sleep. But alas, for now our tent was up, food was prepped and we were ready to go… absolutely nowhere.

See, when the journey's over and the works done and you find yourself sitting around a campfire with your twin, a friend and 2 complete strangers who don't so much as share a language .. shit can get awkward. It's no secret, I love awkwardness but this one was pushing the envelope. For as amazing as these Africans were, at this point they just seemed to mock our every word. To their credit, they're much more comfy in silence than us dumbass gringos.. So when I couldn't take it anymore I came up with this brain busting gem of a question.. "so, you guys from around here?". "soo yoo geys frum rrrround heer?" they mocked and giggled. I deserved that. Let's ponder for that fucking question for a moment shall we? We're 9 camelitus hrs into a desert of nothingness. Not to mention, I already know where they're from for

127

fuck's sake, we came from there. And finally, nobody is from around here! If they were, they'd be baby bones by now.

I punished myself for the stupidity until one of them finally got up and disappeared into the tent for a minute. He returned with some beers and not one but 2 sets of bongo drums. Yes.. Just what this party needed. And with that, the awesomeness was born.

The Africans delighted us with a song and dance for the ages. We clapped along like 3 challenged folk with a "when in Rome" mentality, while making silent pacts to never discuss this with anyone. And with that, they grabbed Matthew.

I don't blame Matthew for his dancing that night. What was he to do? If a tree falls out in the desert..? He had no choice and true to his character he fucking went for it. He jumped, shook his ass and limbs as if joyously exercising invisible demons. As if it were some necessary ritual or rite of passage, he danced his face off. Above a fire and under a desert moon, something changed in Matthew that night. Unfortunately, something was changing in myself as well.

A few hours later we all crammed into the teepee and spooned. 5 dudes. Cold desert. Perfect strangers. Cuddling. Together. All for one?

I didn't sleep well. I can't really describe what was happening to my intestines but it was definitely an issue of immediate concern. I sprang from the warm embrace of the Africans, grabbed a roll of toilet paper I'd brought from Florence and ventured out into the desert. I was already squirting little bits of shit into my pants but I didn't wanna stop til I could barely see the campfire. It was a mere spec on the horizon by the time I pulled my pants off and let err rip. Dudes and ladies..

Apologies for this but in order to understand the sheer magnitude of the affect of eating or drinking shit in Africa that your body isn't accustomed to, you need to hear this. Shit was squirting out of my asshole as if somebody had put a thumb over a garden hose nozzle that was already raging with water. It flew everywhere and anywhere with no rhyme or reason and with the torque of a thousand horses. My stomach wretched and twisted for the next 20 minutes or so. With my pants out off and out of the blast zone, I was slightly bent and blowing up like the god damned Old Faithful.

When I thought I'd finished, I cleaned myself up, buried the toilet paper and headed back to nestle my disgusting ass in between the Africans.. I'd repeat this process 4-5 times more though out the night. I thought I was dying. The prospect of being 9 hrs on camel from any sort of help much less civilization was daunting.

The next morning I woke up to shitty toilet paper strewn about our campsite like garland on a Christmas tree.. The Africans were picking it up, surely wondering which of our sick asses did it, only until they realized I was keeled over in the tent, in tears.

The ride home was unbearable but we made it. We made it all the way back to the village, the bus stop, Tunis and finally boarded our plane. Our seats were next to each other and only then did we decide to open up the god damned "Let's Go Africa!" book. The first page read "WARNING: A Matter of Life and Death!! no matter where you go or what you do, for the life of you do not… if you do you will shit and piss yourself until you die!" or something… and proceeded to essentially list our itinerary. We drank the tea which had tannin levels toxic to Westerners. We ate the food which had microbial strong enough to take down a foreign horse. We drank the water, touched the shit and otherwise ingested, indulged and/or engaged in every forbidden activity listed. Glad I had the wherewithal to not dodge that bullet. Judge me.. I am.

After nearly 9 months worth extraordinary learning and experience, we were headed back to Chicago. There was however, one more magical moment before the trip was through. Being a firm believer in the Universe's energy and omniscnence.. I believe it guides us in the strangest of ways and one of those ways is via "signposts". Signposts are just tiny little serindipotous happenings or events or coincidences that steer, reassure, direct or otherwise show you that you're on the right path.

When we landed at Ohare, it was like 3am and the airport was empty. We went through customs and waited for our bags by the conveyor belt. One by one every suitcase on the planet came and went and soon we were the only 2 left aside from one group of about 4 a few claims down. Upon further investigation it turns out those 4 people we're Billy, James, Jimmy and Darcy of the mighty Smashing Pumpkins. It was insane.
We'd planned that entire trip around seeing them at Reading Festival. Mellon Collie and the infinite Sadness wound up being the soundtrack to the whole thing. I can't express to you how incredibly huge of a deal they were in our lives. We managed to keep our cool and said hello. They were so awesomel I can't even tell you..   and though we only learned a few chords in Italy, we were firmly convinced that music was our calling.

CHAPTER 9
Back to the Doldrums
1996 Indianapolis

When Matthew and I got home from Italy we were dead set on pursuing a musical career. As most kids we were entirely lost when the real world began to rear it's Wizard of Oz ish head. My anxiety at this point was unconsoleable and despite my many efforts to numb it out, or at least shut off the voices, they were efforts in futility.

Amid the flury of noise in my head, the general themes remained consistent. They encouraged me to panic, they relentlessly berated, antagonized, doubted and downright verbally assault me *(and probably even sexually assaulted me.. can one accuse oneself of sexual harassment? Ya know cuz I'm a schizophrenic and so am I? Artsy thought.. where was I? oh yeah, another run on sentence with a lot of comas..)* about everything from personality, character, and stature to thoughts, actions to decisions. I guarantee you, despite any accomplishment, skill, logistical argument or negotiation with myself, I could never win. Oddly though music was one thing that those voices could not compete with. Once I became aware of the fact that I was going to pursue writing and performing music no matter what, I never heard a word about it. The lesson I gleaned was that when a passion is so strong that living without it simply isn't an option, you've found yourself.   And when you find it, grab that fucker and hold on for dear life.

Since we still had college to deal with, we decided we were going to hide out and finish up at Butler while continuing to learn how to play. So we rented an absolute shit-hole of an apartment on the near West side of Indianapolis. We brought 2 mattresses, some clothes, a guitar and a bass and decided to hide out and barrel through. Despite our best efforts at reclusion, however, we'd be back on the radar in a few short weeks.

This apartment complex was fucking hilarious. Our unit was on the 2nd floor and whenever we'd stand out on the balcony to grill or whatever, these little hood kids would shoot bottle rockets, roman candles and/or anything else they could find at us.   We'd laugh along and pretend they were just being friendly, playing with us etc. "ohhh you crazy little bastards! woah, that was close! You know you kids should probably be more careful.." type of shit. Zing! zriang! rockets whizzing by our heads and the occasional 8 year old voice, "fuck you whitey!".

Then at night we'd watch the gangbangers dismantle a random parked car. They'd pick it clean, tires, battery, rims, whatever the fuck. By the time they left there wasn't even a steering wheel left. Inevitably the old white trash racists would come running out with a broom or some shit and try to chase the gangbangers away. It was like a Sanford & Son in a bad "Cops" episode. Needles to say, we were effectively off the grid, though we still had to attend classes.

That Shit was Wack Yo (car jacked)

I suppose most would consider this lovely experience traumatic or at least worthy of leaving a long enough lasting subconscious affect to keep a therapist in business for years. Perhaps they're right but I've never wasted much time on it. Matter of fact, if anything, it's served as quite an entertaining go-to during awkward social moments or when in need of a good laugh. The "bad guys", as it were, and whom you'll meet soon, we're so god damned stupid that the severity of what they did to me is was lost on their ultimate self-incrimination. But alas, let's just get to it: Matthew's and my ghetto fabulous apartment was about a mile off campus and since we were on the proverbial wagon as far as exercise was concerned, we'd drive to class. On October 14th (made that date up out of thin air), I pulled in to the school's library parking lot around 11:59 and seeing as I was early for my 12:00pm class (I just had to ask my wife if noon was 12am or pm), I decided to sit and listen to Sublime's 40 Ounces to Freedom for a bit before I went in.

My window was about 2/3 of the way down and the day was pretty much perfect. I should mention that the night before, we'd decided to go skiing that forthcoming week-end so Matthew and I and 4 dudes from the soccer team went to some giant sports store and bought a shitload of ski gear, all of which was of course still in bags in the back of car, and on top of 4 years worth of garbage and crap. As usual we had zero gas in the tank as well but alas, none of it mattered cuz I was chillin listening to Sublime before class and leaving for a ski trip after.

I remember seeing 2 of them in my side door mirror as they approached. In my 21 years of life, I'd been in enough situations to know that crazy shit can happen on a moment's notice. However, that 6th sense hadn't fully developed yet, which is why when they stopped at my window, I thought nothing of it.

They were two .. earmuffs everybody.. black dudes, who certainly looked and dressed like they meant business. Well, not business per se.. That phrase implies that each party gets something out of the deal. They didn't mean business at all; they meant to (*SPOILER ALERT!*) steal my fucking car. Terrific. (*note; the controversial use of the term "black dudes", has nothing to do with racial predispositions or stereotyping whatsoever and instead was used as a pertinent descriptive for it's eventual relevance to said story.. I think.. I hope.. I'm not racist. I have a black friend.

Anywho.. The first dude says "say maannn, can you tell me what time it is?".. Without hesitation, alarm, or even a moments consideration I said "sure dude, it's 12:0....2." But by the time the "2" came out of my mouth, there was a glock 9mm jammed into my neck.

They say that time seems to slow down in moments like these as the brain ponders it's fight or flight options. Considering there was nowhere to "fly" and despite being a Steven Segal fanboy, my Shito-Ryu (that's "karate" to the laymen) skills were questionable at best, the "fight" option quickly evaporated as well.

I can only surmise that I'd seen enough movies and/or TV to think that my best play was to put my hands up in the air.. in a "don't shoot!" gesture. I may have even said "don't shoot" which would've been wonderful to have on film. I felt uncool about that move pretty much right away. In fact, I often ponder it; usually counting the countless amount of cooler things I could have done/said.

Since it was 1996, my fantasy replays of course consisted of my fav Segal moves where I'd chop the gun out of the dude's hands and put him to sleep in one motion. Or Goonies his ass by grabbing hold of his hand and driving away, dragging him next to my door. But alas, in reality I did neither of those things and instead squirt a little piss into my pants.

With my hands "frozen" up in the air, he then said "Now get the fuck out of the car!".

I've often wondered about my next move as well.. I grabbed the keys and turned the car off. To be honest I legitimately thought maybe they wanted me to get out of the car so they could mug me or something equally as retarded and unlikely. Well, turned out to be the wrong thing to do. This enraged him.

Either he was so fucking stupid that he didn't know how to start a stick shift or I was so stupid that I didn't realize he was car-jacking me (more likely, both. Actually, I'm surprised the 3 of us even managed to affect a successful car jacking) but either way he delivered a swift and gnarly pistol-whipping to my neck.

As completely normal and reasonable as this whole situation was at this point, my next move still baffles me. I apologized. After all, how dare I further inconvenience him by forcing him to have to endure the arduous task of re-starting the car. I'm thinking, damn I should be handling all of this way cooler than I am.

His accomplice opened the door and they pulled me out, shoved me into the car parked next to mine, jumped in mine and took off. I watched through the window his as his knees flailed up and down in search of the clutch. When he finally managed to start it up again, he revved the engine into oblivion, trying to back out but finally did so and squealed away. Since I have an odd co-dependency to material possessions, this pained me greatly. It was like watching someone rape the car you love. We've all been there..

As it screeched out of the library parking lot, 2 more dumb motherfuckers came running from the adjacent bus stop like they just won the lottery and hopped into the back. For my part, I ran to the public safety office just across the "quad" (college). I suppose people could sense something happened to me.. I mean it's not like I was gonna wait in line to file my "complaint" and since it had just happened there was a small chance that any cops in the area could spot em before they breached some sort of perimeter? So I step to the front and say "2 , I mean 4 bla.. I mean dudes.. stole my car!" ....here's the kicker... "right out from under me!". Right out from under me?.. cheeky, classy, literal yet figurative, witty yet nerdy, true yet no so much. Moving on .. Eventually I did say "black" dudes cuz I felt it was relevant and pertinent to the possibility of identifying them (told ya). The Public Safety dudes sprang into action and took off running toward the library. I was impressed to say the least and immediately regretted blowing off a quarter stick of dynamite under one of their campus cars freshmen year. As 2 of them ran to the scene of the crime, another called the Indianapolis Police and a 4th sat me down to get my story. They were compassionate, attentive and extremely helpful, high fives bros.

So I waited around til the Po-Po came and took me over to my friend Neidermeyer's house. He was the only one home and the cops didn't think I should be alone, which I thought was downright adorable of him. I mean I wasn't upset or anything as far as I can remember. If I cried at all it was only for attention but I really don't think I did. Sure buddy.. I didn't really squirt that little bit of piss into my pants neither. About 2 hours later I got a call from the Po-Po. They'd found a car fitting mine's description and wanted to take me to identify it. They picked me up in a squad car and we swung by college to pick up Matthew and my friend Mills on the way, which I thought was cool of them Po-Pos. Then they drive us to the local shopping mall where sure as shit was my car, 3 other squad cars, 2 news teams and 4 bla.. I mean dudes, were standing in front my car with their arms cuffed behind them.

They each graced me with death stares as I sat shotgun in the approaching squad car. The cop driving asks me to point each one out and identify their respective roles. "this is a one-way glass windshield right? surely they can't see me?" I mused. He assured me not to worry and I proceeded to point all four of them out right in front of them.

When I pointed to the first one, he gave me that don't-tell-on-me-faggot-ass-or-I-will-kill-your-whole-family-while-they-sleep look (we all know that look). When I pointed out the 2nd one, he looked at me and said "bullshit, I didn't jack yo ass!". Seeing as I hadn't yet "said" that he jacked me, and further considering that he did, I felt comfortable that THAT little quote was going to be used against him in the court of law.

Moving down the line to our 3rd and 4th "suspects", one looked like he was proud of his first arrest and the other one looked like .. well, he bore resemblance to.. Michael Jackson.. what? He did.

The other cops put them in the back of a 2nd squad car and escorted me to my car to identify the weapons. There were 4 total, 1 under each front seat and 2 in the back. In front, 2 glock 9mm's, in the back an S&W .45, and a Browning 9mm. They were fucking huge guns and that's when I realized it was kind of a big deal. Otherwise, my car was covered in a thick black powder which I'd later learn was finger print dust. The whole car was covered in it and though I'm grateful for their due diligence, that shit wasn't coming off for years to come. Let's take a quick second to bounce into the genius of these perps for a moment. The 4 nit-wits (wha?) who took my car had one hell of a day. After dropping me off in the library parking lot, they took my car to a gas station where they emptied it, cleaned it and filled up the gas tank (much obliged). Then they drove to the local shopping mall where they decided to mug a lady on the way in. That's right folks, on the way in.

Apparently it failed to cross their minds that she might call the Po-Po, describe them and when they ask which way the perps went, point to the fucking mall that she watched them walk straight into. It also never occurred to them that she watched em get out of MY car which at this point they seemingly forgot they fucking stole.

Back in the Po-Po car, it couldn't have been 30 seconds later that a local NBC News camera blasted its way through my window and positioned itself 2 inches from my face. A business dressed 30 something reporter followed it with a microphone, as she blurted out "can you state your name, age and where you're from?!". WTF? Why? No, of course not. Except that it came out of my mouth more like.. "Sure! I'm Nat.."

Fortunately, before I could finish saying "Nathan", Matthew slapped me on the back of the head and Mills drilled his knee into the back of my seat. It took me a second but I eventually realized they were discouraging me from giving my real name in case these thugs had some vengeance seeking gangsta friends watching the news (which I'd file under the ole not bloody likely column, but stranger things have happened.. probably).

"James Hetfield?" I sheepishly blurted out and we proceeded with the interview. "How did it feel to get hit with a gun and have your car stolen?" "well Diane, it was awesome. Just fantastic. I tell ya, you ain't livin til you been pistol whipped and jacked" blah blah.

The next morning my friends were hell bent on taking me skiing, as planned, to get my mind off the trauma that never really took. As our BFF/room-mate Chester NeiderMeyer loaded up the car with his families stash of 70's ski gear to replace the stolen shit we'd just bought, I got a phone call.

It was my friend Lacy who was half asleep. She rambled on about how in the middle of the night she had the craziest dream and it felt so real she couldn't get over it. "You were on the news and you'd just been car-jacked! But it wasn't really you, I think you were the singer of Metallica". You wish.

6 months later...

I must have been sitting in my hot tub (dad's hot tub) or riding one of my go-carts (dad's go-carts) or lounging around in some other lap of luxury when I finally got the call from the po-po in

Indianapolis. Aside from milking the story whenever I had the chance, I'd all but forgotten that I was car jacked but sure enough, the cops called and informed me that I was to attend the perp's trial to testify. Remember, I can't publicly speak to save my life. I vomit, my voice cracks, I sweat, forget what I'm saying, shit myself and am prone to a myriad of other similar symptoms... at the mere notion of it. So now I have to go to court and sit in that little box next to a judge and not only face my assailant but also field a variety of questions from both the State's attorney and his defense attorney. Awesome.

I drive to Indianapolis, pick up Matthew and head downtown to the courthouse. They escort me to some chambers "back stage" and make Matthew sit in the audience. He was the only one there which would later come back to bite me in the ass.

Back in my lil chambers there was a cop (for security I suppose?) and a lady. The lady was a wreck and I felt bad so I struck up a little conversation. In my ultimate adoration for small talk and my complete lack of ability to conduct it, I say .. "So... what brings ya in today?".

I suppose I could have put 2 and 2 together but every time I do, I get 3 or 5 so I decided not to think about this one. Which is why it came as a bit of a shock and no surprise at all when she replied "umm, this guy mugged me on the way into a shopping mall".

I reacted as if our 2 completely different worlds just serindipediously collided by some magical ambition of the Universe. "No shit!? How weird, I'm the guy who's car they stole and drove to your mugging! ... you're welcome.. I mean..I'm sorry.. I mean, hi I'm Nate.". Eh, weird start. Anywho, we exchanged a few more pleasantries.. or unpleasantries as it were when a bailiff walks in.

"Nathan Leon?" "That's LeonE to you Bull, I mean sir".. I wish. Instead, "yes sir, what can I do ya for?" "you're up for testimony, follow me". I swallowed a little barf.

I walked out into the courtroom and sat at the little chair in my box. My face was already bright red as I adjusted the mic with a "check 1-2, check", gave a lil how-do-you-do to the judge and scanned the room. I see Matthew first, who's making this face at me that we've made since I can remember. It's kind of hilarious so here I go already. I pan across to see the State's prosecutor who's serving as my lawyer, shoot a quick high five with my eyes and continue to pan. Then I see the assailant's attorney who looks like he hates his job and life and finally, the cou de gras.. the main event.. the star of today's show.. the effing main nitwit who jacked me.

He's locked up in hand cuffs but somehow wearing this extraordinary Hawaiian styled, short sleeved button up shirt. Despite his death stare, I loved him already.

My attorney begins the proceedings by walking me through a handful of the easiest questions I've ever had to answer. He asks me to recount the events of that day which I do. I'm smooth. I'm on point, no umms, no ehhhs, etc. just rapid fire killin it. "then he asks me what time it is, then he told me to get the f*&k out of the car, then he hit me in the neck with his gun, then he pulled me out and kind of shoved me down..." blah blah.

Then he has the bailiff bring a packet of pictures up to the bench. There were 4 in all and each one was a different kind of gigantic gun that they'd found in my car upon recovery.   He has me identify the ones used against me and I do.. Then asks me if the guy who car jacked me is in the room.

Takin aback by the sudden game of Marco Polo, I manage to say "Yes, sir, he is and right now you're a little cold.. just kidding". "Order! Order!" says the judge as Matthew cheers from the crowd of 1.

   "Can you describe this man?". Now remember, there's the jury on my left, Matthew- the only one in the audience in front of me and the assailant and his lawyer; being the only other ones in there, on my right.   Right when he asked me to describe the dude who was so obviously the dude that it already started to get funny, I looked at Matthew. The face he was making destroyed me and I burst out into a weird muffled laughter. "Order! Order!" .. it was great, just like TV.. "ok, ok sorry your honor". "yes sir, well .. he's that guy over there..". "Can you be more specific?". "I can try? he's wearing a Hawaiin shirt and umm he's got hand-cuffs on and hmm let's see.. short black hair with fluffy, tight little curls..." "Objection your honor! he's leading the witness!" "I am?" "No, not you, your attorney". "Oh, shame on him.. leading me where?" "Over-ruled!, council?" "Yes your honor?" "not you, you're a witness".. "you wish. I mean, you bet" "Order! Order!" . Things get back on track and finally there are no further questions.

The defense attorney stands up for cross examination. This guy knows he has no case. He knows that his job is so shitty that he has to actually try to find some way to defend this nit-wit and he's got nothin. Nevertheless, he sucks it up and decides to grill me. He adopted a bit of an archetypal persona and attitude, convinced he can get me to eff up.

His questions were obvious and absurd and after each answer he'd go.. "hmm, really.. so you're saying.." and then repeat what I'd just said. "Yes sir, that's what I'm saying which is kind of why I said it".

His line of questioning eventually gets to my account of the events just as I was pulled out of the car. I repeat my story yet again.. "and then he shoved me .. blah blah". "He shoved you?" his attorney repeats curiously. "Did he shove you into the ground? into another car? what?" he demands. "The ground" I comply. "Did your knee hit the ground?" "I can't remember to be honest, why does that even.." "Answer the question! Yes or no! Did YOUR knee hit the ground!?" .. I paused for a moment and said.. "ok sir. I'm going to go with "yes", my knee hit the ground".. and that's when it happened. Our nit-wit ass, car jacking, hawaiin shirt wearing fabulous dipshit stands up and yells.. "That's bullshit man yo knee never hit the ground!". "Order! Order!".. just like the movies. Our audience of Matthew, was in stitches. The jury had their collective jaws dropped and the defense attorney could only put his head in his hands. Our criminal nit took a minute to realize what he'd just done to himself.

Needless to say, our formidable defendant had just confessed to everything. I on the other hand, squirt just a little more piss into my now judicial panties.

CHAPTER 10
El Diablo Nella Citta Blanca
1998 CHICAGO

Columbia College
Matthew and I both agreed to transfer to
Columbia College in Chicago to finish up school
and get to work on our future. When he got
back from Indianapolis, we rented a penthouse
apartment on the top two floors of a 22 story
high rise in Chicago's South Loop and registered
for class.

Our high school friends Bart and Bateman (aka
Neidermeyer) lived with us as well as a girl
Bateman met at a coffee shop the day before
signed the lease. She was a model, student,
racist (though she was white, she also hated
white folk) and bulemic. This scenario
provided for some wonderful times.

Bad Trip
*(on a plane to los angeles to shoot a video for
"Never Take Us Alive")*
Here's another one of our "dares" that ended up
quite extraordinary. The penthouse was above
and beyond any of our means but on account of
stuffing 5 people in a 3 bedroom, it became
quite affordable and perfect.

We'd acquired the foosball table Matthew & I
grew up with and playing became a nightly
tradition. We'd usually play 2 on 2 and bet on

the games but when cash was scarce, the ante changed from money to our standard default, "dares".

The real pride in these dares was the creative aspect of the gamble. Like I said, we'd come up with something that so delicately rode the fence of being horrific to have to do, yet rewarding enough to get to watch your friend do, that it was it was worth the risk.

On this particular night we decided that the losing team would have to strip down to the buck nudes, ride the elevator from our top floor to the lobby, make their way into the mail room and steal some form of confirmable proof that they'd gotten there and then head back up. Now it seems relatively harmless enough. Problem was, it was about 8pm on a Friday night, which in our building was high traffic hour. The losing team was pretty much guaranteed to cross paths with a cultural cornucopia of strangers at some point during the sojourn.

I was teamed up with "Bart" whom, for all intents and purposes, was a jockey frat boy type who's only compensation for his insecurities was to be the loudest most obnoxious dude in the room, at all times. The nude aspect of this dare, coupled with the mandatory male partner, was a shot through the heart of this alpha male. It would be no walk in the park for any of us but we all knew if he/we lost, he was sure to be a loose cannon.

Bart's a funny dude. He was the all-star football jock in high school until literally one day his dad punched his mom, took off, they lost their house and he found drugs. That's when we befriended him.

His plummet from the All American, suburban, white picket fence perch, left him with a huge disdain for "society" and a pension for making a jack ass of himself. This was the perfect opportunity to do just that, except for one thing; he's a total and complete homophobe.

The game was one for the history books. With several over-times, in accordance of the ole win by 2 law, it went on for over an hour. Stakes being what they were, none of us were going down easy. Matthew and Bateman had us on the ropes and when Matthew scored the fateful last goal, Bart blew a gasket. .

He was convinced that if anyone saw us on the elevator together nude, that the whole building would think we're "homos". Now trust me, I had no desire to sit in an elevator with that kid either but a dare's a dare.

His engine heated up right away. While he protested with every fiber of his being, I striped down to my birthday's finest and insisted we get this over with. "Faggots" rifled out of his mouth in the dozens per second, even though he was equal parts in creating the dare. Matthew and Bateman of course were loving every second of it.

They decided to position themselves in the mail room for their viewing pleasure. While they headed down, Bart finally stripped to the nudes. I peaked out our door and made sure the hallway was clear before scampering out and hitting the "down" button. In what seemed like an eternity, the elevator finally came. We each had one hand holding our dick-n-balls and the other cupping our respective assholes and boarded the elevator. I hit "Lobby", the door closed with indifferent finality and we were off.

I remember watching the numbers drop as we went from 21 to 20 to 19 and so forth. The building was so huge that rarely would we make it all the way down without picking up at least 2-3 additional passengers on route so when it slammed to a halt on the 13th floor, we braced to accept our fate.

Bart, in all his homo-phobia jumped directly behind me for cover, painting a grim picture. As the courtesy ding rang and echoed for ages, the doors slowly opened.

Just a few days earlier, we'd met this kid Brandon who lived in our building as well. He was a super hip, rave going college loving acid trip and Bart was smitten. His ambition to meet new people and dive into the spoils of college life made him a fan of Brandon right away. We'd hit it off with him and agreed that we should all hang out sometime in the not so distant future.

I've seen a lot of faces and even more expressions but never in my life have I seen 4 eyes so completely and utterly shocked in my life. When the doors opened, Brandon was standing on the other side with a gorgeous girl on his arm. They took one look at us and we could see their hearts leap from their chests. Bart got hysterical as words of defense and justification pissed from his mouth like shit through a sewer pipe. "We're not faggots! umm sorry dude, it's not what it looks like. It's complicated! I mean I'm sorry" etc. I, on the other hand, just pounded every button on the control panel until the doors finally shut again and off we went, again.

The elevator eventually stopped again on the 9th floor and we jumped out and sprinted for the stairs. I've never raced up stairs this fast in my life. While the 9th floor became the 10th and the 14th became the 15th, I'd begun to develop an adrenaline fused dizziness. Coupled with the exhaustion of a full throttle sprint up stairs, I ran out of gas.

Bart wasn't fairing any better and by the 18th floor we'd slowed to a crawl. Lacking even the strength to continue to cover our balls and assholes, there we were; 2 embattled pals, stripped of all dignity, pride and clothing to boot, inching our way step by step up the infinite and arduous climb. Then the 20th floor stairway door opens.

A couple dressed in full work out gear bounces into the stairwell, already jogging in place (as work out folks tend to do at red lights or other various cardio-impeding junctures). These go-etters were decked out in the latest sportswear, wrist-walkmen, running shoes etc. and of course, they froze in their tracks. Like deer in headlights, they stood motionless and silent as we turtled our way passed them without so much as an "excuse me".

When we got about half way up that flight the dude finally says "umm, you guys can't do that!". *Often I ponder his words of wisdom. We can't do what? Climb stairs? Be nude? Climb stairs in the nude? Neither.*

Turns out this effin dude is not only a homo-phobe but a Jesus loving God fearing homo phobe at that. We "can't" conduct male on male stair banging in a public stairwell. Ok buddy, you stop working out in the stairs and Bart and I will stop climbing em in the nudes. You wish.

The real clincher to this one, however, didn't come until the next day. We bumped into our new would-be pal Brandon, who was still scarred from the incident. He proceeded to explain that just a few hours prior to our encounter, he and his new girlfriend dropped a few hits of acid, each. Couped up in his cozy studio apartment, Brandon's girlfriend suffered an acid induced panic attack of the claustrophobic nature.

Despite his best efforts to calm her down, she only grew more hysterical by the second. When he finally agreed to take her outside for some air, they put on their coats, walked down the hall and called the elevator. He cradled and comforted her as the bad acid trip poured tears down her face. He promised her that everything was ok and in mere moments, they'd be downstairs and outside in the vast fresh open air. Then, the elevator came.

With a ding of the bell announcing it's arrival, the indifferent elevator doors began their clunky expanse, inevitably revealing its nefarious secret. I can only imagine what the acid did to her when Bart's and my dick n balls unceremoniously and unexpectedly danced in her face. Don't judge me, judge her?

1997, 1998

Now that we had our footing in Chicago, we only had one thing left to do. Start a band. Minor set back being of course that we could hardly play and didn't even know anybody that did. After much debate, we decided to track down a dude we'd met in 7th grade named Michael Foderaro.

10 years earlier, Michael and a pile of his friends played Metallica's "One" in the school talent show and absolutely killed it.

He was like a fucking prodigy and despite the fact that his band was a disaster, Michael was amazing. So we picked up the phone and made that awkward, totally out of the blue call.

"Hey dude... umm... I don't know if you remember us but my twin brother and I saw you play Metallica in the 7th grade talent show and well, we've recently decided to become musicians ourselves and... um we want to start a band.... And... can we come over?"

Now, we'd been the " rich kid jocks" in High School and Michael ran with the "burnouts" so, needless to say, him playing with us pretty much ran against every social scene principle there was. We knew it would be a long shot, presuming Michael would barf a lil in his mouth and swiftly hang up. However, the Universe would intervene in rare fashion.,

Turns out, not too long before, Michael had actually gotten into his car, chased down his sisters boyfriend and promptly ran him over. In short, he was under house arrest. Bored out of his mind, with nothing left to do and ever less left to lose, he begrudgingly agreed to let us come over..

Since denile is just a river in Egypt, we promptly ignored the red flags and drove an hour out to the suburbs and officially jammed in his mom's basement. At this point, we could hardly even hold our instruments much less play them but we insisted on driving out there 4 nights a week a harassing him til he agreed to be in our band..

that didn't exist.. About 2 months later, he did and we officially had our first band.

Finally. Well... ish. No drummer, no singer, no band name. So we began the hunt. Michael kept mentioning a dude from one of his old bands named Jim Knight. "He's the best fucking drummer in Palatine and we've gotta get him!".

Of course James (hereinafter "Trix") already had a band or 2 or 4 and he was engaged to whiskey so any sort of commitment was off the table. Plus, on account of Michael's band mates being the Leone twins, he wouldn't even come over to jam for fun. So what did our house arrested, super anal, OCD, misanthrope guitar prodigy do? Stalked the living shit out of him. He literally got in his car and followed the dude to his house, work, the bar, his friends house, the mall .. where ever and just parked. He stalked him like a Dateline pedophile.. well minus the cyber flirting with a 12 year old, creepy wiener pic exchange, some flowers, pizza and a 6-pack.

As persistence tends to do, it finally worked. Trix finally agreed to come over and "jam" with us.. once. When Michael called to tell us the good news we were fucking elated. We knew that all we needed was 5 minutes with this guy and it wouldn't matter that we couldn't hold our instruments.. We would turn the flirt on, charm his pants right off and

have his signature on the dotted line the
following day.

When he came over, the 3 of us were admittedly
nervous. Especially Michael who knew he was
selling this kid a shoddy bomb casing full of
used pinball machine parts. We were all
banking on Michael's talent and reputation
combined with our knack for social "fines" and
salesmanship which in the end was a long shot at
best. Since he was such a stunning drummer
and a rare, white-hot commodity, this was surely
our only chance.

He was cool as shit right out of the gates and
when he started to play, I knew we had to have
him.

We played Soundgarden's "Spoonman" which
was one of the 4 songs Matthew and I half
"learned". Prior to Trix's arrival we'd set up
Matthew's bass amp and my guitar amp to face
away from the drums and turned the volume
down on both. Then we set Michael's to blast
directly at Trixs' face to showcase him and mask
our inability. Halfway through the song
Matthew's bass simply dropped from his
shoulders and smashed to the ground with a
muffled thud from the amp.

Instinctively I ran toward it to half cover/half
help him pick it up but instead I kicked a
microphone stand over, tripped in the process
and lit up like a bolt of lighting when my ghetto
ass amp shorted out. Despite the comedy of
errors on our end, Michael was a fucking

machine and his impeccable performance that day sealed the deal.

Wow, we have a real drummer. An insane drummer and an insane guitarist, how in the hell did we do that? We were out of our league. But that's where we've spent our entire lives so rolled with it. Now all we needed was a singer. Singers are all but impossible to find. Nowadays anybody and everybody is a singer on account of technology, auto-correction etc. but a real rock singer who can front a band, fits your genre/style, will commit, is tolerable and/or cohesive enough personality-wise, artistically malleable and has relatively little baggage? Shit.. there isn't one. But alas, we begin the hunt anyway.

Michael managed to find a few to try out. First was an Eddie Vedder/Kurt Cobain looking dude with long blonde hair and ripped jeans who showed up clutching his girlfriend's arm, with his eyes rolled to the back of his head. I was confused, I didn't get it. "Hey bros .. I'm Brent, cool to meet you cats".. he manages to mumble. We exchange some awkward pleasantries and his girlfriend helps him negotiate the stairs down to the basement. We wanted to get right to it to find out if it was even worth another second of this situation. Michael hands him a lyric sheet he'd typed up to one of our 2 originals and tells him to just "roll with it"..

Brent was holding onto the microphone stand at this point just to stay on his feet. He says cool bro you got it and Trix counts off. About 3 seconds later, he collapses over the top of the mic stand.

His girlfriend shrieks and runs to his aid while the PA emits a deafening feedback. This kids rock stardom hath preceded him. In retrospect, heroin. At the time? I was about as clueless as a 12 year old girl with blood in her panties. Eww, you guys are sickos.

Brent manages to stand up again and simply asks if we can start over. Matthew Trix and I were loving it but Michael was raging. Regardless we start again and this dude fucking kills it. He had a phenomenal voice and sang that song as if it had already been a classic. We were stunned.

At this point it was the first time we'd ever heard an original song with vocals and it felt better than anything I'd ever felt in my life. As effed up as Brent was, we could tell that between nodding in and out of reality, he was pretty excited as well. Our poker faces weren't about to take down the big money but it didn't matter cuz Brent managed to sputter out a commitment and we had a full band.

Unfortunately the hi-fives were short lived as we got a call 2 days later from the enabler girlfriend who informed us Brent's rock stardom had in fact preceded him and he'd checked into rehab. That was the last we heard of him to this day.

When Matthew and I get our heart set on something, we go all in.. for better or worse, that thing becomes our entire existence. We wanted to be in a band, write songs and tour the world so we devised a multi-pronged attack toward realizing that impossible dream.

Since we'd spent our 10,000 hours on soccer and not music, we knew we had to learn a lot in a very little amount of time. Once we began our artistic endeavor with Michael, we turned our professional attention toward the music industry. After Florence, we both switched our majors to communications and interned at radio stations, record labels and distribution companies. We pillaged industry books, magazines, contacts and spent every free second at shows.

By the time Brent went off to rehab I was working at Scratchie Records as Head of Marketing & Sales. I got the job by calling every single day for 3 weeks and talking to a dude named Ajay. He worked radio promotions there and was so kick ass to me and my harassment that once I got the job we became the best of friends. As a large Osama meets Sam Kinison looking Hindu, and me being a short white bread soccer rocker, he and I were the odd couple. But to this day I've never met a smarter, more kind hearted, hilarious dude in my life.

It was him who suggested I should try to sing for the band. In fact it was a particularly aggressive rendition of RATM's "Killing in the Name of" during a car ride together that prompted the suggestion. I'm not ashamed to admit. Lol. Of course since it never crossed my mind and I'm plagued with stage fright, it took some convincing to get me to try it but at the end of the day I was so eager to progress as a band that I went for it.

I'd started singing for The Blank Theory and despite my complete and utter lack of ability to do so, we forged ahead and wrote 6 songs in the next 4 months. Matthew and I ran things on the business side while Michael and James held down the musical aspect of being in a band. They were seasoned players and though Matthew had developed an almost immediate style and skill and I'd written the lyrics and vocal melody, they were truly the talent.

We decided to get into the studio right away. I called up a dude we'd met at shows at Double Door and Metro named Bryan Mitchel. He was a pathologist by day and budding engineer/producer by night. Bryan had built an immaculate studio in a small free standing garage behind his house and though he had few clients, he'd managed to hone his craft quite well. Being new to the entire process, Matthew and I jumped in with both feet and booked a week-long recording session immediately.

We had absolutely no idea what we were doing. Matthew showed up with his bass in a god damned garbage bag but fortunately Michael and James were on point and we managed to track 3 songs in as many days. I'd despised my voice and almost sank under the pressure. Not only did we invest everything we had into that demo, we'd also counted on it to book shows, garner fans and shop to labels. It was a brutal wake up call for me and despite managing to wrap a 3-song demo, I started vocal lessons the next week.

"Clean" was a slick, melodic track that Michael had written years before and would be the only TBT song with his lyrics. We rounded out the demo with an ethereal, heavy, groovy ass track called "Broken Glass and an armature punk rock shot at Frat- dudes called "Johnson". Now that we a tangible product in our hands, Matthew and I got to work immediately.

We sent that demo to everybody we could think of from promoters, clubs, bars etc. to an entire music industry directory of A&R reps.

My good friend and now former boss at Scracthie, Jeremy Freeman offered to send it out to a few people he knew in the industry as well and a week later I got a call that would yet again change my life forever.

Luke Woods from Dreamworks Records called me a week later and said he was interested in the band. I asked him to hold, muted the phone while I shit myself and pissed in the dishwasher and returned to the call.

I managed to maintain my composure as he told me he'd heard our demo and wanted to fly to Chicago to see us play. We traded some dates and hung up with a plan. I shoved a fork up my ass to make sure I wasn't dreaming and when 4 little holes opened up with blood pouring out of them, I shit in the dryer and called Matthew. God knows what he did when I shared the good news but for the next week there wasn't much without piss, shit or sperm on it. Christ, what am I talking about? Oh yeah, we were excited.

The thrill soon gave way to absolute mortification. What were we thinking? Not only had we never played a show in our lives, but I couldn't sing, he could hardly hold his bass and we absolutely fucking sucked. This was Dreamworks Records by the way. Dreamworks!! The biggest, richest major record label on the planet. We couldn't believe it. Nobody could and rightfully so, we were from ready for this level but fuck it, we believed in it, went for it and here it was.

I called up Jeremy and told him all the wonderful things I'd do to his anus for sending the demo to Luke. He was explaining that he was quite shocked himself that Luke was interested when my other line rang. I asked him to pause and clicked over.

"Hi this is Kurt from Arista Records looking for somebody in The Blank Theory?", What the fuck is going on here. I loved our band at the time but I can't imagine I was naive enough to think we were awesome. I couldn't sing for shit and though I contend to this day that I can't, trust me when I say at the time I couldn't even whistle in key. This began a decades long yin yang with the music industry that would both elate and destroy us several times over, several times a month. Labels would call and life was magical. They wouldn't return calls a week later and life was a cold cruel hell.

CHAPTER 11
THE REAL WORLD

Matthew and I had recently moved out of the high-rise in the South Loop and into a gigantic, seemingly abandoned loft on the near West side. This place was amazing and awful all at once. Our landlords were a Greek family that owned and operated a restaurant attached to the first floor. Otherwise, there were 3 units, all of which were empty when we moved in and none of which could seriously be considered habitable.

The heat/AC didn't work, there was a mystery hatch on the ceiling of a lofted "bedroom" that flapped wide open in the wind and to further the trusty security, we had a giant freight elevator that opened directly into our space. When we first saw it, there was a giant barn themed bedroom on the left with 3/4 walls and glass windows. On the right was a make-shift staircase that meandered up to a small lofted bedroom. It was wide open otherwise with the freight elevator in the back right corner.

We'd recruited our perpetually unreliable friend Bateman to be our 3rd room-mate and help build out the rest of our space. Since Matthew & I can hardly operate a screw driver, Bateman spear-headed a construction project that would ultimately provide us with a 3rd bedroom and a

4 foot high, 12 X 12 foot stage directly in front of the freight elevator. It was amazing.

The idea was to have parties, which we did approximately 4 times over the 3 years we lived there. Since the rest of the building was empty, we'd load all our furniture onto the elevator and take it down to the 2nd floor. Then we'd buy 10 kegs, rent a port-o-potty for the alley outside our back door staircase, hire a security guard and book bands. The first one we had was on New Years Eve in 1999.

We'd also recently started an independent record label called 4 Alarm Records. Ajay and I left Scratchie and Matthew left BMG to do so and having raised $70,000. in start up capital, we signed the Chainsaw Kittens, Bo Bud Greene, Pinehurst Kids and The Frogs and set up shop in the loft.

Matthew and I were quite calculated with everything we did. Since our driving passion in life was to get our band signed and on tour, we'd structured everything else around us to galvanize our pursuit. Since we couldn't get signed, we started a label and signed ourselves. Since we couldn't get a show, we built a stage in our living room and booked ourselves once.

CHAPTER 12

THE BLANK THEORY

We'd decided to move the band into our loft. It was wonderful for Matthew and I because despite the lovely bonding opportunity that a 3 hour commute 4 days a week provided, driving to Michael's mom's house in Hoffman Estates to rehearse was starting to suck balls. Besides, Luke Wood was now flying in from LA to watch us rehearse and the loft was a much cooler setting than a suburban basement.

We set up our equipment on the brand new stage and pimped it out to all hell. I tormented over what to wear, what to say when I met him, what to say between songs, and forgetting the lyrics. I had horrific stage fright.

You remember the speech class debacle in Italy where I pissed myself into a frozen stupor? Needless to say, my stage fright was downright committable.

Now, I'm about to sing? Words that I'd have to memorize? In front of somebody? An A&R for the biggest label on the planet no less? Not a chance.

Well, the day eventually came and I ended up writing all the lyrics on my arms and hands just n case. I'd never been so nervous in my life and it showed. The showcase wasn't as awful as I'd imagined it would be but alas, you can't hide the truth forever and Luke graciously passed on us. He was honest and blunt and told us everything I already knew in the back of my mind but refused to believe and was devastated to hear. In retrospect, we were soccer players, not musicians. Matthew and I had managed to build up a solid enough mirage to get an A&R exec to fly to our damn house but in the end, we just weren't ready. But now? We had a mission. We'd get a record deal if it killed us. Despite all the buzz and major label interest, we still couldn't get a show. We'd call the Double Door almost daily, begging to get added to any bill whatsoever. We'd gone to the club since we were 18 years old and its legendary status would be a dream first show. Always aiming for the moon, at least at this point, we weren't hitting it. So we decided to throw a New Years Eve Party in the loft.

Like I said, we moved all of our furniture down to the 2nd floor, bought 10 kegs of beer, rented a port-a-shitter for the alley, hired a security guard and booked 4 bands. We even managed to buy Dram shop insurance for the night. Our best friend and partner Ajay had a band called Monkey Paw who'd been playing around Chicago for a few years so we put them on 2nd. 2 other bands we'd known in the local scene called .22 and Fondly played 3rd and 4th respectively and the all mighty Blank Theory opened up.

At 10pm that night, you couldn't even move in that place. The energy was fantastic and by the time we went on, grandpa could have ripped a 30 minute skin flute solo while grandma queefed into a megaphone and the crowd would have still gone nutty. I'm not sure if it was the spirit of New Years Eve, the Universe reassuring us that we were on course or sheer luck but the night was majestic. Of course, I puked for about 45 minutes straight before we played. This while I scribbled every lyric onto my arm again, in case I blanked out. Regardless, when the time came, we took the stage and threw down.

Our loft was absolutely packed to the gills with approximately 600 people. We didn't know where they came from and honestly knew maybe 50 of them so it didn't phase me when I watched some random dude drop his pants and piss all over what just yesterday was and tomorrow will again be, our living room. *It did however phase me slightly when moments later, I did the same thing.* Anywho.. I had gotten myself good and retarded after we played and despite my knowing how awful I must have sounded, I didn't care. We'd gotten our first show out of the way and it was fucking great.

Winter 2000

Even Guido's Need Love, Piss

It's no secret that I hate guides. I'm Italian so I can say that. They're the steroid, Ed Hardy/Affliction-wearing mamas boys that call people like me a faggot. And they absolutely adore the thought of a fight. I'm a mangina. *Wasn't built for battle. I see myself more as a tactical fella in a battle situation. They may be bigger and stronger but I'm smarter and craftier and I will always win. I wish. You wish..*

Anywho, after the first year in the loft, some kids finally moved in to the 2nd floor. We were bummed that we lost the freedom and use of that space but it turned out they were some pretty crafty kids. They started an ISP and completely pimped out their unit, building tiki-style cabins as bedrooms and even put in a hot tub, complete with waterfall, next to the back window. It was amazing.

So the back windows looked out onto an alley just off Union St. About a half-block down from Union was a cheesy ass guido dance club called The Drink. On weekends this place was packed full of monsters.

From our window we could watch them all wait in line in the freezing cold: the girls in tiny dresses and the dudes in muscle suits. Every week-end night there were approximately 5

fights outside this club. The dudes would get first-time wasted and scream at each other, start punching and I-shit-you-not - usually end up crying. *Nothing beats seeing one of these over grown guidos screaming his voice out, messing up his olive oil soaked hair rolling around on the street with another guido and crying.*
The point however is that a lot of them parked in our alley and on the way back to their cars we witnessed some amazing things.

Once we saw a guido buy sex off a hooker, take her in the alley and when he was done he sat against the building with his hands over his face crying. We saw them buy cocaine, get arrested, fight, crash their leased rice-burners, get arrested etc. Always entertaining but what really annoyed us was the fact that every morning after, we'd walk out the back door and step in puddles of their piss. Our doorway was dark and discreet and a perfect place for them to piss before they drove back to their parents house in the burbs.
Anyhow, one night we were in the hot tub and we heard some commotion from the window. Upon looking down we saw a cheesy red Porsche convertible parked right outside our alley door with a blonde bimbo sitting in the passenger seat. Just below us we could see her guido muscle dude walking up to our beloved back doorway for a refreshing piss.

I've always believed in fighting fire with fire so we grabbed a bucket and filled it with hot tub water. Then, thanks to his stage fright we had an extra minute to muster up as much piss as 5 of us could muster in such short notice.

Just as he zipped up and turned around to get back into his car we dumped the entire bucket of chlorine and piss water onto him, his girlfriend and the entire interior of his leased sports car. She got the worst of it and was so confused by what happened that she just sort of starred in a moment of shock and curiosity. He reacted relatively quickly. Not even knowing there was a window above him, much less 5 dudes who just pissed on him, it took a minute for him to look around.. Of course right when the piss water hit, we all jumped back to avoid detection but the giant open window and some hearty laughter gave us away. This guy went berserk. He started screaming so loud that he must have popped every vein in his throat. "You mother&^*ers I'm gonna cut off your heads and shit down your necks!" - type of stuff they learned in guido charm school.

We were about 20 feet in from the window, patting each other on the back when all of the sudden bottles started flying in. He was throwing rocks, bottles and bricks from the alley at all the windows in the building. There's only one thing to do now to put the icing on this proverbial cake. We called the cops.

We told them some psychopath was wasted and trying to break into our building. Knowing the cops would take a minute or 2 we had to keep this guy around so we started taunting him. I crawled up to the window and popped my head out to get a better look. By now his girl was also out of the car throwing shit and screaming and when they saw me they quickly realized I was just a little rocker faggot. We're like kryptonite to guidos. They tend to hate that we're different, they can't stand that we generally have fun with life and they absolutely can't stomach the fact that girls tend to enjoy our company.

The screams got louder and louder and we'd pop our heads out to respond with the occasional "wow, you guys seem really "pissed". and "Urine a lot of trouble!". We were definitely proud of our cheesy little jokes but the most rewarding feeling was the site of this guys leased sports car.

It was totally drenched in our piss, as was the bimbo guidette. She was screaming so much shit that surely popped at least one of the balloons in her tits.

By now, they'd both seen us and the guy simply couldn't take it anymore so he grabbed a 2X4 and rammed it right through the first floor window. I couldn't believe the extent he was willing to go to quench his ego. But alas, the karmic poetry was already in motion and a few short seconds after the 2X4 blasted through the window, 2 of Chicago's finest grabbed him and rammed his head into the brick wall. I love Chicago cops.

We had to lay low so the guy sounded like a gibbon trying to explain to the police that a bucket of piss miraculously fell from the heavens onto his car and girlfriend. But we did get to watch this guy take a breathalyzer, fail and get thrown into the back of a cop car. His girl vanished into the night, most likely just leached on to some other poor bastard in a leased car. The super gay red Porsche convertible? got man handled by a tow truck and disappeared forever. It truly was a triumphant moment.

CHAPTER 13
A Newline on Life
2001

Having Dreamworks and Arista call us gave us just enough leverage to secure management which Matthew and I knew we needed. As we accumulated knowledge and industry contacts we'd realized an A-list manager was the necessary next step. Our challenge at this point was the fact that we were based in Chicago and also, as much as we'd spin, hype and over-state our "label interest", the big time East/West Coast managers wouldn't bite just yet.

We looked for the very biggest, most powerful manager we could get with the relatively little we had to offer. As much as I hate to admit this, one of the few natural gifts Matthew and I were imbued with is the ability to spin. If I'd email a major label asking for their address and get so much as a reply with it? Well hell, that label was interested in signing us. I'd manage to convince anyone I could get to listen that we were the new happenin band that was about to get signed and blow up and they should either get on board or miss out.

In Chicago, Disturbed had just released "Stupify" and it was climbing the charts like a mofo. They were managed by local big fish Roger Jansen. Or at least that was what Roger would have anyone believe. He had the same gift of bullshit that we did. Truth was, he owned KMA Management and when label's started sniffing around Disturbed, Roger managed to convince their manager to sign on with KMA and bring them into fold.

That manager was Jeff Bataglia who was for all intents and purposes was a South side hustler whose best friend was in Disturbed and let Jeff manage them. He had zero experience but loyalty reigns supreme in that camp, respectfully, and they brought him along for the ride.

Jeff teamed up with Roger's partner Dougie to co-manage Disturbed and their star began to rise quickly. *Dougie, by the way used to play bass for Supertramp and turned to management when the band ran its course.*

The music industry is quite impressionable so when Disturbed took off, every major label flew to Chicago to sniff around and find the next big thing. Ever since Seattle in the 90's, music execs have hunted relentlessly for the next "grunge" and Chicago started to look like the safest bet. Roger took full advantage of this and claimed Disturbed for himself, giving him the golden ear. Matthew and I realized this and got to work.

We can flirt with the best of em and though I maintain that we're genuine, integrity based people, we'd definitely turn on the charm when we saw an opportunity. We knew we were playing with fire because the "buzz" our band had developed was largely manufactured by yours truly. Convinced that this is just how the world works, we set out to secure KMA Management.

Not only would KMA galvanize our momentum but it would also qualify our band in the eyes of the industry. We finagled a meeting with Roger and left it with a management contract.

As word got out, more and more labels started to call. We structured a several pronged attack with the band, hitting both the streets and the industry with everything we had. We'd go to as many shows per night that we could, handing out fliers and demoes to anyone who'd take one. We'd promote ourselves to a sickening degree and it started paying off.

By the time clubs would finally book us, we'd started to develop a bit of a following. We took our music and live show very seriously and beyond practicing 5 times a week and promoting 7 nights a week, we also climbed deeply into the art of it all.

Since that very first show in our loft, we were enamored with the live show. Playing had such a visceral affect on us and it became intoxicating. For people like Matthew and myself who require some sort of physical release to go along with our daily existence, performing live replaced soccer. I've always said that soccer to me is an art form. The fluid dynamic on the pitch, creating runs, plays, strategies and the like became a personified chess game in my head. Having switched to music, we'd invest the same physical output but the bonus of performing pieces of art that we created was fucking euphoric. Shows at Double Door turned into shows at the iconic Metro.

Metro is a 1,300 cap theatre in Chicago's Wrigley Ville and has a rich history of hosting some of the world's biggest and best bands. Playing there was enough for us to die happily. When we ultimately sold it out in September of 2000, we'd died and gone to Heaven.

Having picked up instruments only a few short years ago, he we were headlining a sold out show at Metro playing our very own songs. Unfortunately, I'd still suffered from a pain-staking stage fright.

Moments before we'd go on, I would convince myself I could not do it and try desperately to cancel.

I was so neurotic about it that on this particular night I seriously considered pulling the fire alarm or calling in a bomb threat. In the end I suppose I knew I couldn't let Matthew and my band down and though I was quite serious about the fire alarm bit, I knew I wouldn't be able to live myself so I strapped one on and went for it.

The show was insane. 1,300 kids moshing, jumping and generally going off was absolutely exhilarating. By the time we got to the last song in the set, the place was in a frenzy. I'm not sure what inspired me to do so but in an adrenaline infused moment I was already way too caught up in, I decided to climb up one of the giant speaker trusses and dive into the crowd. I was at least 20 feet high and though the landing was brutal, I'd develop a new habit that would take a significant toll on my body for the next 15 years. B y the time I got to our dressing room after the show, there was a sea of industry folk standing outside it waiting to talk to us.

Jeff Blue from Warner Brothers and Daniel Schulman from Island Def Jam were jockeying for position and each vying to talk to us first. I couldn't believe it. Just like so many articles I'd read or stories I'd heard about major label A&Rs being ruthless when pursuing a band they wanted to sign, it was now happening to us. I was elated.

Jeff Blue came in guns a-blazing. He told us that he had put Linkin Park together and had essentially written their first record (*which he didn't*). Warner Brothers had given him his own imprint and he continued the cliché industry bravado that I had just now learned to love. Daniel Schulman was next and he played it much cooler but in the end there was no doubt that we were getting a record deal. Or so we thought.

CHAPTER 14
Judas

In the days and weeks after that show, we didn't hear from either of them. Several more labels would call and feign interest on account of the "buzz" but it never amounted to anything. To this day I'll never understand what happens between moments like the one in our dressing room and the ultimate lack of a return phone call. This was the first of many of these devastations to come but now that we had a taste, we would stop at nothing.

A few agonizing months later, I got a call from Jeremy again who asked me what The Blank Theory was up to. I gave him the typical schpiele about how a million labels wanted to sign us and we were just deciding which one.

He listened intently and asked me to list each label, the A&R and what they were prepared to offer. Uh oh, was this my bluff getting called? Sure seemed like it and I took a moment to consider coming clean. I really do pride myself on honesty and integrity and it was high time I man up and tell it like is.
What proceeded was a 30 minute dissertation of bullshit about how many millions of dollars millions of labels were throwing at us and how lawyers, booking agents and management firms

are lighting up our phone lines begging to sign us blah blah. Well, Jeremy took notes of all of it and when I finished he said, "well, I'm working with a new label called Newline Records and we'd like to throw our hat in the ring".

Just like the now several times before, we were back from the dead. I'd started to learn not to believe anything until I'm coming home from it but starting to learn it and learning it are 2 different things so yet again, I paraded the news around to my band, friends and family as if I'd just come home from the bank.

Jason Linn from Newline Records called shortly there after and we began a courting process. Newline Records was Newline Cinemas attempt at starting their own indie label and run it through the major distribution system that was Warner Brothers. Of course in Matthew's and my minds, we were signing to Warner Brothers. Roger, on the hand wasn't so impressed. In his mind he was humoring our delusion and if he managed to pocket 20K in the process well hell, he won a lottery.

Matthew and I facilitated the entire record deal from start to finish. Part of Newline's pitch was that they would secure the production team of James Iha (from smashing pumpkins) and Adam Schlessinger to make our record. It was a dream coming true. However, with "Disturbed's manager" on board, a fake bidding war and manufactured hype, we had one giant

house of cards.. built on sand… on a
cliff..ready to go.

We officially showcased in Indianapolis where
we hopped on a local bill at Emerson Theater.
Jason Lynn, Adam Schlessinger and James Iha
all flew out and we got along famously. The
following Monday they began working up a
contract.
Newline sent us to NYC a few weeks after Sept.
11 to record a Beatles cover for their
forthcoming "I Am Sam" soundtrack. We
stayed at Jeremy's loft in the financial district.
It was a mere blocks from Ground Zero and still
a mess. The smell of burnt twisted metal and
god knows what else hung thickly in the air and
it was a lot to take in but alas, we had work to
do.

We recorded "Hey Bulldog" and though
everybody was thrilled about it, it got bumped
from the soundtrack because we hadn't signed
the contract yet. It didn't much matter in the
end, as we were back in Manhattan 2 months
later to record our first studio album "Beyond
the Calm of the Corridor".
They moved us into an apartment in Soho for 2
months and we had the time of our lives. We
went in with 15 songs and the recording process
was a blessing and curse all at once.
I was told for the first time that I had to take
voice lessons and that my lyrics weren't good

enough and would have to be "dumbed down".   This sparked a new kind of anxiety in me that would only grow in the years to come. We went home with 11 tracks in the can and though I can't listen to them to this day, I learned more making that record than I ever had and Adam became a mentor to me.

Back in Chicago, we couldn't shake the feeling that our record was missing something so we wrote one more song. Matthew called up a friend and extraordinary producer named Tim Patalin who invited us out to his farm in Michigan to record it. The day before manufacturing, we sent it to NewLine and "Middle of Nowhere" became our first single. Our label managed to get the song placed in a scene of "Final Destination 2" which NewLine Cinemas was about to release. They also made a deal with their parent company that gave us a video budget to simultaneously promote the single with the movie

This was all fantastic in theory. Unfortunately it also mean that we were at the mercy of their producers to shoot whatever video they wanted. The video shot for Middle of Nowhere was yet again, absurd and amazing. The treatment was laughably bad and though we'd protest with everything we had, looking a gift horse in the mouth was hardly an ambition. We flew to LA and checked into the ultra sheik Standard Hotel where my untimely boner was poised and ready to strike again.

The treatment followed the same concept as the movie and had each band member die an ironic death. It didn't sound as dreadful as it would ultimately become but alas, the events that took place during my scene would be unforgettable. Wardrobe put me in a tight pair of sweatpants/pajama bottoms and no shirt. The bit was based off of a tattoo I have on my right forearm of a brown recluse spider. The producers decided it was a tarantula and just before I be-sexed my fictitious girlfriend, a tarantula was going to crawl onto my arm and bite me... to death.

The scene took play in one of our suites at The Standard, of which we had 2. Production decided to use one of our rooms as the staging area and the other as the set. They'd booked this "super hot" chick to be my girlfriend in the scene and dressed her up in some casual sexy night garb and plopped us in bed next to each other. If you'll remember for a moment, I have a trigger happy boner who tends to meddle in my business constantly.

Now this was a legitimate concern for me because I'd done my research and learned that it definitely happened from time to time on movie sets and the like. If it ever happened even once, it was going to happen to me so I set out on another psychological sexcapade with my pap boner. This time I had dad in full dominatrix garb, whipping my ass and stepping on my balls with the high heels he was wearing.

Join me for a quick side note if you will. In the ever changing trends of modern hotels, LA likes to consider itself on the forefront and though often times this is the case, sometimes their ideas fall on the side of cheesy, contrived lamity. In this case, our room which doubled as the staging room, was much like a regular hotel room except that the bathroom and shower just to the left of the entrance had a translucent wall between itself and the beds. In another words, if you were sitting on the bed watching TV, all you had to do was look to the right and you could see the shower and anyone in it.

The scene was split into 2, one on the bed, flirting and the other in the bathroom. In the bathroom I was on the floor dead with a real tarantula crawling up my arm and my make believe girlfriend was on top of me crying. We shot the bed scene first and sure as shit, I popped a god damned boner before cameras were even rolling. The remainder of the scene was the most awkward attempts to deny its existence while the whole cast and crew did the same. This stumbled clumsily into the bathroom scene where more of the same played out. When we wrapped, I snuck back into our room and jumped in the shower. I can't remember if I'd forgotten about the translucent glass or simply didn't care on account of it being my room and assuming I was alone. Either way, I contorted my body to all hell and scrubbed my inner asshole, my balls and everything else that's otherwise unbecoming to watch get cleaned. Once clean, I proceeded to shave each of those parts with equal rigor. Shaving one's own asshole is a challenging feat in and of itself. Without mirrors, custom shaving equipment and/or a friend to help, it's a god damn vicious endeavor. I must have looked like a psychopath to anybody say, sitting on the fucking bed watching me. But alas, I never considered to even look.

While I went on to wash my hair and shave my tits, Matthew & Schabeizel came into the room and walked straight into the bathroom. They asked me how my scene was and what it was like shooting with that girl. To this day I can't be sure if they'd set me up or just also didn't realize, the girl was sitting on the fucking bed watching me fist my own asshole. Regardless, they definitely knew she was there when they listened to me explain my horrific boner problems throughout.

I said some of the weirdest shit I've ever said about it, the girl and the scene. Suddenly, I hear a ruckus in the main room and look to the right, through the glass just in time to see a very distraught young actress shriek in disgust and gather up all her shit. I was mortified.

The dudes of course were loving every second of it and she walked past the bathroom door she simply said, "You're disgusting" and walked out. I cringed about that for a few years to come but in the end, we wrapped a shitty video and went home to Chicago to wait for the million huge tours that never came.

We had a record deal, a major budget video (almost 200,000 all in), a manager and lawyer who all got their commissions and couldn't get a booking agent to save our lives. Despite a costly radio campaign, PR campaigns and everything else you'd need to get a real shot, we sat at home washing the RV we bought with our record advance.

All in, we eventually played 2 radio shows with Trapt on the West Coast and a handful of one-offs but The Blank Theory was a stillborn. As the frustrations mounted, Newline stopped returning calls, Roger gave up with a "see, I told ya so!" heir about him and Michael quit. Trix was an alcoholic and his jeckly and Hyde tendencies had begun to cause a lot of problems. When Michael quit, he followed suit and Matthew and I clung to the facade of having a band. Truth was, we had nothing.

A few months earlier, Roger had signed this band from New Jersey called Reforma on account of their charismatic, writing genius front man named Mateo. He was from Bogota, Columbia and had moved from there to Florida to attend recording school in Florida. In Florida he met Dan Torelli and formed a band that would ultimately move to Jersey. Reforma was a pop version of Refused and much to our chagrin we fucking loved them.

Roger moved them to Chicago to oversee their career and his first order of business was booking them a show as direct support for us at Metro. We were pissed, jealous and keen on destroying them.

At that show, they had colossal technical difficulties and went down in flames. It was difficult to watch but we got to meet them and developed a fast friendship with Mateo and Dan. When Blank Theory lost our guitarist/song-writer and drummer, Matthew and I began devising a long, calculated game plan. The first phase entailed writing with Mateo. Roger was always a fan of cross-pollinating so he jumped at the idea and before we knew it, we had 3 new Blank Theory songs and no band with which to play or record them. We hired Mateo to do just that and soon, Reforma had an expiration date.

The only problem was, Reforma had begun to develop a buzz of their own. Since Matthew and I were the only ones who knew the long term plan, we had to either sit back and pray they didn't get signed or somehow get The Blank Theory another record deal before they did. Since we're the restless type, we went full throttle.

The 3 song demo we did with Mateo managed to garner some significant interest. We were still technically managed by Roger but operating entirely on our own. We'd start packaging the lies and spin and soon convinced a lot of people that The Blank Theory was not dead but in fact on the precipice of blowing up.

I called up an old friend named Rene Mata who had interned at Columbia Records a few years ago and become quite chummy with Matt Pinfield in the process. Matt was a VP of A&R at Columbia in lieu of his hit MTV show 120 Minutes. Rene convinced me that if we paid 20K to record the new demo with Jay Baumgarnder in LA, he could convince Matt to fly us out for a showcase at Columbia. We didn't hesitate for a second.

We flew Mateo out with us and hired famed studio drummer Matt Walker to play drums. Putting the entire undertaking on credit cards, we managed to maintain the illusion that we had reached some sort of success with TBT and since a record deal was inevitable, all was right with the world.

It started to effing work. Matt Pinfield got the demo and convinced his bosses to finance a trip out to Manhattan to showcase in their office. Now, we were spinning too many plates. We had Columbia convinced we were a band, Mateo convinced we were just hiring him to play the showcase with us and Roger convinced we had no intention of breaking up Reforma. It was precarious at best. It couldn't get any better and it couldn't get any worse all at once.

When Columbia flew us out, we were all giddy. They wined and dined us and by the time the showcase came, we were loving life and shitting ourselves. We set up in a small showcase room and waited for the bigwigs. The plan was to play 3 songs, the ones we'd just demo'd, secure a deal, make Mateo and Jeezy an offer they couldn't refuse and we'd be off to the races.

Since we were on thin ice with Roger at the time, we had our friend Ajay come to NY with us and act as interim manager. Minutes before we were supposed to start, he got a phone call. Clive Davis had recently been ousted from the label he built, Arista Records. Clive was the industry's most notorious power player and he started up J Records immediately. J had become one of the biggest labels overnight thanks to the likes of Alicia Keys and Maroon5. Another industry heavy weight named Jeff Fenster teamed up with Clive and now they were calling us. At Columbia Records no less. This was fucking amazing.

Ajay brokered a deal in which J Records would literally buy out our trip to NY from Columbia, paying Columbia back for our flights, hotels etc. and re-booking us into the infamous Hudson Hotel.

Columbia refused but J convinced us to let them extend the trip instead. They'd pick us up from Columbia in limos, take us to the Hudson, wine and dine us from there and have us showcase for them the next day. We agreed. But for the moment at hand, wed have to perform one of the most nerve wracking showcases to date.

The showcase room was about the size of a classroom and it's location next to VP offices and cubicles made it non descript. It was dark and the walls were adorned with fancy awards and platinum records from decades ago but it couldn't escape the board room vibe. Of course my nerves were acting up again and I'd begun scribbling more lyrics on my forearms.
Our keyboard player Schabeizel had a shaved head and when ever he got nervous, it broke out into blotchy red patches all over it. Needless to say, he began to look like Michael Gorbochov while Matthew commenced fisting himself.
We went over the quite simple 3 song set list yet again to assure we were all on the same page. This was critical because awkward silences between songs are death enough at live shows with an audience. In a showcase room like this was a handful of suits standing there? It was about as comfortable as a family orgy. Moments later the execs started trickling in.
With Clive Davis recent ousting, new president Charlie Walk was at the helm at he was another legend in the industry. When he walked in, I pissed myself and we took the stage.

Schabeizel was one of our best friends whom we'd met in 6th grade and as Matthew and I began to war with Michal and Trix, we brought him into the band to not only play keys but also serve as a reasonable buffer between our warring factions.

The problem however, was that Schabeizel wasn't a seasoned pro by any stretch of the imagination. I always admired his creative contribution and he still is one of the best dudes I've ever met but when the pressure was on, he was more likely to queef himself than to deliver.

I've done it myself time and time again so I'm hardly judging him but boy he sure could pick his moments. His only job for this showcase was to start the tape machine. Literally, push "select track", "1" and "play", then "2", then "3".

We took the stage, he hit #1 and we were off to the races. First song absolutely killed. When track "2" was supposed to start, however, out came track "3".

I played guitar in TBT and since I'd already had the "2" guitar strapped around me, this was a fucking nightmare. As the track continued, I nervously chuckled and peeled the guitar I'd just put on, off my neck and just dropped it. Since the vocal was coming in any second, I didn't have time to be smooth about it so it looked ridiculous. Add to that, once something like this derails me, I go into an internal psychosis I can't even revisit with words.

We barreled through that song and I made some stupid joke about the gaffe to the suits who had no idea what I was even talking about anyway. The room was silent and our strategy of cruising between songs to avoid this very misery was shot to all hell as Schabelezeils head lit up like a Christmas tree. The 20 seconds or so it took for him to load the 3rd and final song "2" felt like a god damned eternity.

It's moments like these that I immediately reflect on that fateful last day of High School soccer. We were in the first round of play-offs which was an elimination round. We were seniors which meant losing would be the last HS soccer game we'd ever play. On paper, we were better than St. Viator so when they had us down 2-1 late in the second half, I caved. There was about a minute left and Matthew was fighting like his god damned life depended on it. Me? I gave up. It turned out to be some sort of sick vindication of Coach Pagnani who'd fought so hard to hold me back. As if he had to prove to the world that I wasn't good enough. Regardless, I'd been one of the top goal scorers that year and despite many frustrations with the team and season, I'd played pretty well and here I was, giving up. It sickens me to this day but I learned a critical lesson with that mistake and haven't given up on anything ever since. Well, here it is again.

I picked up the guitar I'd dropped before the last song which was now all kinds of out of tune. I gave that 3rd song every ounce of energy I had. I didn't care, I was not going to let this slip away. We'd come way too far on way too little to give up now. In the end, we nailed it. The execs ushered out of that room pretty quickly and though they weren't blown away, we'd done just enough to get the approval. Matt Pinfield was prepared to make us an offer. Ajay was on the phone in the hall when we all did the cordials. Meeting a bunch of label people and talking shop with the label brass. It was not protocol to discuss on the spot but they all knew J records was on the phone with Ajay in their hallway and they wanted to sign us if just to spite Clive Davis. Matt asked for our attorney's information and just before we left they said the following "We'll beat whatever J offers you, just remember who found you first". I could have tattooed those words on my face for how excited I was to hear them. I couldn't fucking believe it. We did it.

When Ajay got off the phone, we thanked Columbia, said our goodbyes and headed out. Standing on the sidewalk at 550 W. Madison with our guitars, we all freaked out. It was one of a very few in a lifetime moments of absolute elation and we savored it for the mili second it took for Ajay to fill us in on the J Records call. Moments after that a limo pulled up with "The Blank Theory" written in sharpie on a sign in the windshield. This just kept getting better.

J Records moved us to the ultra swanky Hudson Hotel in Manhattan. It was the fanciest hotel any of us had ever even seen much less stayed at. They rented a showcase room for that evening and we'd have an hour or so to check in and drop our bags before heading over to the Chelsea rehearsal studio. They'd already managed to have all of our equipment sent there and waiting as well as every piece of PA equipment on our stage plot. These guys were good. I don't know how it was even possible, given the time frame but when we arrived, 2 of their execs were waiting in the lobby.

Victor Murgatroyd and Jeff Fenster were legends. They charmed our pants off and when we finally played the same 3 songs we'd just played for Columbia, we seemed to already have the deal.

Jeff and Victor were old school industry folk. Victor had only recently become a star in the A&R world for his work on Evanescence but he adapted quickly to all the clichés we'd read about a million times. Big money, big deals, big game.

Fenster was known for his work with Brittney Spears and laundry list of hits. They both loved to hear themselves talk and our showcase was more of a 15 minute break from conversation than any significant audition. In the end, they wanted Columbia's blood. We'd learn much later that Clive Davis' ego played heavily into what was happening here. Jeff and Victor kept railing Columbia and telling us how J controlled the industry etc. They all but threatened to blacklist us if we chose Columbia over them. We were loving every single second of it. When they finally left, Victor said to me "money is nothing to us, Columbia can't compete. You just have to chose between the turtle or the rabbit.". I didn't get it , but I ran to the nearest closet, pissed in it and got into the limo with the dudes, high on life. That night we cruised Manhattan in a J financed limo and had one of the best nights of our lives.

The next day we'd gotten calls from both labels reiterating their interest in signing us and both asking what the other had offered. Matt Pinfield had estimated 250K signing bonus which I relayed to Victor and they came back with 350k. Now mind you, both promised to put it in writing and have to our attorney by days end but neither had done so. We flew home expecting to have voicemails when we landed but we didn't. Convincing each other it would take a day or 2, we buckled down and waited. We wouldn't hear anything for a week. When we finally did, it was only via MTV News. Matt Pinfield has gone to rehab for cocaine abuse and was let go from Columbia Records. Once Columbia was out, J Records had no reason to sign us. We were absolutely devastated.

Making matters worse, Reforma was getting calls from every label under the sun and they'd begun the showcase process just as we had not only years before, but just weeks before again. Matthew and I had nothing.. again. Desperate to cling to anything, we'd call Victor relentlessly and ask him what it would take to get J Records to reconsider.

After several ignored calls, he finally told us we should reach out to his producer friend in LA named Chris Johnson and hire him to make a demo. We jumped on it.

Back in Chicago, we'd quickly become best of friends with Mateo and were now planning to write a couple brand new songs with him. We still had TBT's rehearsal spot at Superior St. which doubled as Matthew's and my office. We'd go there every day to work on music, make phone calls and strategize. Since all of our equipment was set up there, Mateo would come by and we'd sift through riffs and ideas and work through them on the spot.

Matthew and I were like poachers. As Mateo would scroll through his files, we'd be hovering over his shoulder ready to pick off any of them we thought were bad ass. This was precarious as well because technically these were all his ideas for Reforma songs so if we showed too much interest, Mateo might hold on to a particular idea. But one of them jumped out at us immediately and we had to have it.

It was a gritty, hooky, up tempo riff that would ultimately become "Here I Stand". I couldn't contain myself and demanded that it be the first new track we work on. It became part of a 3-song batch that would include "Now or Never" and "One Last Kiss" as well and they came together quick.

The only way to officially lock these down for us was for me to write vocals to them as soon as possible. Once I did, we'd send them out to Victor and eventually Chris Johnson. We didn't have a new band name yet but that could wait. First we needed a drummer.

Dan joined the mix and it was magic. Not only would the 4 of us become inseparable, we'd write some of the best music any of us had ever written. Thus, a pink elephant was born.

Chris Johnson was a hack from LA who'd made some money writing music beds for commercials. We'd learn later than he was Victor's AA sponsor and the $20,000. fee we'd pay Chris Johnson for 3 days in his studio was likely split between them. Nonethewiser at the time, we begged dad to spot us the cash, maxed out our credit cards and flew Mateo, Dan and Matthew and I out to LA.

Sitting in his make-shift little studio in W. Hollywood, Chris Johnson was pathetic. The whole situation was murky at best. Matthew and I were hyping the Victor Murgatroyd situation to keep Mateo on our side. As we incorporated Dan into the mix, we were all too scared to admit what was really happening.

The Blank Theory was dead in the water and Reforma had been passed on enough times to explore other options. Roger, still technically managed both of our bands and all of our friends would be pissed if we folded them. Yet, here we were in LA with Mateo, Dan, Matthew and I about to record a demo with a relatively fictitious record deal for a relatively fictitious band.

We checked into the Wyndam Belage in West Hollywood, just off the Sunset Strip. The fun kicked off immediately. We were living up the cliché Hollywood rock n roll lifestyle at night and went over to Chris Johnson's garage studio during the day. Chris would play the demos over and over again then print out pages of All American Rejects lyrics and tell us, if we could write these lyrics to our music we'd have a hit. Literally, that was the extent of his production.

After 3 miserable days we flew home with the exact demos we brought out there, not having recorded a single note. To further the scam, just before we left Chris told us the songs were now hits. He would send them to Victor and we'd get a call the following week. Needless to say, the call never came. Back in Chicago, we'd uncover one of the biggest betrayals we'd ever experience.

The mystery surrounding the sudden vanishing of both Columbia and J Records was not settling well. We were beating a dead horse by clinging to the Victor Murgatroyd scenario and in the back of our minds knew we were being thumped by him and Chris Johnson. We did however have to maintain some sort of perception that things were still on the up and up to convince Mateo and Dan that we were worth jumping their Reforma ship for.

As we wrote feverishly in order to come up with some tangible value, the writing on the wall became crystal clear. We either delivered some of the strongest material possible and reinvigorated some industry demand or we were sunk. We finished a new edit of "Here I Stand" and sent it to Victor. He called a few minutes later.

The rush of adrenaline from seeing "J Records" on caller ID is something I'd never gotten used to. We craved it like a narcotic. This particular call must have been a difficult one because though he believed in the track, he had much worse news for Matthew and I.

Apparently our best friend and manager Roger Jansen had called Victor right when we got back from New York. He told him that The Blank Theory was no longer a band, that the twins were done and that Mateo/Reforma was the real deal. He told him that any and every one of the new songs we'd sent were Mateo's and tried to steal our record deal from us and give it to Reforma.

Fortunately Victor didn't bite but it had essentially put the nail in our coffins and we'd have to start from scratch. When Mateo and Dan found out what Roger had done, the shit hit the fan. They decided to bail on him, officially fold Reforma and commit 100% to our new band which we'd call Madina Lake.

note- It should be said that we've since made amends with Roger and though I will never forget what he did, I've also learned to forgive.

Our circle of friends at the time included most members of Reforma so once the writing was on the wall it would be a little awkward to say the least. Dave Swick ("Stevo") was one of our closer friends and it pained us all greatly knowing he'd be hurt by this. Another dude in that band named Damon was Mateo's best friend ever since he got to the US and he'd be anther casualty of the merger. On our end, Schabeizel was going to hurt the worst.

A lot of bands had a DJ/Keyboard player role which for all intents and purposes was becoming obsolete. Damon and Schabeizel both knew they were expendable and that the only thing keeping them in the fray to this point was our friendships. When Mateo, Dan, Matthew and I decided to roll the dice and form an all star band, we couldn't afford to include friends as favors to them. As shoddy as this sounds, it was our last shot and we weren't going to fuck around.

Chapter 15
Panophobia
November, 2004

I'm standing on yet another platform but this time it's atop a strange looking truck that's driving 40 mph down a closed off California desert highway. On my left is my twin brother and on my right is Joe Rogan who's relaying real time status updates from an earpiece. It's freezing balls outside, my knuckles are black and blue and my hair and clothes are still wet from the events 30 minutes earlier. I hear Joe say "he can't find the flag! Ryan can not find the flag!". I know better than to get comfortable with the possibility that Matthew and I may be in the process of winning $50,000. for a decision we made solely to make our friends laugh at our expense. But this was getting interesting.
"The wire Joe?" I ask half sarcastically and half to confirm his recent claim that this race was actually close. I remind myself how hilarious it is that these 2 frat boy, jockey, hillbillies had apparently already rented some cheesy club in Alabama for their victory party ahead of the final stunt. I also maintain that Matthew and I are simply entertaining each other with another ridiculous circumstance that we humbly and unwittingly stumbled into.

Though the $50,000. will definitely change things for us, winning or being champions never held any weight and still doesn't. As Matthew said the only real motivation to win was not to be Fear Factor champions but rather to keep that dream from these douche bags who seemed to bank their lives on it.

We could see top of the oil tanker in front of us hauling ass and swerving as if the desolate highway was littered with IEDs. One of the cowboy twins knelt on top of the back end of the tanker clutching a flag pole he'd recently screwed into place. He was yelling motivational insults at his twin brother through some air holes like a trainer in a yuppie gym. His brother was inside the tanker getting absolutely molested by the tsunami like wave that the driver created with his swerving, accelerating and sporadic breaking. See, it was full of about 5,000 gallons of water and while one twin was hand-cuffed inside of it, the other had to climb in, swim to the back to find a key which would ultimately uncuff his brother who then had to swim back for a flag which was hidden next to the key under water.

At this particular moment, the first twin had found the key, unlocked his brother and climbed out to wait while the other was desperately trying to find the flag amid the relentlessly pummeling waves. Gigantic gieser bursts of water would periodically blast through the entrance hole at the front top of the tank while the tidal wave inside bounced back and forth. As Joe's latest time update indicated the twin in the tanker had about 23 seconds left to find the flag, swim to the ladder and climb out onto the top of the truck, shimmy his way to his brother's flagpole at the back and hang it. The math started working itself out.. even if his head pops out of that hole right now, he'd still need a good 13 seconds to shimmy his way to the flagpole. There's no way he's gonna make it. About 10 seconds later his head finally popped out of the whole and the game was on. Fortunately, I under estimated the time it would take for him to shimmy back and hang his flag because he was about half way across when Joe called time. We couldn't believe it. We just fucking won $50,000. on one of America's most popular reality game shows. We're now NBC Fear Factor Champs.

The producers sat us in the back of an SUV to conduct the final round of interview and we had a few minutes to sit and warm up before they started. The first thing Matthew said to me was "So if we hire Ryan Hewitt to produce 3 songs at $10,000. we'll have enough left over to manufacture 20k sampler CDs to hand out at local shows and ship them off to press and labels etc."

I began to do the math in my head and pointed out that this time we're going to do it right. I said that I'd call Ted Jensen at Sterling Sound to see if we can get a DIY rate on mastering and otherwise let's do a relentless myspace campaign offering to send our sampler to anyone who wants it. That way we can build up a mailing list and develop a fan base from the ground up.

Here we were having just wrapped up one of the most epic "upsets" in TV history (ehh well that's probably not true at all), almost died in the process, winning 50K without anybody even knowing we were out here and all we could give a rats about was moving the band forward. It was wonderful.

Since I can remember, life has been one gigantic roller-coaster of highs and lows. Just months before this moment, we'd been on our knees at rock bottom with a couple of shovels digging our way even further down. Of course in our hearts and minds we were simply pursuing the only destiny there was for us and though we'd done nothing but fail, failure was not an option. As things became more and more bleak, I developed an adage that we'd adhere to from then on. "You can't lose if you never quit". Granted, you can be 78 years old and the score could be Life: 344989348659465 to your 1 but if that damned game wasn't over, you still hadn't lost.

We were almost 29 years old and our band had been dropped and subsequently broken up. I remember 2 very specific moments in that time frame that would define who we were, are and will always be. The first was when Matthew and I had gotten a call from Roger Jansen who informed us that the bidding war Matthew and I miraculously managed to drum up for The Blank Theory after Newline let us go had just fallen apart. We stepped onto our balcony and took inventory.

We had no band, no prospects of a record deal and zero future whatsoever. As if some invisible voice beckoned the question: do we throw in the towel and join the real world? With no skills, schooling, or interest in any alternative career whatsoever, this would be hell on Earth. Not a chance. We had nothing and yet we committed to each other that day that we would stop at nothing to make our dreams come true. Or die trying anyway.

A few days later we'd have lunch with my dad and 2 of our sisters. They'd all become quite disenchanted with our refusal to grow up and dead end careers at this point. They knew how prickly of a subject it was for us so they were quite delicate when bringing it up. Dad suggested we give up and consider law school or med school. I said "Dad, I'd sooner slit my own throat than give up". This shocked and terrified him and needless to say that lunch ended in a massive fight. How did we get to this point? Like this...

"Can I Tell Him Who's Calling?"
August, 2004

Right about the time when TBT had officially been put to rest and Reforma was getting lit up by major labels, Matthew and I had become pretty prickly with one another. It was a brutal stretch and I remember driving down Ashland Ave. screaming at each other when his phone rings.

It was an LA area code which at that point is all we would answer, LA or NY (ya know 212, 917, 323, 310, where the labels are). Turns out to be Fear Factor. One of our best friends Schabiezal had gone behind our backs and submit us on line for this retarded game show.

I'd only seen the show once or twice and hardly knew the premise but given an opportunity to make asses of ourselves for our friends, we're all over it.

Now yes, we used to play Division 1 ball back in college but let me tell you we're far from in shape, health conscious, competitive or willing to do things that are the slightest bit uncomfortable. So none of this made sense from the very beginning. We thought it might be hilarious to not tell anyone we were doing it, secretly go out to LA and get our asses kicked all over the place by a couple meaty girls and come home to have a laugh with our friends when it airs. No problemo.

When we got out there they had cars pick us up from LAX and take us to a hotel in Studio City. When we walked in there were these 2 giant cowboy looking frat dudes checking in. I mean these were real men. bodies chizeled to all hell, perfectly V-shaped, muscles even in their faces kind of men. It cut like a knife when we realized they looked exactly the same and dressed in the exact same goat fucker-gone-frat boy outfits complete with cowboy hats. Yes sir these dutch ovens were the competition.

Sitting behind them in the lobby were 2 tall, hot-til-you-get-too-close, blonde chicks and another 2 spitfire black chicks. Weird part is they were all dressed exactly the same as each other. This was the special Twin Edition and holy cow did these twins adore that they were twins.

We've never understood this type of twin. Sure we hang out all the time and enjoy one another's company but these people dress the same, talk the same, go to twin conventions, and practice saying the same thing at the same time. These types of twins give us all a bad name. When I hear the term "twins" I automatically think of 2 douchy nerds that love the fact that they're twins - cuz of these people.

Anyhow we got upstairs and quickly realized that we were gonna get our asses kicked into the next galaxy and it got pretty hilarious. I mean we came up to the cowboy dudes nipples. and to make matters worse they turned out to be scholarship tri-athletes at their college. Couple of xanax later we forget why we were even in LA and flipped through the channels til we passed out.

The following morning we had to wake up at like 6am. Upon first alarm it sank in that we took this joke way too far and fuck this we weren't doing it. Passed back out until a producer came pounding on our door and reminded us that we'd signed a contract, blah blah. So we shook off the morning grouch and headed downstairs.

The lobby was festive with giddy twins who were about to embark on their life's crowning moment. Not to belittle or condescend of course but for us it meant nothing but a possible laugh and now that it was real we had to face the daunting inevitability that we were about to be very uncomfortable.

Some black secret service style SUVs pick us up, blind fold us and drive off. I was immediately lol-ing at the blindfolds but I guess it makes sense because if I saw where we were going i'd text every one of my retarded friends and have em come horse with us. But the blindfolds helped me sleep as we went for a 40 minute ish drive.

When we get to this mystery destination they escort us out of the SUVs and walk us into a trailer. 8 douchy looking twins, all dressed like each other sitting in a relatively small movie set trailer with the blindfolds on. Mind you it's about 43 degrees outside in LA and they come in and tell us to put our swimsuits on. If anyone's

seen my upper body you know that this already
sucks balls and is amazing all at once.

We had to change in front of each other which
was kind of cool cause we got to see 8
boobies. Then they bring us out of the trailer
and line us up with our blindfolds still on.

This is the opening shot of the show where the
Braveheart music plays and they show all the
contestants walking next to each other in slow
motion while the voice overs introduce us. They
record the voice-overs before or after each stunt,
pulling us individually into an SUV so the
producers can interview us.

As they show everybody walking in slow-
motion of course, all the other contestants were
talking about how awesome they were and that
fear wasn't a factor and that they'll be
champions. As we're lined up they finally take
the blindfolds off to capture the "surprise"
reactions of our location. A

lake. woohoo. They call "action" and we all
start walking. Matthew and I were on the far
right end, almost hilariously shorter and skinnier
than everyone else. About 5 seconds into the
walk this fucking helicopter comes up behind us
out of nowhere. I don't know about you but my
first instinct was to dive for cover, which is
exactly what I did.

The camera men, Joe Rogan and all the rest of
the production crew were split between laughing
and thinking WTF have we gotten ourselves

into with these 2.   Alas, we had to re-shoot it...
about 5 times lol.

Eventually we get to the part where they reveal
what the first stunt is to be.
Basically there are 2 platforms, one on each end
of the lake. One twin kneels on one of the
platforms with this harness mechanism (that was
ten sizes too big for us). and the other twin is
leaning out of a helicopter which has a long rope
hanging underneath it. The rope was to be
fastened to my harness and the helicopter would
then lift me and start hauling ass across the
lake. There we're 2 red buoys spread a decent
distance apart sitting in the middle of the lake.
Essentially the helicopter flies a straight line
over each buoy .. when the twin in the
helicopter feels like the dangling twin (me) is
close enough to the first boy (considering
centrifugal force and all, ya know.. an object in
motion stays in motion unless acted upon by an
equal or opposition reaction? or
something?).. he pulls a lever which releases the
twin to then plummet 70 feet into the icy abyss
of the lake. The helicopter twin then has to
jump onto the 2nd buoy (using the same
calculations of course).. When each respective
twin lands, they must grab a flag from their
buoys and then swim a treacherous swim to a
speed boat. Treacherous in that the helicopter
then flies directly over us and hammers wind
down relentlessly.

So then you climb on the speed boat and it proceeds to race around the lake and at 35mh (fast as hell for a boat) and as it passes a platform about 20 yards away you each jump off it, explode again into the water and swim to the platform to hang your flag.

I cant remember exactly when or how I learned to swim and perhaps that's because I never really did. I mean, at this point if you can't stay afloat in water you're either retarded or have holes in your lungs ... all due respect? But staying afloat is one thing, actually swimming is an entirely different matter.

I can swing my arms like they do in the Olympics but it never seems to get me anywhere but exhausted. I can kick my feet but since there aren't webs between my toes that tends to be futile as well. Regardless, I figured since I was wearing a life jacket I'd just start to do both as soon as I hit the water and aim toward the target. There's that gift of common sense paying me dividends again!

As I crouched on one knee atop the first platform, the wind from the helicopter blades was demolishing me. One of the safety dudes had to hold me up as they affixed the rope to my harness, all the while trying to stay out of the camera shot. Fortunately it didn't take long and in no time I was rising above the arctic lake like a wet flag into howling wind. This fucking sucked.

There was a brief moment wherein I thought it might be fun to act as if I'm running in mid-air and sure enough, it was. Until that is, Matthew must have pulled the release lever because even quicker than I launched up into the air, I suddenly plummeted toward an icy abyss. Hitting the water is difficult to describe. It was literally 43 degrees outside and we'd been out there for hours in shorts and t-shirts and now I was topless and plummeting from 50 feet in the air. It felt like I crashed into an atom bomb. The frigid water, high velocity impact and disorientation caused immediate shut down of all essential brain function. Once again, left to the wares of my auto-pilot, I started swinging my arms and kicking my feet.. just like I've seen them do in the Olympics.

Fortunately Matthew dropped me practically on the first buoy which meant I grabbed the flag in the first few seconds and thus began my swim to the speedboat. My body was frozen numb and I could feel my lungs collapsing on themselves. It was very difficult to breathe, not to mention swim but alas, it's what I had to do. I have no recollection of how long it took me to get to the boat but as you could guess it felt like an eternity. When I got there I forgot the rules. My initial instinct was to reach both arms up to a camera man already on it, presuming his instinct would be to pluck me out of the water for an easy hero card. Well he didn't.

Not only did he deny my desperate, life-threatened pleas for help, he declined to even yell to me that I had to climb up myself. So for an awkward few moments I tread water behind the boat until I got my wits about me and arduously climbed up onto the back of it.

I collapsed on the little landing and didn't even consider holding on. At that moment there were so many stimulating things happening around and inside of me that common sense was nothing of the sort.

My body was still screaming from the shock of the impact and all it's implications when Matthew finally arrived at the boat and climbed up.

The boat takes off around the lake in a few short moments later and quickly reaches a speed of about 178 mph. Its true, I swear.

For the 45 seconds or so that the boat raced around the lake I learned a lot about myself. The reiteration of an age old theory that I'm not a real man exploded into reality. I needed to quit. Call 9-1-1, something, anything. Then one of the producers on board the speedboat yelled above the roaring engines and hovering helicopter blades "get ready to jump!". "I can't" I said. "go!" he said. So I jumped.

When I hit the water my lights went out. You know that concussive shock you experience when your head hits something or something hits your head so hard it jostles your inner TV screen? Well that shock can't be over-stated. I felt like I got hit by a semi, kicked by a donkey in the face and fisted by a sumo wrestler all at once.

When my lights came back on, sure as shit I was still in the water and I still had to finish this nightmare. So I did what any other Olympian might do and I swung my arms and kicked my feet

After what felt like yet another eternity, I finally reached the platform. Matthew had jumped off the side of the boat that was closer to the platform so he beat me to it and that just might have been the difference between winning and losing. You see, by the time I got to the platform, I couldn't move my arms, much less pull myself up onto it. Like so many times in life before, I sent out the silent duress signal to my twin and he picked up on it before I even hit the psychological send button. Matthew grabbed onto my life jacket and pulled me up onto the fucking platform. From there I was able to stumble my way to the flagpole and hang it. It was over.

By the time we dried off and were escorted back to Joe Rogan and the rest of the twins, we'd learned that our time was pretty good. We were in the lead and had knocked out both of the girl sets of twins, leaving just the triathlete frat boy cowboys who were up next.

These guys were built for this kind of shit but not made for it. Their bodies were a grossly perfect blend of muscle and shape. Being college triathletes at a major university in Alabama or something put their odds at nearly 100-1 to beat us.

The All American Tri-frat-letes were underway and when the first twin dropped his brother all but on top of the buoy, it appeared that our lead was about as solid as a fart in the wind. As he then jumped out right on top of his own buoy, they were poised to knock us out of the running. *Author's Goat: If I were a real writer, I'd go back and add in or edit anything I forgot to mention or repeated but since I have the luxury of being a self proclaimed idiot, I don't have to do such things so I'll just mention now that this first stunt was a non-elimination round but instead, Capital One Visa donated $20,000 to whichever team of twins had the best time in said stunt.*

When, however, the first twin grabbed the flag of his buoy, something wonderful happened. One of them swam the wrong way. It only took him about 3 strokes to realize it, which for all intents and purposes is maybe 3-4 seconds of a difference but holy shit did it count. Joe Rogan kept the rest of us apprised of their time every 30 seconds until the last 30 seconds in order to keep our audience and contestants in suspense.

They finished, hanging the final flag in similar fashion as we did. We had to wait for them to be shuttled back and dry off before we were told that it all came down to a 2 second difference. Since we were perfectly even when they jumped off the boat, it all came down to that final swim which I wasn't all that confident in. I mean don't get me wrong, I swam like they do on the Olympics but struggling to get up that ladder probably cost me a second or 2.

But alas, Joe announced that the time to beat was our 1:38 and that the cowboys time was 1:40 so we won.

Our sole interest in life and more importantly throughout this experience was to get our new band up and running. Back at the hotel we strategized and passed out watching TV, forgetting entirely about the 20K we won earlier that day.

The next morning we woke up in the same fashion as the day before, begrudgingly strapped on our blindfolds and were off to the middle of nowhere again.

A few hours later, the SUV pulled up to an old barn on a massive farm. They line us up to reveal the stunt and I could already smell death. When they pulled the blindfolds off, a few feet in front of us was a carved out trench about 50 feet long, 2 feet wide and maybe 4 feet deep. It was full of a dark, muddy water and cow parts. Brains, spleens and intestines marinated in the thick stew while a giant plate full of maggot-covered cow jaw bones graced the far end.

On the opposite end was an old fashioned grinder with a pint glass underneath it's spigot. Above the trench hung a pulley system which connected the 2. What in the wide world of sports was this all about? Suddenly, reality hit and it did so like a ton of bricks.

Joe Rogan does his usual bit explaining the stunt while we all starred blankly at the nefarious challenge that lay before us. The 2 blond girl twins bailed instantly, refusing to even dip a toe into the trench. Both twins are attached to harnesses that hung from the pulley system so while one of them is on one side of the trench, the other is automatically on the opposite side. Each twin swims back and forth in synch taking huge mouth full bites of meat and maggots off the cow jaw bones, swims them to other side, spits them into the grinder and grinds. Once the pint glass was full we'd be tasked with drinking the entire concoction. Matthew and I went first which meant we'd have to set the bar.

It was freezing as all hell again and since we'd be getting into a trench it was required that we wear our bathing suits and be otherwise topless. By the time we harnessed up to the pulley system and stepped into the trench, hypothermia was an imminent threat.

Stepping into it was like stepping into that pool at the end of Amityville Horror. A dark, slippery, muddy abyss of death and evil. The smell, the cold and the foreboding task battled the defenses we'd built out of xanax. A formidable opponent at that. My nipples were razor sharp and the more Joe's banter prolonged the inevitable, the grouchier I got. At some point I said, "let's just fucking start already" and off we went.

There were 2 cement blocks buried under water in the trench that we'd have to climb over on our way back and forth. They didn't serve much of a purpose at the time aside from annoying us to all hell. They'd serve another purpose in approximately 36 hours that would dramatically affect several lives. For the time being though, the producers counted down and we were off. About 9 minutes in we'd filled the glass and started to take turns drinking it down. The concoction was nauseatingly thick and since most of the maggots half survived the grinder, we'd be swallowing these whole along with the cow meat and fish juice. It would take 13 + minutes for us to finish.

When we finally climbed out of the trench they escorted us to a water truck where we were stripped down and hosed off like animals before letting us sit in an SUV to warm up. They ushered us into the back of the truck totally nude and gave us a bucket. Remember when I told you about the time in college when Matthew and I had gotten into a fight but I was naked? Well shivering to al hell, naked and barfing into a bucket in the back of an SUV with your twin is a very similar experience. The whole thing was morbid and fucked up.

The blonde girls refused and clocked out, eulogizing their 15 minutes of fame. The black twins harnessed up and began to contemplate following suit when suddenly one of them slipped on a muddy embankment and fell into the trench. At that point she demanded her sister get in it and they gave it the old college try. Their journey didn't last much longer as they quit before even chewing one piece of meat. Alas, it was just us and the cowboys left and they had yet to do the stunt.

They started strong but within minutes one of them barfed all over himself and the trench. This left his brother the task of completing the entire stunt on his own and with our time of 13 minutes, they had no chance. Knowing as much and that Fear Factor couldn't have an episode with only one set of twins left, the dude took 45 minutes to finish. He even barfed at some point which should have given Matthew and I the grand prize right there and then but again, they couldn't be eliminated because we still had 2 stunts to go and we'd be the only ones left. So we got screwed, but alas, we won the 2nd stunt as well and were now 2 and 0.

The 3rd stunt was my time to do what I do best and I queefed all over myself so needless to say, we don't have to get into it.

That night we'd decided we were over the whole thing. The cow trench was fucked up and we both started to feel a little shitty. Not to mention the shtick of the whole thing began to run it's course for us. Yes we were still in it and winning, but it wasn't that funny any more and began to be a pain in the ass. We tabled it for the next morning and passed out.

Several hours later I'd been having another nightmare. It was about 3am, the lights were on and Matthew was saying something to me as I once again bounced back and forth from dream state to lucid.

In my dream state, a man was chain sawing my hand open. When I'd wake, I noticed Matthew putting his clothes on and telling me he's going to the hospital. In these situations my immediate inclinations is to anything in my power to simply get back to sleep and deal with whatever was happening the next day. This time, however, that man chain-sawing my hand open in my dream left a Freddy Kruger style wound for me back in the real world. I looked at my hand and it was mutilated. I begrudgingly told Matthew to wait for me and got dressed.

We got to the hospital around 4am and when we walked in, sure as shit there were not only 2 other sets of twins but also 2 Fear Factor crew dudes sitting in the ER already. The plot thickens.

Essentially, the trench effed everybody up. You know those cement blocks I was talking about that we had to climb over? Well, as we did so, you'd get tiny little nicks and cuts on your hands and feet. Not something one would typically get alarmist about but in this case, whatever rotting carcass fodder for the worst kinds of bacteria to feed on that lay in the cess pool of hell managed to swim it's way into every tiny little cut each of us developed. We ended up with a lethal cellulitis blood infection.

It felt awful, like a flu on steroids. I wasn't really concerned because I couldn't wrap my head around the idea that a little microbial could end up killing 8 of us but when NBC's team of attorneys showed up in the hospital, I began to consider it. Furthering our cause for alarm, they decided to call our parents.

They hadn't quite flown any family out or anything but they were considering which is when things got really shitty. Seeing though, that Matthew and I are opportunists, we began to focus on the positive and after a little bit of math we'd felt like we had a pretty good case for some pain killers.

They began to load antibiotics through our IVs every hour on the hour. I didn't pay much attention to the diagnosis or their treatment strategy. I suppose most people would but I never took things too seriously and somehow assumed that in 2004, modern medicine had a decent handle on infections. Boy was I wrong. Cellulitis infections start with a deep red streak at the point of infection which in our case was any of the several nicks and cuts on our hands, knees, thighs etc. Once the bacteria gets in your blood stream it begins mutilating it's way up your veins on route to the heart. Once it gets to the heart, it kills you. Doctors are able to track the infection by simply following the streak. They would put a little "x" on our skin where the red streak stopped with a sharpie to gauge the infection's progress. Each hour it would move a few inches up the arm or leg marking it's way to ground zero.

It was a critical 24 hours as the few inches became a few more inches in a few less minutes. Every time they marked the spot, they also loaded up the IV bags with a heavier anti-biotic. The fucked up part is that as the hours went on and we all felt shittier and shittier, the producers kept trying to get the doctors to sign off on proceeding with the final stunt scheduled for the following day. By about 6pm, the hospital decided to fly in an infection specialist and NBC finally got the message. They wanted so desperately to wrap the final stunt and send us on our way before this thing got any worse but once they considered the gravity of the situation they began whistling an entirely different tune. Matthew's infection which started at his knee had accelerated dramatically. When it passed his pubic region, heading North we began to get terrified and pissed off. It was a matter of about 6 inches now to his heart and we were all 8 different kinds of anti-biotics deep.
The producers were careful to remind us that we signed our lives away while they became more

accommodating and compassionate. They discussed flying our parents out with the now handful of lawyers in the waiting room. By the time they officially canceled the 4th and final stunt, everybody was scared shitless. The other twins weren't fairing any better. One of the cowboys' infection started at his neck and was barreling south.

In the end it took the 10th anti-biotic to stop the infections. Matthew was a mere inches from losing his life and I was a few inches behind him. They decided to reschedule the final stunt for a month later, giving us time to fly home and recuperate. We flew home but did anything but rest.

CHAPTER 16
I Love it When a Plan Comes Together

It would be over a month until we could reconvene in LA to ultimately win Fear Factor. Since the 4th and final stunt was a month later, this time we decided to bring Mateo and Dan back to LA with us to finish the agonizing session with Chris Johnson. We were disgusted with the first session but not only were we 20K deep already, but the Victor/J mirage was the only sliver of action and/or hope we had going on. Naturally, we wanted to keep it as alive and well as a dead horse can be. It was literally a $20K psychological investment.

When we finished shooting the final stunt, we called the dudes who were hiding out in our Fear Factor financed hotel. We were giddy over the fact that we'd just won 50K which would not only offset the $20K sinkhole that was Chris Johnson, but would also allow us to hire a real producer and make a real demo. None of us could believe we won and that night we went back to Hollywood and celebrated. Things seemed to be snowballing in our direction so when we found out Metal School was playing at The Roxy that night, life didn't get any better. The next day we had our 3rd and final day with Chris Johnson which he spent at the hospital with his kid and we spent sitting in his studio room plotting our revenge against him.

The Disappearance of Adalia

Back in Chicago, Matthew hired a dude named
Ryan Hewit to producer our demo/EP. We'd use
the Fear Factor money to fly him from LA to
Madison, Wisconsin and record 3 songs. Ryan
had been an up n comer known for his recent
work with the Red Hot Chili Peppers. He turned
out to be amazing and by the time we wrapped
our 3 song demo, industry buzz began to rear it's
pesky little head again.

We manufactured 10,000 CDs and started
handing them out to kids outside shows in
Chicago. We also sent them to every A&R we'd
ever heard of or discovered. One of them was a
dude named Ron Burman who worked for
Roadrunner Records. Ron signed Nickelback
and though they aren't exactly the coolest band
in the world, they'd sold enough records to
finance a small nation. Roadrunner had used
Nickelback's string of multi platinum records to
bank roll the label's ambition to cross over from
metal to mainstream. Since Ron was the wizard
behind Nickelback, the label tapped him to
quarterback the expansion. Needless to say,
when Ron called us, we were stoked. He
expressed his serious interest in the band and
when the Fear Factor news came out, he wanted
to come see us play live.

We booked our first Madina show ever at Metro
on May 21st, 2005. We promoted the shit out of

227

it and though we were 3rd of 4 bands, we were the clear headliner that night. It was Madina's maiden voyage and the show couldn't have gone better. 2 weeks later Ron would bring us back to Manhattan to play for the label's president.

We decided to take the van so we could bring all of our own equipment and stayed at a friend's house in Brooklyn. It was quite the departure from flights and limos and fancy hotels but we meant business this time and so did Ron. He'd warned us against trying to parlay the Roadrunner showcase into building an industry buzz in hopes of a bidding war. We made him promise they were serious about working with us and agreed to keep it on the downlow. This time around we'd learned our lesson and since Ron was as genuine as they come, we weren't going to rock any boats. Against our every desire to do so, we didn't tell a single soul. Not our friends, not industry people and not even our family. We'd been down this road before and knew well enough to not believe anything til we were coming home from it. Further more, I don't think anyone wanted to hear about it anymore. We'd been elated and crushed so many times that we were the only people who still believed in ourselves. The fantasy was to go out to NY, secure a record deal and announce it only after we'd signed the dotted line. So we rehearsed relentlessly, loaded up the van and disappeared.

The showcase was at a metal club called Continental and we'd play 30 minutes before doors opened.

It wasn't the first time we'd play to a group of suits in a small or virtually empty room but it never got any easier. My stage fright only escalated with time but somehow, nothing was going to stop us on this particular evening. In our hearts and minds we knew we had something special with this band of best friends and more importantly, we were ready to get in the game.

We blasted through a 5 song set absolutely on fire. The new songs, the chemistry between the 4 of us was undeniable. Dan being one of the best modern drummers I've ever heard, wailed. Mateo, with his latin rhythmic styling's exploded on guitar and of course Matthew, lost his mind. For my part, I hit 70% of the notes which was at the top end of my handicap. More so, I managed to utter a few decent lines between songs that worked for the circumstance and by the time we finished, we felt amazing. We'd learned better than to convince ourselves we were going to get signed but at least we knew we represented Madina to the best of our abilities and now it was up to the suits.

The next morning we woke up to a blaring sun and the sweet sweet sounds of Matthew's phone ringing. Hung-over from the celebratory post-showcase party, the 4 of us were strewn about the couches and floor of an old Brooklyn Brownstone. Matthew leapt to his feet and ran into the kitchen as he answered the phone and all we hear him say was "El Capitano!" which was his nickname for Ron Burman.

Jeezy, Mateo and I were giddy and terrified and giddy. Tryin to eavesdrop on Matthew's call, we eventually resigned to waiting it out in the dingy room we slept in, so as not to make Matthew nervous. After 5 minutes we began to gain confidence because bad news only takes 30 seconds to break. After 15 minutes we started to get excited. When he finally walked back into the kitchen 40 minutes later, Matthew tossed his phone on the couch and says "dudes.. pack up your shit, we're going to meet our new label!".

From Them Through Us To You
We drove to Roadrunner Headquarters in Manhattan and met the entire staff. They were amazing and the whole company was genuinely excited about our band. Not only had we read a million horror stories about the big bad record labels, but we'd also experienced a handful of them ourselves. Roadrunner was the exact opposite. The radio staff, video promotions, publicist and sales staff were all fundamentally passionate about music and the label. They'd built a legendary brand and were proud of it. Now, they were welcoming Madina with open arms.

After introductions, we sat in Ron's office to discuss songs and producers. Mateo was hell bent on recording with Mark Trombino who'd worked with Jimmy Eat World and Finch to name a few. We didn't think in a million years the label would pay to hire Mark so when Ron agreed, we were stunned. Our last stop for the day was at label president Jonas' office.

This guy was a big deal. He ushered us in and proceeded to tell us things that practically had us all nude in a matter of minutes. He committed to prioritizing Madina and backing our record with everything they had. He guaranteed us International promotion, touring and full radio/video budget. It was everything I had not to just drop his pants and start tuggin. By the time we left, we assured them we'd sign whatever contract they sent to our lawyers and guaranteed we'd make them proud.

Our advance was $75,000. with which we were to live for a year while we toured. There was an additional 100,000. recording budget and $40,000. video budget built in. On top of all that, they offered to pay off a douche bag named Dave Chivarri who pretended he was managing us $20,000. to avoid a law suit. Dave was the drummer of Il Nino and was desperately trying to manage us once our band started a slight "buzz". We gratefully declined but his band at the time happened to also be signed to Roadrunner and the label saw that as cause enough to pay him off and be done with it. For us it was just another unjustified fleecing but whatever, we were in the game now. We'd sign the deal a month later and a month after that we'd celebrate by treating ourselves to a good old fashioned Carnival Cruise.

We began to write relentlessly. The sheer elation of having a record deal comes in tandem with the age old panic of losing it. We knew we'd need "hits", and not just songs that fit the stipulations of one. There is a relatively standard arrangement, length and requisite of "singles". They need to be catchy as hell, around the 3 minute mark, have at least 3 choruses and a massive lyrical hook. To this point, we'd known the protocol but only considered it as far as securing a record deal but this was different. We had the deal, now we needed the hit to keep it and cultivate a career for ourselves.

Chicago changed instantly for us. Our group of friends were all in other bands and the scene has always been extremely competitive. Despite the fact that we'd all hang out constantly, most of them were ready to cut throats to get a record deal. When we got back to town, we were essential hated by our peers but that local scene politic bullshit no longer applied. We had a chance and we had to make good on it.

Our A&R finally agreed to green light the studio. His demands of having at least 3 singles must have been met because Roadrunner went ahead and hired our fantasy producer Mark Trombino and booked us a 2 month session in LA.

At that point we'd written about 13 songs. The label needed 16 all together; 13 for the US release, 2 more for International and B-sides and one for incentive packages. They say you have your whole life to write your first record and only months for each additional which is often why bands hit their "sophomore slump". In our case we had about 9 months all in, from when Madina officially formed to when we officially went into the studio. We used them wisely and were thrilled with the material we'd compiled for our first release.

A few months earlier, Mateo and Jeezy came over to Matthew's and my condo in Chicago. We had a balcony on the 3rd floor of it that over-looked the skyline that we used to hang out on almost every night. We decked it out with tiki torches, a grill and of course speakers through which we'd play Pantera, Rage Against the Machine, Muse, NIN and Refused to name a few. On this particular night we'd just began to fantasize about being in a band together. It was one of those bonding nights wherein each would share their own deepest tragedies and struggles with life and it didn't take long to realize we'd all been through very similar traumas. We talked about losing loved ones, insecurities, betrayals, persistence, dreams and friendship. It was the first night we knew that the 4 of us were there for a reason and the idea of our own band became a reality at that moment, whether we said it or not.

We talked about forming a band based around a fictitious town in the 50's. Every song would metaphorically encapsulate each of our hardships via characters and storylines throughout. We talked about an ambitious concept that we'd unfold over 3 records and began to map it out.

Matthew and I wanted to name it immediately because we knew once it had a name, it would become a reality that they couldn't ignore. We reached deep into our lives and childhood and started to list potential names for this "town". Since I was tasked with all the lyrics, I put a lot of pressure on myself to come up with the winner. I didn't pride myself on much in life but lyrics was one thing I was precious about. Of course it was a blessing and a curse because I'd hate myself 99999 out of 100000 times but it was that 1 that kept me going. I thought long and deeply about our band name.

At the time I was reading about a lot of Eastern Philosophy and religions. From The Vedas and Upanishads to Eckhart Tolle and Gandhi. This was giving me a foundation in existentialism and spirituality which I juxtaposed with my obsession with Islam, Persia and the ebbs and flows of ancient power struggles. Through my studies I'd learned that Islam was among the first religions who's growth MO was the ole, "you're either with us or against us". Thus, the religious wars were born.

There is an ancient town in the region called Medina which is where the Prophet Mohamed is buried. Mohamed initiated the rule by conquer mentality which quickly spread across the continent. On the other hand, his teachings were invaluable in many ways deeming him both savior and destroyer all at once. In my heart of hearts I wanted Madina Lake to represent that juxtapose as it parallels almost every aspect of life. The yin yang if you will.

I was also contemplating Matthew's and my life and relationship and appreciating him beyond explanation. We'd been a team our whole lives and I'd always had this nagging feeling that he'd always done the heavy lifting. It's easy to be the runt of the litter when you've got a dude of eternal strength and fortitude by your side. I'd never underestimate this. Especially when in just 5 short years, I'd all but lose him. I decided to submit Madina Lake as my choice for band name. The metaphorically significance of the ancient town teamed up with the acronym sharing my brother's initials, M. L. gave birth to an epic 3 record biography of his and my life thus far.

The van was all loaded up and we said our good byes to family and friends. This was only going to be a few months in LA, but we all knew that we'd start touring shortly thereafter and would probably be gone indefinitely. It was bitter sweet but in the grand scheme of things it would be way more sweet so I pissed in the trunk and we headed out West.

Man Overboard

We'd had the spoils of LA in our hearts and minds and after a lengthy 3 day trek we were just outside the city. The label had sent over the address of what was to be our new home for the next 3 months and we punched it directly into the ole navigation system. "Extended Stay, Glendale". Now, the accommodations we fantasized about had girls in bikinis throwing beach balls back and forth in the middle of a kidney-shaped pool that trickled over a translucent glass wall into a hot tub that over-looked the Hollywood sign. By the time we pulled into the parking lot, I'd already shit my pants from the conflicting bass tones pulsating from several cars that each bounced up and down to their respective jams. There were thugs everywhere.

We'd all experienced some gnarly neighborhoods in Chicago and the like but this was insane. We'd begun to suspect as much on the way in on account of our street. The strip mall patterns are a dead give away; liquor store, fast food, currency exchange, liquor store, fast food, currency exchange, bail bonds, liquor store, KFC, Planned Parenthood etc. Each adorning cast iron bars and cages over the windows. As for our Extended Stay, it featured an empty, delimitated pool, a variety of smoking mini bbq grills in the parking lot and windows with dark smoke stains above them.

A brief assessment in the van dictated that we give it a shot so we checked in. Our rooms had blood stains on the walls, crabs in the sheets and KFC coupons on the table. What? In a desperate attempt to maintain the enthusiasm we'd traveled across the country with, we decided to go for a band run. Why? I have no idea. Aside from the clinging to enthusiasm, we didn't run. None of us ran. We didn't believe in it, enjoy it or see a purpose in it. In this case though, we figured it would provide for a nice bonding exercise as well as shake off the 3 days we'd just spent in the van. We each put on our short shorts and running shoes and headed out for a trip around the block.

I'm sure it was supposed to be a little longer but each step we took further from the hotel lot was one step closer to our imminent rape, mugging and death. There were burnt out cars, day-time drug deals and pick-up basketball games popping off everywhere. What? So we took each of the closest right turns we could til we were back in the lot. That's when shit got weird. There were police cars. Lots of Police cars. Lights on but sirens off. Lot of commotion, seemed like people were running about randomly with no purpose, destination or cause that we could determine. We hustled to the lobby and up the elevators to the 4th floor. Our rooms were next door to one another so we decided to split up, lock our doors and then meet on our respective balconies to discuss and observe.

Now, this particular hotel was designed in a U-shape with the parking lot in the middle. It was 4 stories tall and we were on one of the sides facing the lot, giving us a birds-eye view of the action. Once our doors were secured we went onto the balconies next to each other and tried to grasp what was happening. Much to our chagrin, it was much of the same. Nonsensical screaming and yelling with a handful of thugs running strange patterns around the lot below. As curious as it was, I was in need of some ice so I headed in for the bucket. Jeezy was next door and had the same necessity so when we both opened our room doors, our jaws dropped.

Just as we each stepped into the hall with our buckets, the elevator dinged. As it did, a gangster came barreling out of the stairwell next to the elevator and hauled ass right passed us. When the elevator door opened, 2 cops came

hauling ass out of it and giving chase to the
gangster. Like I said, the building is U-shaped
so when they all got to the end of the hall, they
could only turn right.. eventually right again
and that was it.

Jeezy and I were speechless. It was like a real
life episode of cops and we were front
row. Obviously it carried with it a pang of fear
so we both bolted back into our rooms and back
onto the balconies to watch this thing play
out. Suddenly, the balcony door of a room
directly across from us flung open to much
fanfare and commotion (Think Ace Ventura
when Jim Carrey yells while opening and
closing the glass door).

About 10 gangsters poured onto the small
balcony and were screamin and yelling. We
couldn't tell if it was a fight, a riot or just a
gnarly party but a few moments later, the
gangster from the hall chase wrestled his way
through the balcony door and fucking jumped.
I'd seen one other death in my lifetime and it
was equally as awful. Back in Chicago when we
lived in that high rise we saw a girl get shot and
fall out of a moving car. It was opening night of
that movie "Set it Off" or something and the
theater on the first floor of our building was
showing it. Apparently the film has a racial
edge to it and when the evening showing let out
there was a huge gang fight on our street. We
were up on our balcony and watched this mini
van slowly roll up to the front door/lobby which

was directly below us. As it did so, the side door swung open and we heard 3 shots. The girl who must have opened that door fell out and onto the street. We called 9-1-1 and raced down to see if we could help in any way. By the time I got out the front door, she was already dead. There was a bunch of gang bangers yelling and screaming and the situation was far from alleviated so we headed back upstairs and waited for the cops. They arrived 30 minutes later. It was awful.

So here we were again. Another gang-banger laying dead in the parking lot. Apparently he had a ton of drugs on him which is why he ran from the cops. They chased him all the way up to the 4th floor, around the whole U-shaped building and cornered him in their room. We found out that he didn't intend to kill himself but shit he must have failed a lot of math classes to think he could survive a 4 story leap. Well, now I'm depressed. Let's move on.

Moving is precisely what we did. Matthew called the label and told them what had happened. We were promptly relocated to Heaven on Earth.. ergo.. The Oakwood Apartments in Studio City. The Oakwood's are a legendary franchise of extended stay suites. These Oakwood's in particular were ripe with A, B, C and D-list celebrities who are working in LA temporarily. Our apartment was nestled snuggly into the side of a big hill (or little mountain, as it were) that the infamous Hollywood sign is on. Sure enough, there were bikinis and beach balls and American Idols and Malcolm in the Middle types poppin off everywhere.

We shared a 2 bedroom, luxury for all intents and purposes, apartment. The complex had 2 pools, complete with hot tubs, work-out facility etc. and our balcony overlooked the side of a mountain. We made it. The first night there we picked up a pile of groceries and Jeezy cooked us all dinner. We had clams casino, a few bottles of red wine and vodka martinis while discussing our forthcoming record. The next day we piled into the van and headed back to Glendale to load in to the infamous Mark Trombino's studio.

Based on his illustrious career thus far we were kind of shocked at the quality of the studio which turned out to be a friend of his' backyard garage. We're hardly pretentious or entitled in any way shape or form, we just envisioned a pro studio and this was literally a small, 1 car garage convert. We were even more surprised when we finally met Mark. This guy was a legend to us and having recently made some of or favorite records, we were giddy like school girls.

He met us there a few minutes after we arrived and his reclusive demeanor made him a tough nut to crack. Here we were 4 kids with tied off wieners so as not to piss ourselves with excitement and Mark was just empty.

He confessed right away that his girlfriend/wife was in the process of leaving him. Add to that he was now having to find a new place to live so he'd be house shopping throughout our recording process.

The plan was to spend the first 2 weeks on pre-production which essentially means we go through each song with a fine toothed comb, pick which ones will make the record and make any last second arrangement changes etc. to them. We sat in the control room and listened through together. An hour later Mark said, "well, I think they're pretty good so that's a wrap on pre-production, see you in 2 weeks." We didn't know if we should be excited or pissed but there were a lot worse things we could be doing than hanging out in LA so we went to the liquor store and hunkered down.

We were having a blast but of course I was in a sheer panic about vocals and lyrics cuz it's what I did. By the time we started recording, Mark was slightly lethargic and despondent. Whatever those 2 words mean.

Don't get me wrong, he definitely brought varying degrees of magic to the process but was clearly in another place personally.

Since the studio was in a make shift garage, the sonic logistics were a nightmare. When we finally started vocals, the AC unit kicked in during my very first take and lit up the track with an airy fuzz. Mark decided to order the portable vocal booth from guitar center and spent the next 3 days putting it together. When it was assembled I tried vocals again and sure as shit, the AC kicked in and washed the track. We were on hold again.

The label had budgeted 2 months to record and on account of the 2 weeks of "pre-production" we spent sitting at The Oakwood's, we were now at the 2 month mark without one vocal track. Further more, Mark had zero sense of urgency and now it seemed like he didn't even care if we finished the record or not.

The label had granted us this massive wish by hiring him and they were starting to get pissed off too. Since we spent so much time and energy convincing them that Trombino was the answer to all our prayers, the onus lay directly on our faces. I couldn't take it any more so I called my papa boner.

Zoloft was perfect for me. My whole I'd felt this internal resistance to things. This obsessive fear of the other shoe dropping. Any time anything good happened, instead of embracing it, I braced for the backlash. Perhaps losing mom had gifted me this paranoid refusal to accept happiness and peace of mind. I certainly didn't want to get too comfortable because there was always a monster just around the corner waiting to smash it all away. I'd developed a brain pattern of doubt and trepidation and when the Zoloft kicked in, it all evaporated.

We finally started recording vocals and I'd chosen a track called River People to start with. I liked how my voice sounded against the track and was proud of the lyrics so I figured it would be a good confidence booster. The vocal room was dark and I could see Mark through a window to the control room. He had a dim light on in front of him but the room was made much brighter by the dismal glow of his computer screen. I'd do a take and he'd click the talk-back mic on and say, "again", over and over. I could see the computer screen so I knew damn well he wasn't even listening to me. He was playing World of Warcraft. I finally had it and when I called him out and he left.

Mateo and I had developed an incredible working relationship to go along with our friendship. He was becoming a great engineer and having done all of our demos together for the past 9 months, we had a chemistry. He and I decided right there and then that we'd fake our way through the days and stay over nights to finish the record ourselves. We did this for 2 weeks and managed to pull it off. We'd see Mark less and less for the remainder of the recording I've got nothing but love and respect for him and his work but this extremely frustrating. We didn't want to upset our label or have them question/2nd guess Madina in any way shape or form so we played along like everything was fine.

The nerves and anxiety were already getting to me and the false starts only made it worse. I began to over think every single lyric and melody. I questioned my voice to the extent that I started to get depressed. One by one I had watched my best friends and band mates step up to the plate and nail their parts. Not only performance wise but the writing was phenomenal.

I watched Jeezy bring songs to another Universe with his beats and fills. He literally wrote drum hooks that improved each song immensely. Matthew developed a signature bass style that I hadn't seen or heard and became one of those identifiable bassists who's lines could carry entire songs. He created grove out of space, space out of clutter and melody out of monotony. It was incredible.

Mateo absolutely electrified. His enthusiasm for working with Mark Trombino could not be thwarted and his ambition to impress and/or make Mark proud created some of the most innovative playing i'd ever heard.

There will always be those who see our band as a relatively run of the mill emo or pop punk band and I'm not claiming that we've reinvented the wheel but, Mateo's latin stylings partnered up with one of the best drum and bass sections created a powerful platform. Now it was up to me. Again. And yet again, I was caving to the pressure.

Matthew had to rebuild me from scratch. His uncanny ability to do so is invaluable and especially for me, it's essential. It's not the first time he's had to do so. He carried me through our entire soccer career when I'd hit a downward spiral. He'd pull me through games, showcases, Fear Factor, among other things and now he was pulling me out of the doldrums that almost sank our career.

My confidence was restored and the Zoloft took care of the rest of the rough edges. Mateo and I slept about 4 hours a night for the remainder of the session and just 2 weeks passed the deadline, we finished "From Them, Through Us, To You".

The label flew our team out to listen to the record. It was a perfect afternoon in Los Angeles when Ron walked back to the studio with John G., David Galea and Scott Padell who would become our manager, booking agent and business manager respectively. We all sat outside drinking Starbucks coffee and flirting heavily. These dudes would become our team and each one of them kicked ass. Mark showed up shortly thereafter and we all went into the control room to listen. Ron was floored. When "House of Cards" finished he stopped everything and declared that this was to be our first single.

The mood was exhilarating, especially for as grueling as the entire process was. It felt like we'd finally given birth after an extremely complicated pregnancy and to a beautiful baby.. jesus? *I don't even know where to go with this one lol.* You get the idea.. we were quite proud and so was our business team.

Ron disappeared on the phone for several minutes and when he came back he told us we were going to be shooting a video for House of Cards in a week. That day he solicited treatments from directors and they came pouring in.

Nicolas Hill and Mark Maranaccio are a director/production team and they had a concept that perfectly depicted the intention of the song's lyrics. House of Cards is about a person who's ashamed or insecure about certain aspects of his life to the extent that he feels he has to lie in order to create a perception of who he is rather than just be himself. Since lying can be obsessive, addictive, destructive and pathological, the lies begin to perpetuate themselves. At some inevitable point, they stack up so much that simply carrying on the deceit becomes implosive.

The video took place in an old abandoned house right in the middle of downtown LA. There were homeless people living in it even though at had been condemned years ago. The producers were having a hard time getting rid of them so they decided to just shoot around them. I suppose it provided for an interesting cast at times.

The shoot was fun as hell and simply being in LA, filming our first major budget music video was incredible in and of itself. When we set up in front of the house for the live shots, Ron Burman called up label president Jonas and told him to open up the vaults. In other words, he was so compelled by our performance he insisted to his bosses that they spend some significant money on our band.

CHAPTER 17
Hit the Road Jack

By the time we got out of the studio, we'd already had 3 months worth of tour dates booked. This was a lot to take in given the fact that it was a near decade long pursuit.   After the 7 some years of trials and tribulations with The Blank Theory, we were emotionally exhausted. Suddenly, Madina has a deal, a record in the can, a full business team and now a string of tour dates that seemed to get longer every week, we had to hunker down and baton the hatches.

Roadrunner proved themselves almost immediately. Since we already had the 3 songs we did with Ryan Hewitt, they decided that we should tack on 2 more new songs and make an EP to precede the LP. Even though they'd pay for the manufacturing, The Disappearance of Adalia would serve as a DIY release to build up some cred and the foundations of a fan-base. To support it we'd start touring right away.

2006
Our real touring experience started with a 4 date run from Chicago up to Bamboozle Festival in NJ with a band called Red Jumpsuit Apparatus, & Lorene Drive. We'd fantasized about real touring for years and finally, we were off.

We took to it immediately. At least I did, indulging in every lovely cliché that comes with life as a touring band. At this point it was all innocent and amazing fun but we didn't realize that the partying would become more of a coping mechanism for what is often misperceived as an easy job.

Having played our first 4 shows to about 50 kids total, by the time we got to NJ for Bamboozled, we were shell shocked.

We had a mid-day slot on one of the mid-sized stages and though there were about 10 kids in front of it 5 minutes before we played, there were over 2,000 when we actually started. In the blink of an eye our stage was fucking packed and we were off to the races.

Show was phenomenal. Taking advantage of the crowd size I climbed up a speaker stack about 20 feet up and did a front flip off it into the crowd. I'm not sure what compelled me aside from adrenaline and having made a small habit of that sort of antic. In retrospect it was because I knew we needed those 2,000 kids to go home, after seeing 100 bands, talking about Madina.

Post show was madness. Our merch tent got slammed to the extent that our Tour Manager at the time literally grabbed his suitcase from the trailer and walked off into the sun setting over Giant Stadiums parking lot. He barely uttered a word and this was only his 5th show but as a little insight into the chaos and laborious nature of festivals and touring bands in general, this guy didn't even have the stamina to explain why he was leaving, where was going or how the hell he was gonna get there.

Later we found out he grabbed $100. off our massive merch profits, hitched a ride to Newark and flew back home to Iowa. It was the first example of how grueling the road can be. Bad news for us was that we had to leave Bamboozle by 8pm to drive 30+ hours straight, across the entire country to kick off our first official package tour in Albuquerque, NM. This tour was supporting 10 Years, and thus would kick off the better part of our next 8 years.

Stiletto Formal , Royden, (camping) August/Sept 2006

Our agents wanted us on the road constantly. At the time, so did we and when the dates started stacking up we were loving it. After the Ten Years tour, they'd put us on a package with 2 other baby bands, The Stiletto Formal and Royden.

Everybody has to pay their dues and these type tours were exactly that. Playing to handful of kids in small clubs across the country night after night can be excruciating. At that point though, it's what we'd dreamt about for years and we were making the very most of it. The label was giving us minimal tour support, most of which we didn't want to spend either way. "Roughing" it was kind of in our nature so we'd usually sleep in the van, at strangers houses whom we'd meet at shows or split 1 single bed room at a Motel 6. Until we met Royden.

We hit it off immediately. They were awesome and hilarious dudes and they introduced us to the whole camping scenario. We'd all loved to camp but never really thought about it on tour until then. The first leg ran up through the Pacific Northwest and we found a spot just outside Seattle that was on a river up in the mountains. We each drove our van and trailers along this crazy dirt road until it eventually just ended at which point we grabbed our Wal-Mart tents and coolers and walked another mile or so up to set camp.

They introduced us to a game called frisbeer wherein teams of 2 set up 2 empty beer bottles in front of them about 15 yards apart and take turns tossing a Frisbee at each others. Once you hit one of their bottles, they have to sprint to your side and drink an entire beer while you sprint to the Frisbee on their side and start trying to knock your own bottles down while they drink. If you do so, they have to drink another. Make sense? Doubt it.. I don't even get it. Regardless.. we were all completely shit-housed within an hour.

I can't remember the next couple of hours very well but at some point I found myself in the nudes on top of a kind of ravine looking down on the river and our campsite. There was another dude and girl from Royden somewhere close to me.. I think they were nude too but I'm not sure. The bushes or trees or whatever were too thick to even see each other and I have no idea what the hell we were doing up there. Suddenly one of them screamed "Bear!!!".

Before the scream even got to the "ear" portion of "Bear" I was tumbling down the side of a mountain. Obviously I had obviously tried to react in some way to the threat of a bear but my systems weren't exactly functioning properly. I felt like a giant rubber ball rolling down a patch of thorn bushes. Well I got the thorn bush part right because when I'd finally stopped rolling I was absolutely punctured everywhere. I had little tiny thorns all over my body, arms, legs, asshole, wenis, face, you name it. It took me a minute to get my bearings when I ylooked bank up to the shelf I just tumbled from in time to see a giant blackish brown furry monster scamper off in the opposite direction. Thanks dudes, good lookin out.

Sunday, Roofie Sunday

So we're driving around somewhere out East on route to Florida for the next handful of shows when our manager John G. calls. As usual, Matthew discusses whatever pertinent business affairs with him and just as they are about to hang up, John G. says "oh wait!! Hold on.. you guys are gonna love this". He proceeds to tell us that we've been officially invited to stay at a dude named Chris Kirkpatrick's house after our forthcoming Orlando show. This doesn't ring any bells or garner any enthusiasm until he explains that this guy used to be in that boyband NSync. Things got pretty immediately awesome.

We weren't exactly fans of NSync but a shitload of people, at least at one point in time, were. This meant 2 things. One, he would surely have an MTV Cribs style Orlando mansion which would be funs as shit to stay at, especially vs. Motel 6. And 2, the fact that his dude was once Beatle-mania huge and is now inviting random bands like us to sleep over at his house can only mean something terribly awesome is going on with this guy. We accepted without hesitation.

After the Orlando show, we packed up our gear and hauled ass out of the club to get to the mansion as quickly s possible. Stevo was told to contact Chris' assistant after we load out for further instructions.

30 minutes later, we pulled up to this affluent gated community around 3am and slowly approached a security checkpoint. Something on our van was whistling Dixie when we pulled up and of course we all looked like the "crazy drunk drivers" guy from Back to the Future.

The 2 night guards froze. Each had one finger on their emergency call button and another other on their mace canisters. But after a few phone calls, they finally let us through the gate.

Per their instruction, we followed a winding road til it's end, parked the van/trailer in a massive driveway and headed around back to look for the "pool door". This place was that shizniggetylongduckdongillhaveabananasplithol dmynutscumoniwannalayayaandbtwivepissedine verypoolandorhottubiveeverbeeninhaveyou.

It had a huge pool, hot-tub, grotto blah blah (why do I suddenly have to piss?). Whatever, just imagine the Playboy mansion. It was like that but even had a sea plane parked on the lake off his back yard.

We were loving it but exhausted so we crept in through a sliding glass door and searched, in the dark, for a door to the "home-movie theater", which were supposed to sleep in. We found it and crept in, one by one.

I could barely make out the 10 rows of seats and giant white screen when suddenly I hear a hard thud behind me. Matthew tripped over a mystery wire. In that instant, all these red white and blue flashing strobe lights pop off from everywhere, these jack-in-the-box heads popped out of the walls and all this crazy ass circus themed music blasted out of some hidden speakers.. We all panicked, laughed our ass off and tried desperately to shut the whole thing off when suddenly, another surprise.

From the back row of seats, amidst a symphony of moans and groans, a handful of heads began popping up. Thus, we met the dutch ovens in National Project. Most bands have at least one douchy apple so I try not to blame entire bands for having one but these guys had at least 2 of the most ridiculous vagina cleaners we'd ever met on tour.

We apologized profusely, explained that we had no idea they were even staying there, much less that a secret trip wire would turn the room into a circus. They just could not get ok with it. So they kept bitching like 2nd graders while we rolled out blankets in front of the room and turned the lights off.. 5 minutes later, Matthew rolled over the god damned wire again.

I of course pissed right into my panties and all over my blanket as the National Produce dudes were now standing up with their shirts off, rifling off such classic confrontational questions such as "wanna go man?" and "wanna dance bro?". The madder they got, the more hopeless the notion of containing our laughter became. But it was the kind of course, that you can't display.. like at a funeral or something.. so the more we tried to contain it, the more outrageous the outbursts. We finally passed out around 5am.

We were supposed to head out the next morning but Chris convinced us to stay for their weekly "Sunday Funday" party. Stevo of course knew this was a terrible idea and despite his pleas to the contrary, we were set on it.

Around 4pm people started showing up. Within 20 minutes it became a beautifully cliché, Playboy mansion/Spring Break, Girls-in-bikinis-throwing-beach-balls-back-and-forth-in-the-pool party and we were loving it. It was around that exact time that Jeezy cracked open his first beer of the day.

He drank about half of it and shape shifted into a blubbering, fumbling, exorcist eyed animal. He could hardly stand up, much less function in any way shape or form. We were having too much fun to be troubled by this so we decided we'd rotate Jeezy-duty.

The other 4 of us would take turns looking after him for 20 minute intervals so we could still enjoy the paradise that we'd stumbled upon. Stevo and I sat him down in a beach chair around a campfire of harmless party goers and figured that would be a safe spot for him during our 2 shifts. Well, that was the last time anybody saw him for the rest of the night. Regrettably we didn't even realize he was missing until the next morning.

Once we did, we began a massive search. Chris Kirkpatrick and his friends helped, as we checked every single nook and cranny of the house and his yard. We finally found him climbing down off the top of our trailer. He'd passed out up there at some point and was now throwing up in the grass. The real kicker though, and a mystery that baffles us all to this day, was the fact that he was wearing another man's clothes. Having no recollection of anything beyond the first half of that beer at 4:00pm, he somehow managed to swap outfits with a mystery dude and ended up with an Abercrombie and Fitch rugby top, some good ole frat-boy khaki shorts and Birkenstocks. Awesome.

CHAPTER 18
Supernova

Paramore (Oct, 2006)

As our agents struggled to find us any worthwhile tour, we struggled to garner ourselves some value. It's a conundrum. Bigger bands don' want to take no name bands out on tour because they won't sell any tickets. No name bands can't garner up any drawing power without getting in front of an audience. Add to that the fact that we were just one of a million other bands in our position, all vying for even the slightest opportunity, the odds were stacked against us.

Just as we were threatening to drown in the abyss of obscurity with the other 93% of bands in our position, an opportunity presented itself. As they usually are, it was out of nowhere and had a catch. Paramore asked us to support them on their headlining UK tour.

We of course were pissing all over one another with excitement because even though it didn't stand to benefit our standing in the US, we got to tour in another country.

It was surreal. Mateo and Jeezy had never been to England and it was one of Matthews and my favorite places on the planet. Not to mention this would be the first tour we'd ever do with a guaranteed audience.

With Paramore headlining and a band called Cute is What We Aim For as direct support, we were slated to play first (or often 2nd, after a local opener). At the time, the Emo thing was just about peaking and despite our attempts to avoid it like the plague, simply being on a tour with a band called Cute is What We Aim For even convinced me we were gay, but what the hell did I care, Madina finally had a huge tour and we'd better make the most of it.

It kicked off in Wales and though the Barfly in Cardiff was only a few hundred kids deep, we killed it. I'm not sure if it was the fact that we'd grown up obsessed with all things British, luck or merit but things heated up over there rather instantly. A few shows in and we were making waves from coast to coast.

There was a palpable energy in those rooms and we took full advantage of it. I remember being shocked at the difference between US and UK crowds. In the US, some kids seemed to go to shows with a predisposition to hating a band whereas the UK kids went to shows to go off. They wanted to have a good time and they wanted to find new music to love. To me, that spoke volumes about their quality of life. The more you look for things to love, the more things you'll find to do so and that passion merged in perfect harmony with our ambition to invest everything we had into our music and performances. Once it started to take off, it was gone.

Press started rolling in. By the 2nd week of the 3 week tour, kids started coming to see us based on sheer word of mouth that had begun to spread like wild fire across the relatively small country. As for us, we were coming into our own as a live band. We played with an unbridled energy, of which we'd trade back and forth with the crowds. There began an intimate synergy with our audience that would remain impervious for the remainder of our career.

I remember one show in Newcastle that was particularly insane. The crowd absolutely went off and by the time we were done, it was clear that we'd converted most if not all of the kids in that room. Back stage we couldn't believe it was actually happening. We all knew it. It was a strange but markedly palpable feeling.

Now, after a 10 year pursuit, our success was finally imminent.

This fate was galvanized after the show when we headed out of the dressing room on route to the bus and security had to set up barricades and escorts. As we passed, hundreds of screaming kids surged against it and one of them turned to me. "Jesus, are you lads like the damn Beatles or something?". Not exactly, but we're lucky as f*ck and that was truly a life changing moment. By the time this tour got to London, I'd sang my voice straight out. London is always the most important show and accordingly Roadrunner flew press in from all over the world to check out their new darlings. It was at Mean Fiddler which was just underneath the infamous London Astoria.

We went on and the crowd went bananas. I could hardly project a tone much less a note but the kids didn't care, a testament to how amazing the UK would be to us for many years to come.

We were invited back to the UK in Feb. of 2007 to support Gym Class Heroes. Madina had started to get tons of press over there from the Paramore run and we were growing rapidly but pairing up with GCH brought a bit of a divided audience.

At a show in Oxford, I accidentally climbed up a speaker again and jumped into the crowd. This time though, when I landed, a dude in the crowd grabbed my shirt and threw me face-first onto the floor, exploding my lip open. I finished the set bleeding all over myself and my band and eventually got 7 stitches in my lip. It was the weirdest thing and I quickly learned that for as fabulous as the UK audience is when they like you, they're brutal when they don't.

This time when we got to London, we went on to have one of the best shows ever and it seemed to seal our good standing with the press and kids of the mighty UK.

Give it a (Name April 28 2007)

We continued ping-ponging from the US to the UK and things were starting to pick up everywhere. In April we played our first

massive festival with a slot on the main stage of
Give It A Name Festival with Brand New and
All American Rejects in front of 15,000 kids.
We also started popping up on the radio, TV and
on magazine covers. Life couldn't get any better.

HERE I STAND VIDEO

In May of 2007, Roadrunner had slated an
August release of our 2nd single "Here I
Stand". With the momentum we'd garnered with
House of Cards and relatively strong record
sales world wide, the label decided to go for
broke. Our video budget was huge and once
Roadrunner solicited treatments, they came
flying in from everywhere. We must have
gotten a hundred treatments from directors,
producers etc. who all smelled the money a mile
away.

One blessing and curse about Roadrunner was
that in many ways they still operated
accordingly to the music industry of 10 years
ago. Hundreds of thousand dollar recording
budgets, video, radio promo etc. It was great of
course to get the best of the best but it also
accrued a massive debt that Madina would have
to earn back via record sales. At the end of the
day though we figured if Roadrunner breaks us,
we're probably not going to starve so who
cares. Plus, success only comes from going all
in.

You have to be willing to sacrifice anything and
everything for what you believe in. Our passion

for Madina has always been impervious so we weren't about to hedge any bets. Plus, they say the second you have a plan B is the second you're going to need it. *Or maybe I said that? I doubt it, that sounds a bit too sophisticated for me.. where was I?   Oh yeah..*

We picked a treatment by Dori Oskowitz in large part because we were able to incorporate our band's entire concept into his idea. The trilogy we set out to write as Madina Lake was an arduous undertaking just among each record, much less having to tie it all together via video, live show and the like. So the loose storyline worked perfectly.

The tour we were on was winding around the East Coast at the time so we kind of had to cherry pick a shoot date and location that coincided with a day off. We decided to shoot the vignettes at Needham Broughten High School and the performance parts on a picturesque Lake Crabtree just outside Raliegh, North Carolina. The production team hung gigantic white globes in the thick forest of Beech trees just beyond the lake and built a giant floating stage for us to perform on the lake. It was majestic.

We were floored at the amount of kids that came from all over the country to hang out and be a part of it and that made it one of the better times we'd ever had as a band. Getting to spend hours chillin and getting to know the kids that support our band in an atmosphere like that was

surreal. Accordingly, we captured a pretty
unforgettable video.

Now We Bawlin

I can't remember exactly where we were when
we found out about Projekt Revolution by I
know that it was while we were on a relatively
dismal headlining tour and somewhere in the
South West ish part of the country. Our A&R
called us up and told us to pull over. Obviously
we were on a long highway in the middle of
nowhere but this kind of request could only
mean something awesome was about to happen.

Stevo pulled over at a rest stop and Matthew put
Ron on speaker phone. He proceeded to tell us
that of thousands of submissions, Linkin Park
hand picked us to open their megalithic Projekt
Revolution tour. P-Rev was the biggest tour of
the summer and the odds of getting asked to play
it were seemingly insurmountable and a much
needed life line in the US. I pissed a little with
excitement and we got back on the highway.

The good news kept coming. MTV had reached
out to our label and asked if we would be
interested in hosting a segment for an MTV 2 bit
called "Road to the VMAs". They had
ingratiated our first video and now cast us to
document P-Rev as it made it's way toward

Denver, then fly to Vegas to be correspondents
for the VMAs. We were rollin now.

P-Rev
By the time we pulled into the White River
Amphitheater parking lot in Aurburn, WA for
the dress rehearsal of P-Rev, our van was falling
apart at the seems. Of 9 bands total, we were the
only one in a van which always looked hilarious
parked in the row of 2007 Prevost buses. On
this particular morning, we'd instead be driving
loops around the row of buses cuz our AC only
worked if the van was moving. Since we pulled
in around 6am and the first production meeting
wasn't until 9am, each of us took shifts driving
in circles while the rest slept.
At 8:30am we got up and headed toward
catering. We were floored. Linkin Park had set
up the most elaborate catering I'd ever
seen. Chefs were on hand to prepare omelets,
cut roasts and/or custom make just about
anything you could dream up. There was an
entire section of just teas, vitamins and other
health conscious items so everybody on the tour
could take care of themselves. In one corner
was a one-stop vocal care section with Throat
Coat, Voice Spray etc. just so the singers on the
tour could maintain strong performances. It was
so awesome.
When we got back to the van, Brad Delson
drove up on a little golf cart to introduce
himself, welcome us to the tour and give us a

band care package. Couldn't believe it. The biggest band in the world treating perfect strangers like kings.

The shows were insane. We opened each day and played to anywhere from 1 to 3 thousands kids. The crowds were nutty and we were going over super well. After our set we insisted on doing a signing and determined to stay at the booth until every single kid who wanted to talk, meet us, get pictures or signatures etc. got em. Typically we'd stay for about 2 hours. Under the sun it was exhausting but the adrenaline from the shows and general high from being on such a massive tour kept us strong and grateful as could be.

During P-Rev we were selling about 4,000 records a week which for that time in the industry was apparently pretty impressive. Roadrunner meanwhile was prepping for our biggest radio/video campaign yet. Their initial strategy of releasing "House of Cards" as a soft single to set up "Here I Stand" was working perfectly. The tour was getting better and better and we were heart-broken to learn we'd have to miss 2 of the Florida shows. Until that is, we found out it was so we could fly to Japan for Tokyo's biggest summer rock festival Summer Sonic.

JAPAN, SUMMER SONIC
We literally played Charlotte on Aug 9th, walked off stage and went to the airport to fly to

Osaka, Japan on August 10th. I'd been to Thailand once several years earlier for a random vacation adventure. Stepping of the plane on the on the other side of the planet is culturally shocking to say the least. The air, the sights, sounds and smells are unlike anything on the Western side of the hemisphere. Prone to panic attacks, it was thanks to xanax that I was able to deal with it at that moment. Once relaxed I fell head over heals with the region. Now we're in Japan to play 2 rock shows with our very own band in front of 20,000 Japanese kids. Unreal. We collected our bags and equipment and headed through customs. It's always interesting walking through that final gateway and out to the throngs of family, friends, limo drivers, foreign exchange student host families waiting to meet their new rent-a-gringo etc. who are all crowded up against a nylon security rope snapping pictures and cheering as the passengers walk out. You can't help but feel special until of course the inevitable reality sinks in that nobody is there to greet you.

So as the cheers and flashbulbs went off, red carpet style, we put our heads down and headed briskly toward the exits. I did managed to sneak a glance up at the crowd and just about shit an onion role when I saw a home-made "Madina Lake" flag. We'd never been here before yet somehow there were already at least a handful of Madina fans waiting for us at the god damned airport. We were stunned.

Stopping for pictures and autographs, the fan-fare continued outside at the bus and again at the hotel. I was absolutely smitten with the place. We already know that I just want people to like me and here it seemed they did. They're also, by-n-large, my size. Height, weight, body, stature etc.. I fit in with the Japanese like a god damned glove.

.

The shows were insane and it was at this point that we started to feel like things were changing significantly for us. One second we're grinding it out to 30 kids in small US clubs and suddenly we're flying all over the world, playing to massive crowds and turning up on magazines, radio and TV in foreign countries. As amazing as it was, along with the excitement and gratitude, we'd each start to feel a personal internal melt down.
It's such a strange proposition. The impossible dream was coming to fruition for us and though we were still flying high, the road and constant fear of the proverbial other shoe dropping was beginning to take a toll. But alas, that wouldn't be an issue for quite some time.

KERRANG AWARD
The Linkin Park tour was all it was cracked up to be and more. About 3/4 of the way through we found out that we'd won the highly coveted

Kerrang! Best International Newcomer Award. We even got to film an acceptance speech from P-Rev which was broadcast to the Awards show in London.

Many of the rock and roll clichés had already begun to tickle our pleasure detectors in both hedonistic and alarming ways. At the time though it was so new and fresh that instead of taking it in stride, we shoved our faces between it's tits and motor-boated it. *I'm so white trash. Well I grew up a poor... I mean.. as a kid we never had... sure buddy.*
The last show in Denver was yet another juxtaposition. Super sad that it was over yet knowing we're on route to the VMAs in Vegas made it all just a bit more palatable. Linkin Park invited us to join them on stage for their last song which of course is all of our favorite.. "One Step Closer" (don't deny it). I was so drunk by the time they played it that when we all ran out on stage to fiddle with the fellas as they played, I kicked Rob's in-ear cable right out. This essentially cut off his ability to hear anything, much less a click track, effectively de-railing the whole band. I, of course, mistook the look of terror on his face for a reassuring pair of celebratory devil horns and continued stumbling my way around the stage.

VMAs, Sept 9th, 2007

In Las Vegas we met up with our favorite
Roadrunner rep... let's call him Kevin.. and
headed to The Palms. We checked into one of
the nicest suites they had, courtesy of our heroes
in Nickelback. This is when shit got cra cra..
Kevin you see, is an animal. A beautiful, well
intentioned, man of instinct. As such, he had
innate, carnal necessities to tend to and didn't
waste any time doing so. While we explored the
endless number of luxurious rooms, balconies
and otherwise fanciful spoils that a Las Vegas
suite affords, Kevin was on the phone getting
our evening sorted.

We didn't know who he was calling or what it
was for because we had the blind trust and faith
that as a respectable representative of our record
label, we were in good hands. Turns out we
were in the best and worst of hands they make.
Fast forward god knows how many minutes but
not many, a knock on the door. Each knock
might as well have been the sound of a hammer
nailing our coffin shut because the rest of our
time in Vegas was a glorious, gluttonous, sinful
smudge of things I'd only ever read about.

To grace you with an example, let's just say that
as our band of relatively sheltered kids giggled
our way throughout the suite with our jaws on
the floor as each room was ablaze in various
forms of hedonistic indulgences. What do they
say? Sex Drugs RockNRoll or something?
There were drugs. There were hookers. There
were even drugs on hookers... if only for a

moment before an eager nose hoovered em like the vacuum cleaners you rent from a home improvement store. It was wild. Though some of our crew may have indulged to very mild degrees of adolescent splendor, we also developed a bit of a concern for our future. This wasn't us and if it was part in parcel with becoming a rock star, we wanted nothing to do with it. And if you believe that, you might have a learning disorder.

The VMAs were an amazing experience. Since we were correspondents for MTV2 we spent the next day or 2 interviewing various celebrities I'd never heard of. Most of them were conducted at The Palms pool cabanas which was pretty fantastical. There was a moment out at the hotel's front entrance when a sudden hurricane of people blew by us like a fucking... shit, I already said hurricane.. like a .. tornado? Eh whatever.. a hundred paparazzi flew by us, screaming yelling fighting and generally going insane. In the eye of that storm was Britney Spears. I couldn't believe the aggression and fury that celebrity incites. It was honestly scary. But alas, I'm bored. The next night we put on our Saturday's best and headed for our first red carpet event.

The Palms was a pretty cool venue for the VMAs. Through the massive front entrance was a flurry of journalists, photographers, reporters, anchors etc.. all packed against a velvet rope facing the red carpet and MTV VMA logo-emblazoned wall. Just ahead of that was a team of ushers quarterbacking the whole thing. They'd stop each person, check their credentials and if worthy send them along to the next check-point. Once you've cleared that one, the next usher stops you and positions your group. At the appropriate juncture they open the velvet rope and send you through.

Once on the carpet, your world explodes into a strobed chaos. Journalists and photographers scream at you while the rapid fire flashbulbs blind your entire existence. In our case of course, the avalanche was generally followed by a "who the hell are you guys?" but heyy who's counting.

Our table was in the front row direct middle of the 2nd floor balcony giving us a perfect view of Britney queefing herself and a fight between Tommy Lee and Kid Rock over Pamela Anderson which went down during a commercial break. We got drunk, I met Adrian Granier and then we had to leave for the airport.. as slightly different gentlemen.

Mayday Parade/We Kings Tour + Radio Shows Nov/Dec. 2007

After the VMAs we headed straight out on a headlining tour of the US. Don't be fooled, we had no business headlining and yet again this was a matter of not being able to land any other tours. As agencies do, our booking agent sent us on a long dismal jaunt across our massive country with a handful of other bands nobody wanted to see.

We had Mayday Parade as direct support and a newer band called We the Kings open. In light of our new found "fame".. just kidding.. we decided to treated ourselves to an R V.

The more I remember this RV tour, the funnier those memories get. For example, one night we decided to camp and picked the coolest, relatively desolate site we could. It was somewhere in the Southwest and there was a river, that's all I remember. We decided to stop at the local Wal-Mart to load up on camping supplies, bratwursts, Ice, beer, pellet guns, goggles.. you know, the usual. That's right, we had 6 pellet guns, each complete with a set of goggles. As soon is it got dark we set a couple of ground rules (which nobody paid any attention to anyway) and split.

For the next 3 to 4 hours, the only interaction you'd have with your band/crew mate was blasting or getting blasted by a bullet that stung like a motherfucker and seemed to come out of nowhere. It was most often followed by the shooters proud cackle, followed by his screams and shrieks because his cackle just gave away his location and he started getting blasted by everyone else as soon as he blasted you and laughed about it. Anyhow that was amazing fun.

Matthew got shot from 3 feet away right in the middle of the tip of his nose. He had to spend the rest of the tour with a dark red, bullet sized crater directly in the middle of his nose. The real hilarity, however, showed up after we finally tired of shooting each other.

We remembered that a few hours back we went through a checkpoint which means your vehicle could get randomly searched by border security. Well, we didn't actually go through it to our knowledge but we saw a sign that said "Border Security Checkpoint 1.5 Miles". I don't know much about measuring distance but I know that from that moment, I'd be at the checkpoint in approximately 67 seconds. Being the driver at the moment I did what any good band driver should do and ... well.. I panicked.

Sounding the alarms, screaming and waking everybody up I implored everybody to get rid of anything that may be frowned upon by Border Patrol Agents. As the good band dudes they all are, each one sprang into action immediately and dove for their backpacks, toiletry bags, shoes, screwdrivers etc and started a rigorous search for whatever they knew they had hiding out in pill bottles, wrapped up socks, stashed behind a vent under the RV shower or what-have-you. Schproket gathered his refer and a handful of random anxiety meds we didn't have scripts for and put it all in a baggie. With a tear in each of our eyes and a void in his heart, he flushed said salute down the RV toilet. It was an emotional time for him but we re-grouped and anxiously awaited the Checkpoint.

See they mostly are looking for Mexicans and/or drug runners meaning "whitey deluca" can usually coast right through. Unless of course you're band dudes, then you get the fists up your asshole and your vehicle strip searched. But alas as I pondered all the exciting things that were about to happen to my asshole, 2 minutes went by.. then 4... then 10 and next thing you know we were positive we passed the 1.5 mile mark and this elusive ghostly mystery checkpoint never happened.

Anywho, that was a very depressing hour but knowing we were about to camp was enough to keep us truckin. By the time we'd finished shooting the crap out of each other it dawned on schprokit that he flushed a salute of stuff down the RV toilet and that technically .. it was still down there.. in that hellish abyss that is a rental RV toilet.

Nobody was gonna go down without a fight but somebody was gonna have to figure a way into that toilet. This is the point where you can usually identify which of your lovely friends has the strongest genetic predisposition for addiction. Don't get me wrong, this was gonna be a close race with our group.

See, between the 6 of us, we'd get addicted to a piece of shit if it sat next to us in the van for too many days in a row. I thought I had a fighting chance to win this thing but alas, before I could even offer up my shit-diving services, Sporket was already duct-taping garbage bags around his arms and chest.

We'd all seen MaGeyver as kids, I was a huge 24 fan and Burn Notice was just getting traction but between all of our creative capacities, we seriously lacked any sort of ingenuity when it came to a project like this one. Best we could surmise, we'd position Sproket underneath the RV on his back. We'd then disassemble the hose that transports the shit from the tank to the disposal hose on the side of the RV. At that point, upon Sproket's cue, we'd switch the release lever, ideally causing a mellow stream directly from the bottom of the tank. Now Sproket was covered in garbage bags, he had some movers gloves on and a set of those snorkel mask goggles on. We wheeled him under just like any ole mechanic and counted down.

Upon his word, Jeezy flipped the release lever and behold.. a virtual Niagara Falls of vile blue, brown, yellowish liquid exploded on him. It was spraying like a wild hose with no rhyme or reason. I remember the noises Sproket was making.. I remember the rest of us running for our lives to avoid the ever expanding shit flood as it squirt with relentless force everywhere and anywhere.

God bless that sproket because even though one could argue he might potentially drown in his own shit, that mother fucker, though squirming and moaning and cursing the gods, stayed focused and motivated. His thick glove remained in a cup position under the nozzle. And though his goggles were being annihilated, he kept an eye on the stream throughout it's entire disposal.

The whole tragedy lasted about 4 minutes and when the stream finally slowed to a drip, he began to sift through the muddy pool of hell in a desperate attempt to reclaim any sort of drug he could.

If you're not like us and retain even the slightest bit of common sense you could probably deduce that whatever that thick blue RV toilet liquid is, it's main objective is to kill and/or dissolve stuff. Piss and shit gets their shitty reputation from the bacteria's they contain.

Ever since humans learned that, they'd devised scheme after scheme to protect us from those bacteria. From washing your hands to septic tanks, there is an entire industry built around disarming the wicked affects of shit and piss. Common logic dictates that any sort of pill, refer, tiny plastic baggy etc. wouldn't last a second in that blue bacteria killer. All of it had dissolved, likely upon impact but definitely before Shproket dumped it all on himself.

Watching him was like watching a scene from one of those movies where a character dies and his or her loved one continues to give the corpse an over-emotional CPR and mouth to mouth because they simply refuse to let go.

It was sad, depressing, concerning and utterly hilarious. When he finally came to grips with reality and shimmied his way out from under the RV he looked like a human soft serve ice cream cone. Since I'd never seen one of those before, I squirt some piss into my pants.

Poohdini

Like I've said, probably more times than a real author with a real editor would allow (or any editor for that matter), our "dare" punishments are sacred. Sacred in many ways of course but most importantly in the sense that, refusal to deliver would mean end of friendship forever, period. Not that we're really that shallow, we just have to know we can count on each other in a pinch. You have to be able to trust that your willingness to affect said punishment is equal to that of your friends. If you're in the trenches fighting a war, you want to be sure that the pal fighting next to you would in fact hold a piece of your shit for 5 minutes if he lost a dare to do so. It was a big deal for us to get out of the van and we've always been the camping/at one with nature type of band so the RV was wonderful. We also took advantage of the fact that we could now delve into a whole new world of white trash living.

While most RV bands would find a Wal-Mart parking lot or just park at the next venue, ML made a point of finding trailer parks. Not the run of the mill family RV park, we're talking the RV parks that have permanent residents and crystal meth labs. The kind of RV park where most of the RVs were up on stacks of bricks and had weeds growing out of them. The kind of RV park where the RVs didn't even have engines. The kind that you see on "Cops" or any sort of television show or documentary dealing with meth labs. The kind of RV parks that were in fact, neighborhoods.

So we found one once in Arizona or something and as exhilarating as these places could be, they were also quite terrifying. Not being the type of band that prefers fear to pleasure, we'd usually get a bottle of whiskey, start playing cards and just get retarded which destroyed the fear and bathed us in pleasure.

This particular park didn't have any bathroom facilities, not even an outhouse of sorts. Just a couple holes in the ground that a professional recreational vehicle user would know you're supposed to stick a hose into to drain you're RV crapper.

Now I can't remember if I told you this yet or not but Matthew and Mateo both have IBS. Irritable Bowel Syndrome. If you're that curious, Google it. If you're like me, just try to enjoy it. Before the night got started, Matthew had found a tree in the back corner of the park and laid out a fresh terd next to it.

So we start playing cards and having some shots of whiskey and we're thoroughly enjoying ourselves. Just when things get to this wonderful cruising altitude, someone comes up with a dare. To be fair, it's usually Matthew. When the idea comes up, everybody panics, contemplates and sweats bullets all the way from the time of idea conception to the very end of the game determining the winner/loser. One might think, why waste all that stress and hassle when things are already fun as could be? and you know, I don't know but I do know that I've seen some of the most hilarious shit in the world and also had to do things that I can't even write out for you.

So, let's pause this story for a second to familiarize yourself with one of the characters that will come in to play. About 4 months earlier we were on tour in Australia and on the way to or back from, we got to play a radio show in Hawaii with Yellowcard and Matissyahoo.. It was one of the best 2 days of our career so far because the radio station put us up in a ridiculous hotel in Honolulu overlooking the ocean and gave us each our own suites. Shame on them.

The night we got there we went straight to the bar downstairs which was half indoors, half outdoors and overlooked the most beautiful ocean in the world. It was a wonderful night and we met tons of kids, locals and had a blast.

A few hours into beveraging, a group of kids come up to our table and said they were into our band. Naturally we ask em to join us and buy em a round.

A few minutes later, another local kids who they must have known comes up to the table and asks if he can show us some magic tricks. Ummm, yes of course, absolutely, sounds wonderful, doooo it. So this dude grabs a fork straight off the table and holds it up about 1 foot away from each of our eyeballs.

He began to do that magician thing where they twitch or roll their eyes to give the illusion (pun intended) that they're channeling some higher force and low and behold each of the whatever you call ems on forks began to bend in different directions. It was insane. Then he asked for a quarter and made it float above the table. This kid was for real.

Anyhow, we kicked it, gave him some tip money and he left us his card in case we were ever back in Hawaii. Flash forward to our RV party. In case you forgot, we're at a real deal RV park, Matthew has laid a fresh hot terd by a tree in the corner and we're all retarded drunk. So the dare is this: there are 2 losers, 4 winners.

The first loser had to go to the tree and pick up Matthews shit. The second loser had to then call the magician and try to keep him on the phone for as long as possible because the deal was, loser #1 had to hold the shit for the entire duration of the call.

So, our TM Stevo was loser #1 (absolutely no pun intended of course) and loser #2 was Matthew. Matthew calls this magician with absolutely no justification for calling and muster up as much small talk as he possibly could to make the hell of holding the shit last as long as possible.

Many if not all of you may fail to see the humor in this and I understand. It's weird, immature, without reason, sense or precedent (I hope, for humanity's sake). But I gotta say, watching one of your best friends hold your brothers pooh while your brother stands next to him with a cell phone asking some random Hawaiian magician if he's into penguins just tickles all the right pleasure detectors.

It's no secret that we used to enjoy the occasional pharmie. Ya know, vicodins, percocets, darvocets, adderal, oxys, roxys, Meppergan-fortis, dulauden, methadone, subutex, suboxone, xanax, ativan, Klonopin ... to name a few. *We'd always been very gentle with these kinds of things. An occasional Xanax or a violin definitely helped the stress and physical toll touring takes. There's always an excuse when you need one but the fact of the matter is; toward the end of Warped Tour 2009 I was in so much pain that I started taking vacating almost daily. It was the weirdest thing that I didn't even realize was happening but soon as I did, I went to a doctor and got off em.. high fives. I know, I've never been accused of being proud of myself. Anyway, say no to drugs. Cuz if ya don't, you just might do something like this...*

I Hate that Shit but It Smells Wonderful
*warning, not for the faint hearted

Well it was December and we had a handful of radio shows scattered throughout the country. These are always awesome because you get to fly everywhere, the shows are usually fantastic and since you're on the radio in whichever city you're playing, people want to party with you.

We played in Salt Lake City and had to be in Dallas the next day. Well after the show, someone be-gifted us one giant green violin for the trip. Usually it's me Matthew and Jeezy who occasionally enjoy these types of things together after a particularly physical show. By my count that's 3 of us and we only had one big chunky delicious violin (say no to drugs).

Matthew points out that recently he was reading an article about how the anus is the best part of the body to absorb medication through due to it's sensitive skin and various pleasure receptors. We of course drilled him about the fact that he was reading an article about anus and pleasure but alas a brilliant idea was born. It was rather simple really. We'd crush the giant delicious vbomb into powder and split it up into three separate capsules (which we got by emptying some other useless vitamin capsules). Then we'd take turns going to the airplane laboratory and shoving each respective capsule straight up our assholes.

Before the plane took off, literally in that 15 minutes or so from when you board to when you have to turn off your phone, we researched this idea thoroughly. To our delight, we'd confirmed Matthews newly acquired information and started to get excited. There's nothing really like chopping up a big green delicious violin on an airplane fold out tray. Nosey neighbors and concerned stewardesses made this bit a little more complicated but we pulled it off.

One by one we took the walk to and the walk of shame back from the laboratory. When I got in, I dropped my pants and cleaned up my butthole with a moist towellette and proceeded to stick a capsule up my ass. I pushed and I pushed. It didn't want to take so I had some convincing to do and used sheer force. I think half of my pointer finger went entirely inside the shaft of my butthole. I felt strange about myself. I felt ashamed and dirty, yet had a small sense of pride for the commitment to the cause. I scrubbed my finger for a good 4 minutes and then walked back to my seat looking like I just bare-backed a bull.

As we each got back and sat down it was hard to look at each other for a second. Ya know like, hey buddy, drummer, bff - I know that you just fingered your own asshole. And I know that you know that I just fingered my own asshole. eh well it was a nice bonding experience and we spent the next 2-4 hrs debating whether we felt anything or not.
" oohhh yeah I think I feel something!" "eh, maybe not" "hmm it feels kind of funny, uncomfortable but funny" "I can't tell if it's dissolved yet but I definitely feel like I have to take a shit".

 This went on the entire flight and by the time we got to Denver I for one was hellbent on crapping. Turns out the radio station got us these lovely suites in downtown Dallas and I threw my bags down and headed straight for the fancy bathroom.

I proceeded to pooh out several thin, squirrelly looking logs.. It kind of hurt but not too bad and

I thought I was in the clear. I took a swipe at my first wipe and low and behold I felt something chunky. Whether you admit it or not, you look at the toilet paper after your first wipe (at least). Well so do I and mine was bizarre. It had quit a bit of pooh smattered about the toilet paper. Normally I expect a relatively straight thin line of pooh but this one was all over the board; Several lines, in all different directions and a few chunkier mounds.. Upon further investigation I saw a maimed capsule sticking out of one of the pooh stacks.

The capsule looked like it had been through hell but seemed to be intact. Yeah it was squished. Sure it had pooh all over it. But I wasn't convinced that the goods were destroyed. This is the moment when you reach down into the depths of your soul and you demand an answer to the very question every man struggles with every single day of his life: are you a man or are you a mouse.

Now I know I'm not a man. Can't change a tire. Don't fight, Can't build or fix anything, I balled my face off watching The Notebook, I share clothes with my wife, shave everywhere and for about a week each month.. I'm like a total bitch. But god bless it, I can pull a shitty maimed, giant green delicious vbomb from the depths of pooh-pooh hell, pull it apart, line up the possibly tarnished powder and snort that shit up my nose faster than a real man can do anything else.. And that's exactly what I did. don't judge me, love me.

note from Arthur- I debated adding disclaimers for a long time. I have to remember that those who don't know me well can't always tell when I'm joking so some are just necessary.
DISCLAMIER: I don't generally snort things and urge you not to either.. unless of course it came from a piece of your own shit.

KERRANG! TOUR
Jan 2008
Ahh the infamous Kerrang! Tour.
This particular bill was riveting. Opening was a band called Fightstar. Their singer was a dude named Charlie Simpson who had previously been in one of the UK's biggest boy bands. He'd sold out arenas around the country before finally realizing that might not be the coolest thing in the world and quit to start a metal band. His voice is phenomenal and being one of the rare, legitimate talents out there, he made a seamless transition into one of the better rock bands on the scene. It didn't hurt that he was one of the coolest motherfuckers ever and had a pension for animalistic partying. We were pleased because we got to share a bus with them. More on that later..
2nd on the bill was US-press darlings Circa Survive. One of the better bands we'd ever been

288

privileged to tour with, they also happened to be super bad ass cool.

Their singer Anthony Green had left a band called Chiodos just as they were starting to blow up and formed Circa. Admirable I thought. His heart wasn't in the music so he bailed on a promising career to face the daunting task of starting over. Well, when ya got it you got it and Anthony's gifted voice & proclivity for melodic made me a fast fan.

We were 3rd on the bill and though it was billed as a co-headliner, Coheed & Cambria headlined the whole tour.

I was a fan of the band despite hearing less than charming things about their singer Claudio, I resigned to suspend judgment and instead looked forward to a wonderful time.

Kerrang! Tours are a big deal and the press surrounding them is even bigger. On the first day, we all had a ton of interviews and photo-shoots but the main focus was on a shoot with just the 4 singers. I despised being separated from my band in any way shape or form but when Claudio, Charlie, Anthony and I got together in front of the stage in Ireland, there seemed to be a pretty good vibe about the whole thing. In retrospect, that picture is one of my favorite to date on account of all the chaos that would soon drown the tour in drama.

It kicked off in Belfast, Ireland. Absolutely amazing city and the show was insane. We blasted into our set and they reacted instantly. They must have oversold the venue because despite the many mosh pit attempts, instead the whole crowd lurched back and forth, to and fro as one giant body. Imagine an ocean with sporadic swells.. no rhyme or reason as to the direction but all moving as one. The energy seemed to increase with each song and by the time we threw out 15 giant balloons filled with confetti, they went off. Which is why it probably wasn't the best idea for me to climb the speaker stacks and flip into on top of them. I suppose it was a bit unexpected and by the time I landed on the crowd, I knew I'd done funked up.

The chaos ultimately led to disaster when about 200 kids that I was on top of fell over. There had to be about 3,000 in the venue so this quickly became a serious safety situation. I was one of the ones on the bottom and it was terrifying. Through the jungle of body parts I could see several others getting trampled. I felt horrible and immediately tried to get to each one. Under that kind of mass and energy, with the added psychological stimulation of what had just happened, the crowd was out of control. I pulled 2 girls up to their feet, despite being still buried and trapped myself. I'm such a hero it's disgusting.. can you even get enough of me? I can't.. (no sarcasm was hurt in the writing of those sentences).

This carried on for the next 15 minutes. Obviously the band stopped and security didn't really know what to do. In their defense, not much could have helped aside from letting it die down. I was trying to get kids up while other kids were ripping my shirt, pulling hair, grabbing and squeezing my dick n balls like 5 fingered vice grips.

Eventually the kids realized the danger of the situation and switched from nutters to rescuers and I managed to climb my way out, back onto the crowd and up to the stage where my band just stood there relieved to see me again. When all was said and done, the show was fucking fantastic.

Btw, allow me to back-track cuz I'm too lazy to find an appropriate spot to add this all the way up there. Before doors opened, as all 4 bands back-lined their equipment, Coheed refused to strike their drums. Fair enough, as headliner that's common but the amount of room they took up was quite ridiculous. We didn't think twice about.

Anyway, their stage manager also taped little foot prints where each of them was supposed to stand... so when they walked to their respective marks, there they stood for the entire 2 hour set. . Not one of them taking 1 step in either direction, it was terribly exciting.

Afterwards their stage manager asked us for a quick chat. "Follow me boys" as he walked on to the stage and over to the little tape foot prints. "See that?" he asked as he whipped a flashlight from a hip holster. Aiming the light on Claudia's "designated area" lay 2 tiny white pieces of confetti.

"We see it... awesome right?" we light-heartedly mused. "No more. You're hereby informed that you will no longer be allowed to use your confetti balloons for the rest of the tour". "what?".

The next day we spoke with the Kerrang! folks who shared our shock and humor at the request and promptly told us to ignore it. We promptly ignored it. As you can imagine things slowly but surely escalated. Trust that none of the gaiety of all this is lost on me.. Yes, our balloons were taken away from us and no, we didn't like it. After all, it's just balloons.. but they started it? Jk

There was some fist pounding and proxy bitching via managers which always hilarious. First they suspended our balloons. Then they took away our dressing rooms, claiming they required a 2nd room for their production crew so we had to share with the 2 openers. That was fine of course by us but 3 bands crammed into 1 tiny dressing room is just ridiculous and un necessary.

Next they cut our shower privileges. You heard me. We were no longer allowed to shower after the show because there's a slight possibility that by the time their big singer showers there'd be no hot water left. What the!?

Anyway, next they started fucking with the equipment. They'd set up the drum riser as close to the front of the stage as possible in attempt to leave us with a foot of space so we couldn't move around during our show. This of course affected all the bands as well. Despite their best efforts to fuck with us, at the end of the day we brushed it off and delivered.. night after night. Truth be told I think they were just jealous of our fan base. Not because it was huge or we're so awesome its sick or anything but because those kids were fucking amazing and even if CC turned all of our equipment off, our kids would still make the night mental.
 We're so proud of the kids that support our band... best in the world. Naturally we kept our focus on that and the tour was phenomenal. About half way through Coheed decided to cut the Kerrang! crew from catering. Mind you, it's the Kerrang! tour and aside from the privilege it is just to be on it, they also provided the effing catering! Of course we were asked the same thing and the next day Kerrang! finally blew the whistle on their diva antics.
 I'm sure they traded a pile of tearful emails with their management but alas, they could do nothing about it. That night however, we did decide to dine out in Cardiff

anyway. Regrettably I'd soon become sicker than I'd ever been.

Remember in Africa when I shit myself in the desert? Child's play. Whatever I was infected with had me pissing out of my asshole every 3 minutes. This is a nightmare no matter where you are or who you are. If, however, you're on a tour bus that you can't shit on and you happen to be the singer of a band on one of the bigger tours of their career.. well that's just awful.
I'd lay in my bunk in a fetal position with boxes of garbage bags into which I'd shit and or puke every couple of minutes. I'd then have to take the garbage bags down to the front lounge and drop em out the window. I've never been in such misery in my life. When we got to Norwich our TM took me to the hospital who said I'd had a 102 degree temperature and shouldn't so much as get out of bed for 2 weeks. Canceling simply wasn't an option for me. If I did, we'd disappoint the kids, bum out the band, lose a lot of money and likely piss off Kerrang. Of course that damned memory of quitting my final high school soccer game danced around my head like Richard Simmons on American Bandstand so I decided to go for it.
I was totally bed ridden and 10 minutes before the show our TM tapped my shoulder to alert me. I foolishly grabbed my white jeans and top and headed for the dressing room.

I was sweating profusely and everybody was encouraging me to bail based solely on how horrific I looked. I'd committed though and I was going to at least try to get through a few songs. The crowd in Norwich was fucking insane. We came out to a packed crowd of thousands who seemed to have been eagerly awaiting our arrival. A tiny shot of adrenaline poured through my body as Jeezy counted down, for a brief moment I thought I'd be ok. Instead, upon the very first beat I shit my pants.

I couldn't be certain as to how much shit, what form it was in and/or what kind of a nuisance it would turn out to be. I knew the white pants weren't going to do me any favors but I hoped that if the shot was showing, at least it was only visible from my behind me so I could just face the crowd at all times. I tried to subtly ask my band mates during the song to have a look and make sure it was all good but it's hard to communicate that in that situation. There aren't many universal signs for "hey dude can you have a look at my asshole and see if the shit that just bullied it's way out of there is visible?". So I trooped on, and by song 3 I forgot about the shit and just wanted to die.
My goal was to get through at least 5 songs but this was going to be arduous at best. We started the 4th song and the crowd was going so berserk that I had a temporary lapse of judgment and or conscience because I decided to jump into the

crowd. It didn't take long to remember that I'd shit myself just 13 minutes earlier and as if I was swimming from Jaws himself I panicked my way across the top of the crowd to the barrier and made it back on stage. Terrified and having no idea if I'd just smeared shit onto the heads of half the crowd, if so were they aware I did so? and if they were, did anyone get pictures of it? Those torments gave way to the agony I was feeling and as graciously as I could muster, I said thank you I'm sorry and goodnight.

Eventually I recovered and the tour continued to be amazing. The last day was in London at the infamous Brixton Academy. We'd dreamed of playing this place since I can remember. Add to that London is always the biggest and most important show, we decided we were gonna do our full production whether Coheed approved our not.
We had nothing but love and gratitude for Kerrang so we made sure they were ok with it, then asked the venue and got the go ahead from everyone. The general consensus was that it was the final show of the tour, whatever fit Coheed would ultimately throw would fall on indifferent ears.
Shproket was our stage tech and he recruited some street team kids to help him with the balloons. We blew up about 30 gigantic white, confetti stuffed orbs and stashed em in one of the upper VIP balconies. We neglected to

consider the possibility that Claudio and his
gibbon guitarist would decide to systematically
search the entire 5,000 capacity venue just in
case we tried to pull a stunt like this.

We go on and the crowd is insane. Kids were so
amazing and fired up, we were having the time
of our lives. Unbeknownst to us, up in the ole
VIP balcony, Claudio pulled out a switch blade
in a maniacal tantrum and proceeded to stab
each and every balloon, scaring the shit out of
our poor street teamer who was holding one of
them when he did it.

We of course were already on stage having the
time of our lives, totally oblivious to what just
happened. The 5,000+ kids were fucking
incredible and by the time we got to "House of
Cards" the show was going off. We usually
throw out the balloons during a quiet section in
the bridge of HOC and when the time came.. no
balloons.

I'm not ashamed to say it; I love those damn
balloons so needless to say I was quit
disappointed. I'd managed to turn around just in
time to see a heroic Shproket running on stage
with a handful of confetti he'd decided to throw
on his own as some sort of artistic statement of
principal haha.. it makes me smile laugh and
love him every time I think about
it. Unfortunately, 2 feet behind him was a
gibbon giving chase. Just as I turned around, the

gib had caught up to him and proceeded to punch Shproket square across his jaw.

It was of course, Coheed's stage manager who'd spent the whole tour crying about every little thing under the sun. I didn't have time or the volition to process what was happening but the simple fact that our dude just got hit was all it took. I dropped the microphone and charged at him. What a man I am. How impressed are you right now? Yep.. That's what I thought.

My entire band followed suit and we proceeded to beat the piss out of their crew. When I went after the initial gibbon, he Shproket and I all went down in an entangled heap. I hit my head on the hard wood floor which rattled me for an instant but by the time I came to and turned around, I saw the gib stagger to his feet. An instant after that I saw Matthew.
He was literally horizontal and in mid air complete with bass strapped to him. He was flying feet first and he drilled the gibbon in the chest, cracking his ribs.
Not sure it was exactly the professional thing to do, nor was shproket's brilliant idea but none of that mattered. I regret that the 5,000 kids had to see something like that but at the end of the day, family is family. The gib had no right whatsoever to run on stage during our set and clock our dude.

Anyhow, of course the biggen singer was nowhere to be found. As if he'd even consider getting his hands dirty. Gibs like him talk a big game but when their bluffs called they tend to let thier cronies do their bidding.. or take the ass beating as it were.

When the dust settled I was on fire with adrenaline and enraged that they would actually fuck up our show like that. At least that's what I was thinking at the time.

I realize now that it probably could have ben handled in many better ways. I accept responsibility for my part and apologize for it. In the heat of the moment.. boy did I let it all out. Grabbing the microphone, I proceeded to dismantle Coheed for the next 5 minutes with a likely incohherent stream of word diarrhea. I can hardly remember those couple of minutes but eventually Jeezy started the next song and we finished our set.

Brixton was exploding in a cacophony of boos and cheers. Literally, 50/50. Half the crowd was Madina and the other half Coheed. I've never heard anything like it. We finished without further incident and walked off stage. There were police and security guards everywhere and as we passed the Coheed section, the first gibbon was being treated by a medic and screaming about how we broke his ribs and he's going to sue us. It was a very alpha male moment.

Up in our dressing room, the promoter came into ask us to apologize. He's an amazing dude and despite the obvious fact that it was entirely there fault, we agreed and wanted it to just be over with. Apparently in their dressing room they were already plotting our demise. The kind of shit talking so many people like to do from behind the safety and comfort of walls or their computer or whatever.. They technically "refused" to accept our hollow apology which is hilarious.

We eventually got back to the bus and took off to the local Tesco where the whole fleet of buses would park for the night before flying home the next day. With an amazing tour in the books we hooked up with the Circa and Fightstar dudes and celebrated. I lost track at some point and passed out.

At around 5am I got up to have a piss and when I looked out the lounge window I noticed Coheeds bus next to ours. Upon further investigation I noticed that somebody had dumped a 4-foot mound of confetti in front of their bus door. How awesome is that.

Friday, June 15th, 2008
Castle Donnington, England
"What's up Download, we're Madina Lake!" Since just moments ago, my mind had toured the cosmos, from Mars to Pluto to the Kuiper Belt and I had no idea if it would return in time for

the first song. This was a gamble I'd made several times before on account of my shoddy and unreliable nerves. It usually came down to split seconds and only then would I know if words would come out of my mouth or if I'd instead freeze. Those nano-seconds become torturous with 80,000 people in front of your face. In the nick of time, I returned to my mind and was fully engaged.

We'd come to expect monitor issues so when I didn't hear any bass whatsoever, I prayed it was just that. It didn't take long to remember that just moments before my mind's cosmic tour, there was no bass coming out of the amp during line-check. Perfect. That lousy Murphy's Law cruelly dictates that when something just can't happen, it most certainly will. We finally make it to the main stage of Download and our god damned bass doesn't work?

It's been moments like these that instantly remind me of that last high school soccer game that I gave up on and more importantly my subsequent vow to never to do it again. So I pushed the disaster gently aside and gave the show everything I had.

Regrettably, the bass never quite made it. A few songs later, the guitar disappeared leaving the front of house with only our drums, electronics and my mediocre at best voice. Mateo managed to disconnect his wireless pack which was shoddy and plug a reg. guitar cable into the amp. Thank the heavens it worked but since the cable was only about 10 feet long, he was more or less attached to his amp on a stage the size of a football pitch. Ugh, this was getting brutal. I managed to keep my focus on the massive crowd and the significant portion of it that seemed to be into it. It dawned on me that we'd watched tons of bands get an absolute blizzard of bottles and shit pelted at them and that we were hardly getting any. This is a fantastic sign. Keep on truckin.

We blasted through "Adalia", House of Cards" and "One Last Kiss" in an epic battle of wills to keep and or convert the crowd. I could tell Matthew was livid. He'd take it all out on Stevo of course who for all intents and purposes really pissed all over this one, but is more than entitled to fuck up from time to time.

I just hoped with everything I had that Matthew could at least fake his way through the moment because at that point there is nothing else you can do. Techs would work on his amp throughout the entire 30+ minute set, to no avail. I'd dodged 2 or 3 bottles, which I was thrilled about but suddenly out of the corner of my eye I saw Matthew buckle and hit the stage floor in the manor that accompanies taking a shot to the balls. That's in fact exactly what he did.

Someone whipped a plastic can of yogurt from at least 30 yards away and got Matthew right in the balls. Making the fantastic moment even better, the yogurt exploded upon impact, spattered all over the stage beneath him and with one pivotal step, Matthew was on his ass.

I'll never forget the rage in his face at that instant because it was the beautiful rage that is tantamount to who he is. The rage that makes you laugh and laughs along with you. The rage that says, god damnit why must I be a perpetual victim of such injustice while it also thanks the universe for providing such diabolical hilarity, if at his expense. The rage that says, as pissed as I am right now, I can not wait to eventually enjoy this with my best friends... if that makes any sense.

Anyhow, he manned up and recovered just in time for "Here I Stand" which was probably one of our more popular tracks. At Download it also had the added benefit of $20,000. dollars worth of confetti cannons that would create a virtual blizzard throughout. From my vantage point, it was a spectacle to behold. Matthew had always been in charge of our creative production and since the festival was paying us more than enough, he finally had a budget to play with. That effing dude rented a fucking blizzard machine.

*A Word From Art- I realize we're not Motley Crue big, nor is this The Dirt so I get that we're

303

not snorting heroin and banging 10 chicks on
stage in front of 100,000 fans.. but damnit we
are making it snow… in June.. whats up….. "oh
ed, you sounded like dirt hairy just then"
"really? Pshh, Thanks grace"

Through the snow globe of confetti, I remember
seeing an endless ocean of kids moving with
flags, banners, smoke bombs, etc. that I'd only
previously seen in magazines, now right in front
of me. Groups would splinter off into sporadic
mosh pits, others were screaming the lyrics back
at us while others just seemed to revel in the
majestic UK festival atmosphere.
It dawned on me in that moment that it didn't
matter if the bass or guitars cut in and out, didn't
matter if the press reviews were good or bad and
it certainly didn't matter if we were considered a
successful band or not, this was a gift we'd all
savor forever.

We all knew that despite the outcome of that
show, we'd come to the end of our professional
road with Stevo. It wasn't even our decision
after all. Our label had spoken to our
management about what happened and there
wasn't much we could do about it. It was brutal
parting with Stevo. He was and is one of our
best friends and brothers who'd been with us
through the best and worst of times. We'd all
come to the same conclusion though that the
road was killing him and though it was also

killing us as well, we couldn't acknowledge it. If we did, it would devour us so we pulled our collars up, swept it into the ole denial section of our minds and continued on.

quick word from Arturo: he's since returned to the UK, this time as he should have been, playing guitar in his own band. SHFC supported our farewell tour 5 years later.

ATTICS TO EDEN

We finally finished out the first record cycle. All in we hadn't done too shabby. With a decent pile of records sold around the world and were even pretty close to household name in some parts. Thus we were tasked to write the often dreaded sophomore record. You have your whole life to write your first record and a mere months to write your second which is what often times leads to band's "sophomore slump". Well we'd been working on ideas and riffs in hotel rooms for a few months so by the time we got back to our rehearsal spot, we were already rollin.

The first track we worked on was an idea Mateo and I came up with in a hotel room outside St. Louis. After a show there, he'd called me down to his room to listen to a riff he came up with. It connected instantly and I had the lyrics and melody 10 minutes later. He recorded the guitar part into pro-tools but we didn't have a mic so he'd hit play on his computer and I'd sing along into my iPhone voice memos. When we got home the 4 of us tracked it and it became "Welcome to Oblivion".

All of us wanted desperately to escape the "emo" tag we'd been branded by the press but also didn't want to write against any pre-determined restrictions or rules so we just went with every idea we had. Mateo came up with a the bit for "Let's Get Out of Here" at a late night session and it instantly conjured up an image in my mind. This is typically how I write lyrics. I hear a piece of music and if I like it it's usually because an image or scenario develops in my mind that I then transpose lyrically. For some reason when I heard this riff I pictured the 4 of us driving off a cliff, Thelma and Louis style but landing on an island paradise. I don't know you figure it out. Actually I think I just did... I'm gay.

Anyhow, believe me, just like you I feared I might recap the entire writing process as well but fortunately I just bored myself out of the idea.

So the label wanted us to record with David Bendeth. We certainly weren't opposed to the idea but for different reasoning. See, labels like to chase whatever's happening at the moment. If Bendeth just produced a record with a hit single on it, hell, he's the guy. For us, his records have a certain shine to them that I for one

wanted. He's the master at slick, almost over-
produced, perfect sounding records and by that
standard we were in. He's also an incredibly
gifted musician with a unique understanding of
music, regardless of genre, style or artist. He
knew it all, got it all and loved it all.

Turns out he's a god damned
psychopath. Genius and amazing in every way
but psychopath no less. Once again we moved
our asses into an apartment, this time in New
Jersey. It was almost official at this point; if we
were married by virtue of living together for so
long, we were definitely becoming the stereo-
typical married couple.. or quadruple I should
say. These husbands, though I love them all
unconditionally, they sure didn't give out HJs on
a stressful day.

The first day we got to Bendeth's studio he sat us
down in his office to discuss the forthcoming
process. He opened with; so I hear you guys
like to take pills. wtf? Next he points to Mateo;
I hear your wife is insane. points to me; you're a
terrible singer, go get lessons before you even
think about recording (I was on a train to
Manhattan 2 hours later for my first
lesson). points to Matthew; so you're pretty
confident you're going to record on this
record? doubt it.

He proceeded to pick us apart both individually and as a group until we were all crying and confessing molestations as kids that never happened. He wasn't shy about his Machiavellian intentions (you try to spell it). His goal was to break us all down to our absolute core in the interest of extracting the best of our abilities. According to my math, the numbers didn't really work that way but what the hell.. ya only live once. Let's go there.

We'd talked to other bands that made records with Belvidere (we called him Belvidere from the get go) and they told crazy stories of the damage he'd done. It always ended the same way.. "but..in the end it was worth it because he always got the very best record possible out of each band." It was never without incident. Whether he'd force band members to quit, kick them out of the process, or just drive them insane, he is a controversial producer. To me, that's often what it takes.

Jeezy finished drums on his birthday and Belvidere definitely found this cause to celebrate. He told us we'd be staying late and that he had a surprise in order. I walked out of the guitar room around 10pm and all the couches in the lounge were rearranged into a perfect square. In the middle was a towel on the floor in place of the usual coffee table. Wtf.

Before I could even ponder it, 4 black stripper hookers were ramming big black dildos into one another's privates-that-aren't-vaginas-but-the-other-holes.

That night made men out of some of us.. fortunately not me. As per my usual panic attacks, anxiety over lyrics and vocals put a bit of a dark cloud over the next couple of months but eventually we wrapped what we considered our best record yet. After a slew of press and photo-shoots, we were right back on the road. This time with Anberlin in Canada.

"Attics to Eden" came out on April 28th, 2009. Before we really launched the touring cycle, Roadrunner sent Matthew and I on a press tour of Japan, London and Paris. Afterwards we'd fly to Los Angeles to shoot a video for "Never Take Us Alive" and head right back out around the world. We were excited about the video because Roadrunner approved a bad ass treatment.

The 4 of us would be secret agents trapped in a building alla "Die Hard" (sound familiar?). Throughout the vignettes, we'd narrowly escape capture from metaphorical versions of life's adversities via "bad guys" chasing us. It would climax with us climbing up to the roof and jumping onto a helicopter as the building explodes.

I was skeptical of thier ability to pull it off based solely on the budget. Roadrunner gave us a massive budget but the treatment sounded like it would take a fucking million dollars to pull off. I spoke to the director before we flew to LA and he assured me they could pull it off. We were stoked.

Our schedule was insane so when we landed, we were shuttled straight to the set where we'd learn the entire treatment had changed. Suddenly there were all these kids there, one dressed as a boxer, one as a ballerina or something and one as a baseball player I think? The crew did an amazing job but in the end, I couldn't even watch the video.

The only cool part was a dilapidated playground that was made for the performance part. It had an amazing Tim Burton esque feel to it but in the end it wasn't enough to save the video.

As we took off back to the UK for a headliner, "Never Take Us Alive" struggled to ignite and Roadrunner decided to scrap it and move on to the next single.

In the UK, our label instead went with "Let's Get Out of Here" first and were getting massive traction on BBC1 which is their be all end all of radio across the country. It climbed up to #2 on the charts so Roadrunner did a quick audible and scheduled a video shoot for "Lets Get Outta Here" in London at the end of the tour.

We shot that video and flew home to prep for Warped Tour. When RR got the video back they loved the performance parts but weren't crazy about the vignettes so while we boarded the bus and headed out West, they had a whole re-shoot in LA without us even knowing!

Simultaneously they wanted to adapt the track to fit better with the US radio climate and hired all these "it" producers to do remixes. They were spending a fortune and as much as I don't blame them and appreciated their efforts and commitment, we started feeling really uncomfortable about the whole thing. Especially how much money they were spending on us.

WARPED TOUR 2009

In the Summer of 2009 we'd finally been slated to do the entire Warped Tour. After a few 2 week stints on previous Warped runs we were thrilled and terrified. It is one of the greatest touring festivals of all time and with that, the greatest fun a band can have. They call it punk rock summer camp and for the mostly 20+ and 30+ year old band dudes and crew, life rarely offers such spoils. On the other hand..there are some statistics about bands that do the whole 3 months that are less than promising.

They say approx. 80% at least lose a member before all is said and done. 30% drop off the tour at some point. 20% break up. And considering 90% of all statistics are bullshit on top of the fact that I probably made all those numbers up, I wouldn't take any of these to the bank anytime soon.

Either way, point is, it's grueling. Most of the shows are in 100+ degree heat, as it's routed through the hottest parts of the country on the most sweltering days of Summer. It's a significant amount of work, setting up merch, dragging gear for miles, playing, signings, press, etc.

Since your set time changes every day, you can't get into a routine. One day you'll play at 5:00pm and the next 11:00am. Then there are the infamous Warped Barbeques. Almost every night, the tour hosts a post-show barbeque in the parking lots of stadiums and amphitheaters. They're simply too fun to miss. Anyhow ..

We'd had a few days off before we started Warped and Matthew flew to LA where he had an apartment, Mateo flew back to Columbia where he had a family and Jeezy, Shproket and I were in Chicago packing and prepping. Our bus was set to pick us up at our rehearsal spot where we'd load, board it and set off on the 3 days ride out to LA for Warped Dress Rehearsal. Matthew, Mateo, Bobaboeey and Sprok's friend Buddy were all going to meet us there.

Our bus was part of a fleet from the same company and the plan was to have each of the 4 buses pick up their respective bands and meet in the middle of America somewhere.. I forget maybe Oklahoma or Little Rock or Nashville or something. Anyway.. our bus was fucking amazing. First we'd had in the US and those first 3 days were unforgettable. We linked up with the other buses and proceeded to party our balls off. Since we didn't have any shows to worry about and our whole operation was already coming apart at the seems, we swept it into the ole Nile River and did whatever we had to numb it out. Mind you, the tour hadn't even started yet.

The buses met in a warehouse parking lot In Tulsa or Atlanta or Nebraska or wherever and since the drivers needed some sleep, that's where we'd spend the first night. 2 members of Chiodos crew hopped on our bus and introduced themselves. One of them was their TM who's name I can't remember and the other one was this girl.

She was Chiodos keyboard player Brad's wife and band's merch girl. Though I was intrigued right when I saw her, I didn't' think twice about it. Obviously being married put her off limits and being married to Chiodos put her in the absolutely no fucking chance pile. Not to mention I had every intention of focusing on my band and the tour and was despising the person I'd inadvertently become from time to time. The band dude clichés made me sick but the weeks of touring turned to months and had now become almost 5 years and I was slipping.

Nevertheless, we had a blast that night. It was all innocent fun but I'd be lying if I said I didn't enjoy the girl's company. She was funny and easy to be around and though it would be many a months til I fell for her, a seed must have been planted that night.

I ignored, shot down and/or denied any feelings for her whatsoever because I'm not that guy and would never EVER do that to somebody. But as the days went on, she'd begin to confide in me that their marriage was over.

Officially, they were separated but since they'd long ago planned for her to do the band's merch on Warped they decided to keep it civil and bring her along. Regardless, I wanted nothing to do with it.

As the tour eventually kicked off, there was an amazing energy throughout. On a tour like Warped you'll often encounter a band or 2 that just blows in every way shape and form. I say that of course not even referring to their music but more their attitude and pretension. Some band dudes ironically still play the high school style popularity game and try so hard to be "cool" that they waste the entire essence of Warped. There are over 100 bands each with crew, egos and alcohol or drugs. There are band-whores, star-fuckers, divas, wannabes etc. Drama is inevitable and unavoidable..

One day our label called me and insisted that I start a blog. Since I tend to live with head in the sand I had no idea what that entailed. Our A&R explained that I should just do

a daily summary, diary style and post it on one of the bigger blog sites. Ok Capt.. so you just want me to basically write down what I did that day and maybe add some thoughts? No problemo. Well that first day I happened to stroll by one of the stages and stop to watch an all girl band called the Millionaires. They were getting a lot of buzz with their assinign-to-the-point-of-irony cheesiness and push the envelope marketing. 3 teens, rapping some HS smack talk, dressed in not sexy slootwear and it seemed to be taking off. I had no preconceived notions. To be honest I was indifferent but either way, when I stopped by their stage as they'd just begun I saw one of the coolest things I'd ever seen.

A dj in the back with fake vinyl records spinning while he hit play on a DAT machine or something kicked off the set and the girls went into a choreographed rap/dance routine while singing along. What was odd though is that even though none of them had instruments, each stepped on a foot pedal at various moments throughout the song. I couldn't help but notice those moments happened to line up with each time they addressed the crowd.. like.. anything that wasn't a part of that particular song. My tiny little brain started to piece together what was happening. The foot pedals turned their mics on and off so they could lip synch, yet pretend they weren't by throwing in random comments. Awesome.

By the 3rd song this car wreck was getting fabulous. About half way through, sure as shit, the karma gods hath fluttered down and queefed upon their faces and their tracks skipped. When bands sing to playback tracks or lip synch, they're well aware of this risk. Despite how reliable the equipment guarantees itself to be, inevitably, you're gonna get busted. When it skipped, they had no idea what to do. A curious crowd just stared as they unsuccessfully attempted to get back in step with one another. Just as it looked as if they might be alright, it skipped again. This time though it skipped all the way back to the first song in their set. Man it gives me the willies just remembering it ha.. Eventually one of the girls looked at the other 2 and says "umm this is ummm retarded".. I disagree of course but alas.. they left the stage. I on the other hand headed back to my bus, totally inspired to blog.

I truly never meant any harm though I have to admit, I have a real disdain for bullshit when it comes to music. In this case however I was just doing as I was told to do by label and sharing my day. hah. So I wrote an objective, thoroughly accurate and matter of fact account of the Millionaires show. Woops. My first effing blog ever gets picked up by every music news sites on the world. Well, in our little music world anyway.. and suddenly it's an issue. I of course did what any real man would do and dove under the covers to hide. I steered clear of the internet, of catering and of any texts, emails or phone calls for a good 2, 3 days.

Apparently I'd unwittingly met and befriended one of the Millionaires just a few days earlier. I truly have a problem remembering people, faces, names etc. It's a terrible problem and I'm ashamed but honestly.. I've introduced myself to people I've known for years, label people I've stayed with, sheit I even introduced myself to my own god damned papa B over Christmas. well not really .. but you get the idea.. So yeah, I met a Millionaire.. really enjoyed her. She was super sweet and cool and we hung and everything. Now I feel like a total asshole.

We heard the re-mixes for "Let's Get Outta Here" about halfway through Warped and couldn't believe our ears. Despite their best efforts I'm sure, the re-mixes were bloody horrible. Now we had 3 videos for 2 songs, one with a million remixes and the label had spent a fortune. We were starting to freak the fuck out. They had to be at least a million into this record and hadn't released anything. Then they decided to scrap all of it and move on to the big single, "Welcome to Oblivion". Our paranoia was only slightly cushioned with the fact that now committed to another massive budget for a yet another video.

With 4 days of Warped left, everyone on the tour seemed to come full circle in an emotional, reflective and sort of bonding capacity. The bands all shared a mutual respect and commorodery based solely on the fact that we'd all survived it. Relatively speaking I suppose. There were plenty of loose ends and lingering feelings in the air, especially with the regards to my situation with that girl and Chiodos. We'd become closer than ever and started discussing a relationship. After the last Warped show, she headed back to Michigan, while I went straight to the airport and flew to England for Reading/Leeds.

Reading/Leeds

Almost 14 years to the very day we came as fans and left with a new dream, here we were playing the main stage of Reading. There were nearly 90,000 kids there (as far as you know) and this would be the biggest show yet.

Our sister Paula and Papa Boner flew out and watched from the side of the stage. Paula of course was with us in 1995 when the dream was born as we all watched the Pumpkins. It was pretty damn majestic.

When we finally got back to the US we swung by Los Angeles to shoot a video for "Welcome to Oblivion". We didn't know what the hell was going on. Roadrunner had us shoot the "NTUA" video, not one but 2 videos for Let's Get Out of Here" plus a pile of expensive re-mixes and now this. They'd used NONE of the previous videos, singles and now were sinking another fortune into WtO. Regardless, we loved the video, had a blast shooting it and flew home to kick off a tour with Silvertein.

.

CHAPTER 19
Black Hole

We got home from Reading/Leeds and I did what anyone with my IQ would do and had that girl I met on Warped move to Chicago and into my loft. Dad always said decisions are the most important part of creating a happy, successful life. The good ones will take you there, the bad ones will fist you with a jackhammer, bitchsmack your balls while a boat motor chops your dick into paper thin sheets and queef lil puffs of methane and discharge on your generally psyche. I always thought he should copyright that.

As the glutton for self punishment I am, I made wrong after wrong decision. Cheeky bastards those wrong decisions can be sometimes .. this one went deep undercover for 4 months before fisting my anus. And the downward spiral began picking up momentum.

We went out on tour with Silverstein in the US and by now our foundation was thoroughly cracked and the road had beaten us down. We got a call from Ron who had some terrible news. The accounting department at Roadrunner had done a comprehensive year end financial analysis and discovered what we'd long ago since discovered. With the amount of money they'd spent on recording, videos, re-mixes and more videos, Madina Lake was hemorrhaging money.

The label was also about to go on the market and needed to trim the fat to appear a lean profiting venture before they called it a day so Madina was officially let go of our US contract.

It was a devastating blow but in retrospect, when they closed their doors a few months later, it wouldn't have mattered anyway but here we were exhausted after years of touring, established in many other parts of the world but struggling for air in the US and now we had no label. Fortunately, we had a big European headliner coming up that would lift our spirits.

Arlene's Balls

Mateo is a curious case to say the least. Despite an unprecedented talent in several musical aspects from writing to producing and engineering, he certainly lacks certain functional capabilities. His charm and beautiful heart continue to remain endearing enough to put up with some of the most asinine of his shortcomings. Let's see, he'll steal your favorite DVD (24 Season 6 just before Jack Bauer saves the world. Lost Season 5, just when you simply can't wait another second to see what happens next) and bring it in to the shower to shave with. As if that didn't damage it enough, he'd then leave it at the hotel to never be seen again. He'll guarantee reimbursement and forget it ever happened. He'll beg Roadrunner for the only existing masters of the entire Attics To Eden recording and leave it on the back bumper of the van, where it gets stolen hours later. That type of shit, but in the end, he's always proves himself worthy of every crisis he set off. Case in point;

Mateo is from Bogota, Columbia where they make a lot of cocaine. Accordingly, a Columbian passport is among the top 3 most difficult in the world to travel with. According to that, arranging and securing his VISAS for all out of country travel is extremely difficult.

It takes several months to get approved, tons of paperwork and is super expensive. So months before we're set to leave for our Arlene's Ball headlining tour of Europe and the UK, we begin his VISA process. He was in Columbia at the time so many of the tasks were on him to take care and though he swore til he was green in the face that he took care of it, he didn't. Of course we didn't find out til we were packing to leave the next day. Crisis.

We had a whole slew of dates across Europe that couldn't be missed and Mateo was refused entry. Scrambling, we called up our good pal Seth from the Audition and insisted that he pack and fly with us the next day. He was tasked with learning our songs on the plane just by listening to them on his iPod. The 8 hour flight should have been plenty of time.. except not really.

We were flying to Paris for the first show of the tour and despite Seth being a loose cannon of multiple sorts, we were confident that we had a night to prepare once we landed. That of course turned out not to be the case.

Upon landing at DE Gaulle Int. Airport in Paris, our label reps picked us up with the good news that we'd been invited to head straight to MTV France for a live interview and performance. Say what?

They had an acoustic guitar with them and once we all crammed into a taxi, he started plucking out chords in attempt to pull off at least one song. He was nervous of course so I offered him a xanax. I suppose I was used to taking them and they help in moments like these so why not? I'll tell you why not. Tolerance. Seth has zero tolerance for drugs of any sort. It certainly doesn't stop him from indulging but it definitely turns him into a blubbering animal... at best.

Before we even got to MTV, Seth was a mess. Uncontrollable laughter, nodding out heroin style, mocking every French person who spoke. It was a nightmare but we were all kind of loving it.

Our fabulous French Roadrunner Reps Sabrina and Karina were terrified. They of course knew what we were about to confront. We had no idea.

The cab stops in front of yet another fashionable French building and we hop out. MTV. Getting through security and into the studio was a to-do in and of itself but we accomplished that much. Inside, we were greeted by a lovely staff of production people, engineers, and the host who showed us to our dressing room.

Seth and I tried to practice for the 5 minutes we had until they came in and ushered us into the studio. It was full on. There were 5 stools set up, one for each of us and one for the host in front of a super trendy MTV production stage. Escorted to each of our seats, we were then mic'd with those tiny clip-ons and asked to sound check them. Unfortunately for Matthew, they ran out of clip-ons and instead outfit him with a god damn head-set... Brittney Spears style headset. It looked amazing and we started the giggles right there and then.

Seth of course was sliding out of his chair and running his mouth about god knows what. The MTV crew was beginning to show signs of concern when the producer suddenly informs us we've got 2 minutes til we go live. WTF.. Seth has lost control at this point. "Se De Minute

Mercy Boucup ze faggoot" type of shit word barfed out of his mouth as the count-down began. I started to lose it a little myself..

The host suddenly springs to life with the enthusiastic energy burst you'd expect from an MTV host but of course, she was speaking in French. This proved too much for Seth who completely lost his mind. She managed to maintain composure for another few moments until finally addressing Seth with a question.

"So how do you like here in Pariee?". Seth replies: "How do you like here in Parieee?" and there goes me Matthew and Jeezy. It was the worst time to have one of those laugh attacks you can't contain but we were far gone already.

Matthew desperately tried to regain his composure and took the question: "Well you know, we're just so lucky to be here..." and suddenly his head-set falls from in front of his mouth to under his chin where it nestled and moved with his jaw. It looked extraordinarily hilarious and we were done. The whole segment derailed before it even had a chance and they frantically cut to commercial.

We apologized profusely and tried to explain that Seth was a hired friend who took too much medicine blah blah and ultimately convinced them we'd be ready for the next segment.

They decided to go straight to our acoustic performance to avoid another charade.. little did they know. "Bonjour mes amies! rendezvous après la MTV France au jou dui nous allons au chante rock group dan les etats unis Madina Lake!" or something like that.. and then all stared at Seth and I. We froze.

After a few excruciating moments I looked at Seth with a "start the song asshole!!!" look. He cocked back his arm and swung his hand down toward the strings of his guitar. They collided like in a symphony of clashing notes, creating one loud hideous chord. Thing is, his hand didn't stop there.

It continued down until it's momentum pulled his entire body off the stool where he essentially passed out. Cut to commercial break again. We were asked to leave.

Walking out of the MTV building we of course apologized profusely to our label reps and promised them we'd get it together and make it up to them. Our group of 6 continued toward the street as they half reprimanded and half suggested it just might turn out to be the best segment they've ever had.

We'd arrived at the curb to hail a cab where the apologies continued and just as we promised to be professional from here on out, a spaced out

Jeezy looks the wrong way, steps into the street and gets absolutely pummeled by a fucking biker.

Of course he and the bike fly 100 yards in 2 different directions and without the capacity to even ask if they're ok, I fucking pissed myself.

Once the meds left his system, Seth killed it. He carried us all the way through Europe and flew home the day we boarded a ferry from France to England. Mateo met us in Portsmouth and proceeded to have the best UK headlining tour yet.

a word from Arty- now that I think of it, its entirely possible that I'm getting my tours mixed up and all this happened a year earlier but who knows.. and who cares..

Back home for a much needed break, my relationship was paradise for the first couple months. We spent weekends with her parents in Michigan, I flew her to England for Arlene's Ball and we even threw around the "m" word. Aside from our label problems, things were seemingly perfect... until I went down to Florida to work on Dresden with the dudes for 4 days. The night before I left, we had the time of our lives and were closer than ever. She called the day I got to Florida and told me she's moving back home to Michigan. I was shocked and totally devastated.

The death blow with her was how absolutely suddenly it happened on top of the fact that I couldn't make sense out of it no matter how hard I tried. It literally defied logic and reason. Fortunately for me, I'd eventually discover why.

People who suffer from bi-polar disorder experience extreme highs and extreme lows to varying degrees of time. This emotional swing can volley back and forth within minutes or for as long as 6 months to a year. In this case, she had just flipped from a 6 month high. So quite literally she was "high" throughout our entire relationship. Then one day, sure as shit, the switch flipped and she lost all control of her emotions. I mean of course it had nothing to do with me.. I'm awesome., how could you not love me? Idiot.

But whatever, I've already spent too much time on her.. Short of it is, going through that on top of the band struggles and a myriad of other personal blows, I was on course to self destruct. The irony of what was about to happen next wasn't lost on me..

The days week and months that followed were brutal. I had flown back to Chicago and was alone in my loft trying to deal with it. It was difficult to get off the couch and even more so to be on it. I had no idea what to do with myself. When Matthew got back to Chicago, a friend of ours named Ryan Manno invited us and our other bff Chris Mason out to see some WWE event. Wrestling. He knew how effed up I was and wanted to help/get me out of the house. Unfortunately, I couldn't imagine anything worse so I gracefully declined the invite and retreated back to puking and crying and feeling sorry for myself. Anyhow, they ended up going and Ryan invited a new friend of his to take my ticket. That friend happened to be my future wife, Jenna.

The 4 of them went and had the time of their lives. Afterwards, Chris, Matthew and Ryan each text me relentlessly about how hot and cool Manno's friend was and insisted that I meet up with them at a bar. I refused.

They wouldn't take no for an answer and eventually I put some clothes on and me them at Deluxe. The moment I saw her I was in love. hahaha. Can you believe me? It's true. I sat with them, ordered a drink and proceeded to cry my face off to her all night about my Ex. Of course, I was falling more in love with Jenna for every tear I dropped on her and by the end of the night I got her phone number.

We started dating pretty soon after that night and I spiraled into a nearly unrecognizable blob of emotions and psychosis. I did what my doctor advised me to do and became an alcoholic. Stupid doctors.

My downward spiral turned into a double helix and finally one night I drank myself into the hospital. My sister Paula, friends and Matthew were worried sick. As I tend to do in life, I managed to hide the majority of it from my new girlfriend to save some face. Meanwhile, Matthew and Chris insisted we take a vacation. From my ex to Roadrunner to my drinking suddenly being a problem, I figured what better way to get healthy than to go to Jamaica with my best friends and lose our minds for 5 days.

Jamaica June 5

I tracked down this ghetto ass all inclusive resort in Montego Bay and we booked a 3 night, 4 day (which btw is such bullshit.. it's 3 days, you're not fooling anybody) trip. We didn't sleep the night before the trip because well we were partying our balls off. So much in fact that I convinced myself I wasn't gonna go. Our cab was coming at like 8am and at 6am I was wondering the streets by myself wondering who and why I was. By 7 I stumbled into my loft and threw a pair of shorts and t-shirt in a bag and walked to Matthews. Chris met us there and I argued against going on account of me having to barf. When the cab came I was so miserable I would have opted out of life given the choice. But alas we already paid and I forged ahead.

Matthew and Chris weren't in much better shape than I was. We'd had a rough couple of months which is why we booked the trip in the first place. All 3 of us had been kicked in the ribs chest neck and head by life and ultimately realized if we didn't get out of Chicago something terrible was gonna happen. Little did we know.

So we get to the airport at 8:30. Hardly made it past security. We wreaked of liquor and depression and hadn't slept for days. We were all 3 drunk when we went through and surely the karmic gods gave us a pass that morning.

We found our gate and as soon as I saw a row of chairs I crawled under 3 of them and laid down using my duffle bag as a pillow. This was not time spent asleep but rather time spent negotiating away the pain and immanent vomiting. My head was throbbing, body unresponsive at best but my mind... the real devil.. was annihilating me.

As you probably know by now self-loathing is right up my alley. Except it's not self loathing so much as the "other" guy in my head being a complete dick. Cuz at the end of the day, I really do tend to like myself. My behavior is questionable, discipline is shite but otherwise I enjoy my own company. I'd invite myself to a party.

Anywho.. we finally boarded the plane at which point I was on the brink of having a full-blown panic attack. Something about the misery I felt conjoined with the notion that we'd be trapped in a tubular metal death machine flying over water. Shark infested water, mind you. So I laid under those seats. As passengers continued to board I was hiding under Matthews, mine and Chris' seats. On account of our condition, the stewardess' didn't say a word. It was probably best for everyone on the plane that we pretend I don't exist. My almost certain breaking point came as the plane sped down the runway but a handful of xanax had just begun working it's magic and about 20 awful minutes later I fell asleep.

By the time we landed I was back in action. Amazing how quickly that can happen with a hanger. It didn't hurt that we'd landed in Montego Bay, Jamaica and walked off the plane straight to the dude that holds the "Apple Vacations" sign with the name of our hotel on it. Oh yeah.. it was called Breezes Trelawney or something.

Anyway, so of course he's dressed in the cliché Caribbean wares, tropical shirt, leighs or whatever . So yeah, as we approached, we watched a pile of Griswold type tourists enthusiastically surround this Apple guy. There were families, singles, couples, pairs of friends etc. just basking in the experience when all of the sudden the Apple guy approaches us and god damnit if he didn't put a bag of booger sugar in my tit pocket. He says.. go try it out in the bathroom mon.. The fucking Apple Vacations Tour Guide guy! I wouldn't even know how so.. No gracias. *Woops except for the incident on the plane with that capsule and the butthole :/*

We get on the rickety ass bus with the rest of the tourists who are snapping off pictures of everything and nothing all at once, entirely oblivious to the open market drug trade. Driver gets on the PA and starts his routine of jokes for the 10th but not last time that day. We're sitting in the very back, removed from the rest of them and this dude comes back. He starts negotiating a price for cocaine.

We eventually cave to peer pressure but manage to shift his wares to refer and begrudgingly agree to buy like $15. worth. The dude signals the driver who's watching us in his rearview mirror and a giant white smile spreads across his face. Shit, the whole company's in on the racket!? we're gonna get arrested.

A few minutes later the driver hops back on his trusty PA and tells the tourists that lucky for them, they're going to stop at an authentic Jamaican bar so they can all get Red Stripe Beers! Oohs and Ahhs chirp from our vacationers who have no idea they're being lured into our drug deal.

The bus pulls off the road and up to a shanti shack with a few cokes and Red Stripes. The frat guy of course steps off to get himself and his girlfriend one because hey, he's cool enough to drink during the day and why not.. it's Jamaica mon.. gay.

We're ushered to the back behind the shanti where some Rastafarians open up a tinfoil bundle of refer. We exchange the cash and the drugs and hop back on the bus. By now, our vacationers are starting to feel like a part of the culture and are just soaking up every dime's worth.

When we finally arrive at the resort, we got absolutely mobbed by drug dealers. They even knocked on our damn room door every 5 minutes. It was insane but we no longer indulged and the vacation was fabulous.. But the real reason I brought you into this one is to tell you about the last night.

Our best friend Chris flew home a day early so Matthew and I were able to hang out and reconnect by ourselves. It was one of the better days of our lives and it stretched late into the night. Off the back of our resort there was the standard pools, tiki bars etc that lead to the beach and ocean.

Jamaica is stunning and the crystal blue waters of the Caribbean have healing powers that can't be measured. About 50 feet off the beach there was a tiny crescent shaped island that you could walk to in the 3-4 ft. deep water. It had a handful of beach chairs and umbrellas to lounge about in but the back side of it consisted of giant stacked boulders. We'd climb down them and find a suitable spot to hang out in and stare out at the ocean and up into the Universe. It was indescribably serene and amazing.

So on this last night, Matthew and I ended up out there on the rocks at about 2-3AM. We were engaged in some pretty deep conversations about our lives, the career of our band, our relationships, our mom etc. He'd been especially worried about me as of late because I was drinking quite a bit and displaying some rather destructive behaviors.

Truth is I was entirely self destructive. I'd felt like my entire world, life, soul had just imploded on itself. Both of us knew we were at another one of those impossible crossroads in our tandem lives. We'd been here before. At approximately 4 times to be precise and for as excruciating as each phase one, we'd always managed to climb out of it. However, the later in life we get, the harder and more daunting the prospect of standing back up gets.

We reflected on our handling of the past crossroads and tried to identify the steps we took to find our way out. For as 20/20 as hindsight supposedly is, we couldn't identify any tangible wrong decisions or strategies we'd previously implemented.

We did however realize that throughout our entire lives, buried mostly in the very very back of our hearts and minds, was a blind faith. Not in the religious sense of the word but in the "universal conscious" sense (no idea why I put

that in quotes.. nor do I even know what I mean). Somehow, for as dreadful, grim and hopeless the future seemed at those particular moments, we knew we'd get through and be ok. At the literal moment we'd shared this conclusion the craziest effin thing I've ever experienced happened (and as you know, I've experienced some pretty ridiculous shit).
We could see the pristine Jamaican coast extend from behind us and wind around our right shoulders in the distance. It was lit by an extraordinary moon and billions of stars. As the vast ocean sprawled calmly but infinitely out in front of us, a massive, dark blue shadow began to rise up from it. It was surreal and happening no more than 20 feet from our perch.

A majestic blue whale rose up majestically and slammed back into the water with an unprecedented elegance. Now, I get that people see whales all the time but this was different. Not only was eerily apropos to the conversation we were having at that moment, not only was it practically arms reach away and even splashed us, but at the time a blue whale sighting in the area was simply unheard of. It was exhilarating and though I can't explain how or why, it was as clear a message as we could possibly have gotten. Unbeknownst to us, we were about to face a tragedy worse than we could even imagine. And as ridiculous as it sounds, that whale instilled a strength, hope and faith we'd need to survive it.

We got back from Jamaica and my downward spiral only picked up speed. I could tell it was pulling Matthew down and that devastated me but I was in no condition to even help myself. I had been putting all of my energy into my new girlfriend Jenna and though I thank the angels I did, at the time it probably wasn't exactly helping matters.

Her and I both were pretty fresh off some pretty dismal breakups so the rebound aspect was cliché as they get. We didn't care. We were also both coming off of pretty reckless and wild lifestyles so as we adjusted to everything all at once.. things got nuttier than a fruitcake, hold my nuts.

Disneyland

It was the first night I'd spent at Jenna's and in retrospect, it had an ominous serendipity to it. There wasn't any real reason to stay over there aside from the fact that we'd spent every night at my place thus far and only seemed to fair to mix it up. I couldn't have been there for more than 10 minutes when my phone rang. I picked it up just as AT&T dropped it. A dalliance that would occur several more times before I finally got my brother on the phone. He asked me why he was in an ambulance.

Sparing you the emotional devastation that followed, I'll just say that seconds later I was driving 110 mph down the Kennedy barfing out the window. When I finally did arrive at the hospital and sprinted into his cordoned off section of the emergency room, I barfed again.

I'll never be able to accurately describe the flood of emotion and pain that comes from seeing your twin brother in that condition. For those of you who aren't aware of what happened, Matthew was nearly beaten to death after saving a woman's life, who, ironically, was being beaten to death.

A male (note; not a man) had caught his wife whoring around on him decided to beat her on a sidewalk a few blocks from my loft where Matthew was hanging out. He'd left to meet a friend a few blocks down the street when he encountered the pussy beating on his whore wife (her behavior would only grow more and more despicable as the story rolled out).

Being a real man, Matthew interjected and stopped the cowardly sociopath but only until he turned around to call the police, when he was hit from behind with a brick. What proceeded was too difficult to recount but needless to say, my brother ended up in an ambulance.

A few minutes after I arrived, I could tell there was significant trauma and I was forced to make a scene. The ER docs had scheduled him for an MRI/Cat Scan but didn't think to rush it. As the minutes dragged on and nothing was happening, I ran into the haul screaming and yelling until they brought him in. Minutes after that we were in another ambulance on our way to UIC Hospitals where neurosurgeons were assembling for a life saving operation.

Matthew's brain had been swelling at an unprecedented rate , forcing the removal of 1/3 of his skull. He flat lined briefly during this surgery but thanks to the shear strength my brother embodies, he pulled through.

The events that followed are almost too gut wrenching for me to revisit and in the spirit of this book, I'll only briefly touch upon them.

When Matthew went into surgery I was in some sort of shock. I could literally feel him in need of strength, which I knew he'd come to me for. Battling the devastation of what was happening to my brother against my necessity to be strong for him was a precarious reality. As common sense would dictate that some part of me should at least prepare for the possibility I'd lose him, the wiser part of me mostly refused that option. Except of course in a weak moment when, for the first time in my entire life, I considered the unthinkable. If I lost Matthew, I'd surely have to take myself out of the game as well. The scariest part of that moment was the fact that I was fully prepared to do so.

To the extent one can control his or her thoughts, there were a few that imposed themselves upon me. One was that effing blue whale in Jamaica. We knew there was a massive significance to it and now it was finally starting to make sense. Call it spiritual, faith, existential, universal or whatever you'd like but that whale appeared to not only prepare us for what was about to come but also to get us through it.

Though he survived the first surgery, he was in a brief coma. I hadn't left his side since they finished operating and wheeled him into his room. When he finally did come to, he was unrecognizable and regrettably, as far as he was concerned, so was I.

There's an impossibility about the notion that your twin brother, best friend and soul partner doesn't recognize you that I'll never wrap my head around but here it was. I'd spend hours crying and pleading with him but it wouldn't be til the next day that he'd come around. Fortunately, when he did, the first words he'd utter would prove to me that, though his filter would need some work, he was still Matthew..

at least somewhere in there. Here's how they
came out..

The Pusstache

Anywho.. so a bit before Matthew's
incident.. he and I and a few others (I'll not
mention names in the spirit of.. whatever)
decided we were gonna have a bush growing
contest. We had the rest of the summer which
was a good 3 months .. to grow the most
creative, obnoxious, beautiful bush we could
possibly come up with.
Rules are as such.. nothing is off limits.. grow
that mofo like you were born to do it. Upon
deadline, we'd take close up, HD pictures and
have 2 outside random judges judge based on
creativity, cut/groom and all around style.
I decided to go with the standard 70's afro bush.
Most popularly known in the 70's as the hair
style of African Americans throughout that era
but also inspired by very own mother who's bush
I remember seeing in the shower once or twice
as a young gun. *People get super weird
whenever I say that.*

So I was grooming mine and presumably
everyone else was either grooming theirs or had
forgotten about the contest.. we never updated
one another on our bushes but I'm pretty sure
everyone was fully engaged. But to be perfectly
honest, I kind of forgot about it. Don't get me
wrong, every time I took my pants off for one

reason or another I had to look at it this thing but otherwise, forgotten.

My puss looked like an over-fed ChiaPet w no rhyme, reason or shape. I fully intended on having a stylist pimp it out for judgment day but otherwise it was just a nuisance. Getting back to the real star of the story.. Matthew...

The very last thing on my mind while Matthew didn't recognize me was our Pusstache Contest. My twin brother, soul-mate, other half was in a coma and I was holding his hand w one hand and a gun in the other just in case he decided not to pull through and I had to shoot myself.

The nurse had come in with a fresh gown and a bucket to wash him.. As I tend to do I offered to help right away. So of course I was asked to help her take his gown off. As I gently lifted him, she pulled his gown off and that's when it happened.

His wiener flopped out first.. but as the gown made it's way north, it displayed the most amazing thing I've ever seen to date. His pusstache. He had been grooming one of those long mustaches that curl on the ends. I can't remember what decade.. maybe the 20's?

The only thing that trumped this moment was just a day later when he came to and uttered his first words back .. the lucky nurse was inadvertently struck again when she walked in to his room and Matthew curiously questioned her .. "did you queef out your tampon yet?".

He's back.

I called my new girlfriend that night to break up with her. Truthfully, I was in love with her and I couldn't possibly ask her to go through this with me so the idea was to spare her. *I thought that pretty manly of me, don't you?*
  She met me on the steps in front of the hospital with cheesecake, grapes and a card and refused to let me let her go.
I knew at that very moment I would eventually marry her but I didn't know how absolutely essential to not only my but also my brothers survival she would end up being. For the next 6 weeks, he was in and out as we waited for the swelling of his brain to subside. Word began to spread about the incident and we were suddenly blanketed with an international out-pouring of support from family, friends, fans and perfect strangers alike. I can honestly say, this was as responsible for his survival and ultimate recovery as the surgeons who operated on him. Our gratitude can't be expressed in words.

There was one more majestic moment that came during the 2nd surgery 6 weeks later when Matthew would flat line yet again. I was in the waiting room of course and though I'd been up for days, I was inexplicable full of energy. About 30 minutes into the operation, I suddenly became weak and nearly passed out. 10 minutes after that I was fine again. We wouldn't hear until later that at that approximate moment was when Matthew flat lined and though there's no medical justification for his pulling out of it (aside from the angels that are his doctors), we did hear a theory.

One of his surgeons confessed that, though they'd never discuss publically, the only theory that made sense to his department was that he survived because of a quantum exchange of cells from his twin brother. So at the end of the day, who's the real hero here? That's right, me. And of course I'm kidding because as you'll see, I'm may be many things but a hero aint one of em..

CHAPTER 20
THE BUILDING OF CHAMPIONS

Matthew was eventually able to come home and we began the long, arduous road to a full recovery. I set out to make sure Madina had a record deal to make sure he did so. In the weeks and months to come we'd endure some extraordinary highs and lows throughout this process that will require a second book (which I'll get to work on next) but eventually, our fans, family and friends saved our lives and now we had to do right by them.

We got to work on officially recording our 3rd record and eventually signed a new record deal with Razor&Tie/Sony. We'd already written and recorded a decent amount of it before Matthew's incident. In fact, in an eerily prophetic moment, Matthew recorded his bass parts to "They're Coming For Me" the day before got hurt. He and I also recorded the lead chorus vocal together which I wrote on the spot..

"I feel the angels coming for me, but I'm not ready to leave, I've got a promise to keep. I feel forever slipping away but you know I'll fight this disease. I fight it every day for you"., The song has given me chills ever since.

It would be several months after he got home before he could pick up his bass again but once he did, the record poured out of us. As did many majestic moments and opportunities. Among them, we had the chance to write with our idol, Billy Corgan who not only raised over $80,000. for Matthew's medical bills but also invited us to his studio in Sedona, AZ to where we wrote "Imagineer".

Matthew was also recognized by the Governor of Illinois Pat Quinn and presented a plaque declaring July 27th Matthew Leone Day in the official Illinois Law books. As all this was happening however, life wasn't exactly getting any less bizarre.

There's Only One Hero in this Family
Now, remember what kind of summer we've had to date. I'd also gotten stuck in my elevator on New Years eve., had my car towed, got pulled over by the po-po about 4 times without getting one ticket, broke my nose and broke 2 fingers in separate incidents and then some. Here's how a few of those things happened..

Anyhow so our friends in Papa Roach came to town to play at Congress. It's an old ass theatre in Chicago and while the dudes were playing we were hanging out on the fire escape outside their dressing room window.
It's one of those firescapes that has iron landings on each level and the stairs that retract in case of emergency. I hadn't had many drinks (ish?) but

for some reason I leaned against one of the iron fence bars that turned out not to exist after all. I was talking at the time of my "lean" so a good 5 people's worth of eyes were looking at me when I went down.

The best way to judge a fall like that is by the length from which it starts to ends. My fall off the stage in Houston on Halloween was to date my best of all time but this one was a close second. I fell for about 4.3 seconds when all was said and done.

Weighing in at just under 10 pounds, it was actually my spazztic, flailing momentum that caused the emergency stairs to dispense. In a slow motion, adrenaline fueled moment, the giant old rusty iron stairs began to drop down toward their 45 degree angle forcing me to cling to the railing. Of course, I made the whole thing way more dramatic than it was and clung to that rail like I'd just been dropped off the Titanic. Nobody could stop laughing for long enough to buy my urgency so I cut the act and pulled myself up quite easily. Little did I know, this was just the beginning of a nightlong, self-inflicted comedy of errors.

With an exaggerated limp and my confidence all duct-taped together, we headed back in through the window, made places to meet back at my place and left. When we got to the parking lot, I found out my car had been
towed. Awesome. Took a cab home with some

friends and went to the rooftop for a nightcap. This is where things really kicked off. It was about 2am and 6 or 7 of us were hanging out having a drink waiting for the P-Roach dudes to come over when all of the sudden, the adjacent rooftop exploded.

My building is an old-school U-shaped wooden loft. it looks like this .. ====) - -   woops, I mean, like this " I_I " . So we're on one of the sides when someone behind me suddenly yells "holy shit, black smoke monster!"

I followed the tip of his pointed finger to the adjacent roof and in a matter of milliseconds, the black smoke monster erupted into a towering inferno. People often wonder how they'd react in "crisis" situations... well I always wondered anyway. Naturally, we paused for some killer Facebook pics of us holding our drinks up in front of the fire and only then called 9-1-1. Here's a taped recording of the 9-1-1 call.. kind of..

"hello, this is 911, what's your emergency?". I said "umm.. smoke monster! Exploded! Umm building exploded, gotta go bye!", and hung up. "God damnit you idiot, you forgot to even tell em where" I said to myself.   So I called back. Anyhooter, we ran down to my apartment, my girlfriend grabbed the cat and I grabbed a bunch of pills bottles and we left. We pounded on every neighbors door on the way out and then proceeded to call everyone from the buzzer downstairs, which I thought was pretty heroic. Ok, I had nothing to do with that, my friend Brian and his gf did it.

The firetrucks came pretty damn quick I must say. I decided to call my neighbor Matt to make sure he got up and out and he was like "what's up bro! I'm at this party in Pilsen it's awesome!". I responded "yeah? cool tell me about it! Ohh but wait, before you do .. our building exploded". This is when he popped the question. "what!?! dude you have to go get Spencer!" ... his dog.

I read that book "Blink" by Malcolm Gladwell and he talks about how when you're in a crisis situation, your brain instantly riffles through every moment that it's ever seen/witnessed/learned about that has anything to do with your current crisis and responds accordingly. (I don't know if I made any sense and it was probably boring but I don't re-read and/or edit so.. sorry?).

Anyway, my brain flashed to the 4 or 5 times I'd met Spencer and each one of them consisted of this asshole maniac dog attacking the shit out of me for no reason. On the elevator, in the hall, in his apartment and on the street. My favorite was when Matt's ex go (who was a cunt btw.. all respect to cunts) walked into the hall at the same time I did with her dogs and Spencer.. (4 bitches. Whats up).

Spencer yanked his leash out of her hand and hauled ass right for me. He's a big bitch and I was holding a Starbucks Carmel macchiato which flew right out of my hand as he mauled my arm. Matt's cunt didn't even react but instead simply said, "Spencer, stop".. I was on the damn floor, literally. *She didn't say a word about my coffee much less apologize. The nerve?*

While my mind played its reel of horrific Spencer moments, I had a bit of an epiphany. "Wait a second.. Matthew's the big hero of the family these days... maybe.. just maybe this is MY hero moment?". The fantasies of a ticker tape parade and our mayor presenting me with a key to the city danced in my head for a moment and I said fuck it. I'm goin in.

I waited til the fireman guarding the front door of the building turned around and ran for it. Undetected, I raced through the lobby to the staircase and ran all the way up to the 6th floor, stopping for a short barf break on the 4th (I'm out of shape and had been drinking). I ran through the now desolate halls to my neighbors door. He'd informed me that there was a key hidden in the janitorial closet across the hall from him. I opened the closet door and it looked like the Space Shuttle's engine room with wires and buttons and switches and crap. I was like wtf do I do with all this!? So I called him and he answers "whats up bro?" as if it were a social call. "oh not much" .. I was sweating, barf all over me and being chased by a fire (as far as I knew). "Dickhead, where in this maze of pipes and electronics is your damned key son!" He was like "oh yeah, the fire! well key should be taped above the door".

When I finally found it, I nervously fumbled the door open and ran inside like a panicked circus clown yelling "Spencer, Spencer! the building's on fire, we gotta get outta..!!". Before I could finish explaining the dire situation to a dog who doesn't even speak English, I was mauled.

This son of a bitch annihilated me.. again. Not only was he screaming, yelling/barking and biting the shit out of me, but he also had this crazy move of bitch slapping my with his long ass dog face. I wrestled him for about 4 minutes and finally got his leash on him and we ran down the 6th flights of stairs to safety (pausing of course around the 2nd floor for another quick barf).

Admittedly, I expected a heroes welcome when I got there but instead, I wasn't even noticed. I glanced around at the various pile of neighbors with a prideful grin, fishing for praise and compliments but they never came.

Instead, the adrenaline wore off and I finally noticed my hand. It was covered in blood and 2 of my fingers were broken. My efforts only grew in futility when I learned that the fire was contained to that one, other side of the building and not even so much as a puff of smoke reached our wing.

My neighbor pulled up a few seconds later and I presented his damned dog to him with a splint and bandages on my hand. He grabbed the leash and says.. "oh cool, thanks bro".   My pleasure.

Operation: CandyGramForMongo
Aug., 2011

It all started when a few of us were working on a project over by my sisters house… I mean my neighbor's house?   any who..we dubbed the project "CandygramForMongo". Unfortunately it's classified, so I can't get into specific details but I will say that a key ingredient required in said project was…   hmm .. it's hard to just say it.. but uhh .. well it was human feces. don't love me, judge me.

Being the inspired go-getta I aim to be, I graciously volunteered my own for the job. Only problem was I didn't have to go. So my sister, I mean my neighbor, took action and whipped up a concoction of Epsom salt and hot water that ultimately proved too big for my size.. being none-the-wiser, I took down the whole cup in seconds.. and this just a mere moments before she recommended I sip sporadically so as not to "overwhelm the bowels".   thanks for the advice twisted sister.. I mean neighbor.

We all stepped outside to hang out on the patio as we waited for the concoction to take affect. It was a beautiful night and the lunar cycle had just let go of it's month long full moon. A perfect temperature of 77 degrees and some good conversation essentially dissolved "CandygramForMongo" from the forefront of our minds. Quite frankly, I forgot all about it until I felt a sudden twist in my stomach that can only be compared to a grouchy, 30 foot Boa Constrictor squeezing and slithering it's way through my intestines. At the time we were discussing the trials and tribulations of relationships and it had started to get a little tense. Seeing as tension tends to make me feel uncomfortable and squirmy, often when presented this scenario I'll do something outlandish to change the topic (for example: there was that time at our friend Schabeaschels lakehouse when Madina was fighting like crazy so I decided to stand up a picnic table, fully clothed in broad daylight and piss myself. That one kind of backfired cuz Schaebezel got mad that the piss ran down my jeans and onto his parents deck.. he ran to get a towel while everyone else just stared at me... eh ya win some, ya lose... more?).

Anyhow. I realized this snake squeezing my intestines had seemed to fill my stomach with a significant amount of gascious pressure. To the extent that, really.. just a slight push would likely do the trick. so I went for it.

Well… turns out that ever so slight push unleashed a sonically abrasive, pungently relentless and substantially curious explosion of everything that had ever visited my stomach. In other words folks, I shit myself. now many in this case are probably picturing a "shart" - (pronounced "shh uu ART": A "shart" often describes a fart that releases a spattering of pooh into ones clothing's… the term had its rise to fame in the early 2,000s when it began to appear on the silver-screen and has since been an internationally recognized, though somewhat over-used word-celeb. Personally, I'm over it.) But alas, mine wasn't a shart.. I swear some shit from an 80's chicken macnugget probably made its escape with this thing.

There was a deafening 3-4 second silence and the stunned looks on everyone's faces ranged from shock and horror to confusion and numbness. My animal instinct kicked in and I immediately sprang up and began my sprint toward the door and eventual bathroom/shower. I must have been going about 64mph (which is pretty fast for a human) and as I approached the door it appeared open so w one swift leap-step I launched toward it. This is when everything went black.

You know that feeling of having your proverbial bell rung? When you either collide with something, get hit by something or otherwise knock your head? I felt like an old fuzzy TV that a giant just smacked the shit out of in attempt to improve reception. My mind's entire navigation screen went out for an instant and was now re-booting. As it did so, I began to assess the situation.

My face felt cold and wet and my nose throbbed with a the subtle, slow-tempoed pulsing of a jackhammer. I could see both a ceiling fan on my southern horizon and countless stars on the northern. There was something in my pants. It was also wet and heavy. The entire scene from my vantage point was distorted by a blanket of non-sensual mesh netting and an eerie silence deafened the moment.

As memory slowly began to return and accompany what I was now seeing, feeling and hearing, I started to put the pieces together. I shit myself, ran through a screen door and broke my nose.

Dad used to always say that winners never quit and quitters never win. So I sprang back into action, with blood on my face and shit in my pants I leapt to my feet, climbed through the massacred mesh of the screen door and bolted into the kitchen. Without so much as a stutter in my step, I picked up the FedEx box on route to the bathroom where I proceeded to get the job done.

I'd be lying if I said there were no more casualties. Her bathroom carpet got the worst of it but I also lost my underwear and jeans in the ordeal. Nonetheless, we finally had an armed package, ready for deployment. Matthew and I covered ourselves in black clothing and under the cover of night, crept to "Mongo's" house where we ultimately delivered his Candygram.

AN INCOMPREHENSIBLE PROPOSAL

The now 2-year downward spiral had been hemorrhaging so much peace that I was on a slippery slope. At that point your life becomes a perpetual manifestation of negativity.

I learned a shitload from this period and as much as I wouldn't wish it upon my worst enemy, I don't regret a single moment. The biggest lesson I learned was the devastation of negative thinking. I believe that there is an extraordinary power in thought. One that can literally change present, future AND even past events by their psychological perception and/or focus. I believe in telekinesis, levitation and of course, manifestation of destiny.

Having said all that, once stuck in a negative rut, you are dangerously close to a life of eternal doom. Expecting the worst will affect the worst. Assuming the worst will bring out the worst and so on and so forth.

It would take many a hard lesson over many a years to grasp the magnitude and principal of the power of thought and will likely take many more. As soon as I begin to waiver, I force myself to remember a few potent examples. I met my wife while I was in one of these ruts. From band/label/career pitfalls and heart-break to Matthew's incident, my life dove off a cliff. I was angry, bitter, spiteful and convinced the world was hell on Earth and I was being punished for something. Then I met Jenna.

Her spirit was literally contagious. Her compassion, empathy and unbridled lust for life served as a power source I haven't felt since I lost my mom. The strange part is though I knew she was amazing, it was my subconscious that knew she was a necessity. Like a tree grows toward the sun, I headed straight for her.

Unfortunately, while I was in this rut, I became addicted to pain. There was so much of it and it nothing made any logistical sense. Label drops us right in the middle of a million dollar investment and just after a #2 single. My ex vanishes out of thin air. Then of course, Matthew.

So when Jenna and I started dating, I was convinced that she too was out to get me. It was inevitable that she would hurt me and so I set on a path to see to it that she did. If you look for trouble you'll find it. I cringe in retrospect because if it weren't for her strength and resolve, I would have lost her.

But I didn't. There were many growing pains in the relationship. Surely, enough to feed my pain addiction but there was also a guardian angel protecting the very thing that was saving my life. We laughed, we ventured and explored and we grew into one entity.

Eventually, I stopped getting stuck n the elevator, pulled over by the cops, towed etc. I stopped expecting, seeking and manifesting the worst in things. I began to love life again. So when I finally asked her to marry me, I didn't care that I made a complete jack ass of myself doing so.

Ill Jew Berry Be

I have a whole-sale diamond dealing friend who took me around to various bank vaults to view rocks. This dude had a family operation which included a brother who fished diamonds out of a river in Africa and sent them uncut to their bank in Chicago. Then another brother collected and cut them and finally my friend would sell them to jewelry stores. So when I went to the banks, I was looking at dirty chunky rocks. I picked one and had it cut and set and I was good to go.

In the same manor that I'd write lyrics on my arms and hands out of paranoia of blanking out, I wrote a 4 page "proposal" letter. I took Jenna on my scooter to this little spot on the Chicago river that I loved. It was perfect, until I pulled out my 4 pager and read the 3rd page 1st, the 4th page 2nd, the 1st page 3rd and the 2nd page last. It was amazing. I was shaking like a leaf, slurring my words, swapping my lirst fetters etc. In the end, she was cool as a cucumber and I got the thumbs up.

We got married in May of 2012 and I had my whole band, crew and best friends stand up with me. It was slightly convenient that we flew in from Japan the afternoon before my wedding. Having just played Tokyo and Osaka and flying straight to my wedding was a pretty magical feeling. Aside from the obvious it also drilled a nail into the coffin of a brutal 3 years.

People always say what rises soon shall fall. I've made a habit of saying what falls shall rise again. Regardless of the path my life will take at this point, I'll always feel like the luckiest person in the world. We've all made mistakes and will always learn along the way but after all, it's the journey, not the destination. Anyhow, you've already taken up enough of my time *skeet skert*. Thank you again and again for your support. Live well and prosper, blah blah... as for me? I got another book to go live.

THE END

Prologue

Hindsight is a riveting concept. Most tend to think the perspective provides a crystal clarity. I'd always had a hard time buying into that because for as many circumstances that it had proved accurate, I could never get comfortable relying on it in the present. Here's where blind faith come in to play.

There are moments in life that are difficult to explain. They're the ones made up in large part of feelings and/or perceptions and many of them don't make any sort of logical sense until they're reflected upon later in life.

Such is the symbology we experienced with that effing whale in Jamaica. It had such a comforting certainty to it and though we knew at the time it felt significant, there was no way we could know how it was about to get us through a tragedy of relative epic proportion.

While Matthew lay unconscious in that hospital bed and I clung to his side knowing that realistically there was almost no chance he'd pull through entirely, I also knew that surrealistically, everything would be ok.

There's a reason that whale kept coming to mind as a reassurance from the ether that we'd survive this and for as fantastical as that sounds, it proved itself true.

Credit for Matthew's survival and ultimate full recovery lies in several places of course; the genius and capabilities of his Nero-surgeons (Dr. Sergei Neckrysh and team), the love and support of family, friends and fans, Matthew's innate strength and will and of course that one X factor. The "lighting" that strikes when everything else lines up perfectly but still falls just short of ability to succeed.

For as long as the human capacity to think has existed, this X factor has also existed. Some call it miracles, the grace of God, karma, etc. and the truth is that it is all those things. And the one thing that all those things encapsulate is "faith". Faith in the existential belief that things are going to be ok. That you will survive, heal and get through whatever tragic adversity you encounter. In one way shape or form, it always proves a worthwhile investment. So, I present to you that for as much as we all know life can be impossibly difficult at times, never lose your faith. Accordingly, faith will never lose you.

THANK YOU !!!

Thank you all so much for the support, loyalty and dealing with my "special" tendencies.

Adore you all.

Amanda Dixon

Black Velvet Magazine

Laura-Marie Lonstrup

Will Bourne

Nic Dalton

Andrea Simon

Adam Lazenby

Anna Zawada

Rebecca Atkinson

Lindsey Pitts

Jill Leone

Sundae M. Ford

Emily Atnip

Claire Gellatly

Fran Hodson

Jinx

Ryan Ford

Kellye

Jeanne

Jackie Mott

Joy Leclerc

Arlette Leclerc

Rachel Taylor

Jamie Rogers Pham

Louise Alexander

Charlotte Redrup

Caitlin Rose Manov

Eileen Orloff

Jen Tornabene

Ajay Gosain

Mike Stricker

Aparna Modi

Michele Mele

Marcy Fox

Jaret Reddick

Finger Haross

Anne-Julie Madden Vandenhove

Effie Taormina

Harumi Humasaki

Charlotte Ribar

Fisal Ahamed

Sarah McSheffrey

Greg Allan

Bryan Deziel

Roshene McClintock

Jaqueline Ram

Sandra Giles

Chelsea Thompson

Adam Wilde

Brian Vaugn

Cristal Andino

Karyn Bonder

Allison Voehringer

Zac Bonder

Sami Westwood

Nick Boynton

Chris Mason

Lyndsey Massie
Aimee Croucher
Alyce Hunt
Tyler Hancock
Amanda Olejar
Emma Kemble
Erin Casey
Josh Beebe
Vickzstar Beauchamp
Laura Arthurs
Mel Phillips
Sonya Giles
Joy Leclerc
Arlette Leclerc
Danny Santucci
Lyndi Koehn
Rini Bonus
Christina Hartless
Holiie Pocock
Lyall Campbell
Michaela Elliot
Kyle Cogan
Nik Starr
Beth
Jamie Kerr
Kerry Duggan
Jade Williams
Andrew Haas
Alex Layton
Tara
Tommy Wilde

Liliana

RenRaven- Shaman of the Obsidian

Alistair Lawrence

Rose Walker

Mitsuru Kohno

Shannon Herbert

Daniella Hackford

Chloe Hayes

Haley Avey

Emily DeWitt

Roxy Simons

Julio Martinez

Suzie Ostrowski

Peter Bailey

Liana Pujol

Wayne Stanford

Nicki Nangla

Dan Reeves

Kathryn Cleary

Davud Wahab

Robert Gresh Jr.

Brenna Flanagan

Melanie Kern

Zak Einstein THICK RECORDS

Meagan Manfull

Nicholas Conlon

Seb Zapata

Mark French

Danielle McAuley

Diana Dassler

Lulu Bell

Quyen Le

Marissa Moore

Kristy Angstadt

Hanna Wilde

Christine Nelson

Leila Overthemoon

William Archambeault

Eugenia Flores

Erin Walsh

Marjorie Tang

Carrie McMillan

Carrie Drebenstedt

Chris Thedunced

Andrew Morgan

Riley Olson

Terrance Tremblay

Paul Knight

Robin Harris

Rachel Bokina

Nicole Egbert

Louise Rapson

Andrew Topliss

Dawn M. Price

Lisa Bulwan

Christina Jones

Jacob Brett

Sian Gander

Matthew James McCann

Kelly Collins

Tina Sourounis

Chancy Howard

Sophie Whelan

Janet Rogers

Rebecca Rabin

Katie Carrier

Melissane Guigou

Thomas Lee

Claudia Tremblay

Scott Florek

Deborah "Jinx" Patton

Sophie Louise Moore

Chloe Heyde

Laura Hoefer

Abby Chew

Tegan MacMillan

Jessica Homer

Emily

Cassandra Eberhart

Marisa La Course

Amanda Henry-Johnson

Michelle Kerr

Kirsten Sprinks

Ewelina Konieczna

Chris Harris

Simon Williams

Lizzy Marsh

Sarah Beck Jorgensen

Kirsty Furey

Maria Castaneda

Ashley Cooper

Anna Vasilyeva

Theresa Carrico

Erica Burns

Kayla King

Morgane Bois

Laura Puskar

Amy Farren

Jordan Ellis

Jonathan Brettle

Carly Bigham

Sarah Lenaerts

Jenna Jones

Taylor Coffman

Arlene Wilt

Austin Collins

Dana Stowell

Lyn Marchluk

Eri Tani

Joanne Tunley

Annaliese Scott

Stephanie Lussier

Bridgette Wirkus

Holly Gordon

Esther Kudron

Kate Daly

Zoe Wall

Yvette Elonda

Jessica Rose

Calum Martin

Daniel Crickmer

Jared Azulay

Rachel Coyle

Sarah Kidney

Alexander Borg
Brittany Robertshaw
Jordan Snow
Felicia Crispin
Craig Croucher
Shawn-Ray Dalinsky
Brianne McMillan
Jamie Eytcheson
Stephanie Spaight
Anna Bodymore
Yoko Hirano
Emma Garner
Dan King
Tracy Briggs
Janina Friedrich
Melody Thompson
Monica Spaunhorst
Sarah Tremblay
Mick Collier
Steve
Victoria Barr
Shannon Anthony
Alexis
Lilianna Vetter
Sam Bull
Stephen Pavlik
Alexis Anthony
Mark Beasley
Kara Beasley
Katie Mother Fucking Keller

2 (ish) PAGERS:

As many things in my life these days, this book wouldn't be possible without the incredible support and contributions from my family and friends. And you all know when I say friends, I'm talking to every one of you. As part of my Kickstarter campaign to get this book done I asked a handful of you to contribute 2 pages worth of content that I'd include in it. The content of those pages was left entirely to the writers and accordingly I got some amazing contributions. Here they are and thanks again:

SANDRA GILES:

Born Into Darkness by Sandra Giles

An ear-splitting screech tore through the night, startling residents out of their beds and prompting them to tighten security. Another noise followed, shocking because it could be heard so clearly. Everyone stilled, fixated on the sound of scraping, clawing. Something on the move, agonisingly pulling itself along. It was a sound from countless films and many nightmares: a closing-in sound that echoes from all sides, confusing the senses and ensuring no one can locate the true source. The sound of a predator. Never has a town been so quiet. Everyone strained their ears, waiting for more from this amplified beast. Couples huddled on beds. Children hid under duvets. The most curious of people pressed their noses against windows, searching for an explanation. It seemed there was none to be found.

A thump, small and insignificant in the daytime, punched the silence like the heaviest of hammers. Certain it was from an assault on some unsuspecting victim, a few brave residents climbed to their feet and grabbed whatever weapons they could find: knives, bats and, in one case, an axe. Whispered reassurances to petrified family members sounded like a soft wind, calming all who heard it, even if the words were not distinguishable. Men and women entered the unknown, one trembling step at a time, meeting with others as they made their slow way through the streetlight's orange glow. Despite no one knowing where the sounds had emanated from, everyone knew where to go. The graveyard. The very place they'd expect to find death and destruction, more so because this particular graveyard wasn't nearly as restful as one would hope. Many disturbing sounds have materialized from its depths, leading residents to believe it is in fact haunted. Even the dead fear the place. The wills of the more recently deceased request that their bodies are buried elsewhere, for fear of rising alongside the ghosts that haunt the place, never resting, never ceasing.

As predicted, the group discovered a figure sprawled across the ground of that very place. It was a tiny figure, made to seem even smaller by a blanket of dirt, shielding this tragedy from the view of those drawing nearer. Everyone stopped just feet away as though scared of touching it.

Many seconds passed before the group inched closer, analysing the victim. From the size and congealed dirt-encrusted blood it looked new-born. Beside it was an opening in the ground, presumably to dispose of the dead. The creator clearly had not cared that this was already a grave belonging to a lady. Part of her corpse could even be seen through the gap.

"What kind of monster would ditch a stillborn in the grave of another?" someone asked. The others did no more than shake their heads in horror, seemingly too repulsed to talk. The speaker proceeded to bend down in order to retrieve the baby, and only then did everyone fully appreciate the extent of what they were witnessing.

The supposed new-born was in fact a child, wasted away to mere skin and bone and pale with.. Only it wasn't dead.It moved. Not a sound was made, not even the drawing of a breath. Limbs just started thrashing, the earth around it rising in a cloud of violent lashing. The crouched figure hurriedly lifted it up, trying to offer some small comfort to the poor thing.

Taken to a hospital and welcomed into an orphanage, the child had a second chance at life, and was provided with protection from the horrors of the night and from whatever monster had sought to kill it to begin with. This tale has been told many times, and no one seems to know how it began. No one, that is, except Finlay, for he was the one to start it. Many believe it all began with a woman and her mistake. The woman was said to be a runaway, perhaps no more than a child herself, left to care for an unwanted baby.

She struggled for a couple of years but soon gave in and ditched her undernourished burden before it couldperish. Or perhaps she wanted it to die, hence placing it in a graveyard. Well the first was true. There was a woman, and her mistake had been in stealing Finlay's heart, and through it his caution. They unwittingly made a child together, something they discovered when she grew large and could no longer diet to keep the pounds at bay. Only when they realised what had happened could Finlay act.

He killed her. Finlay felt he had no choice. She couldn't have the child, not with him as the father. She had to die, and take the baby to the afterlife with her. It was the only way, and he has grieved every day since her death. At first it was for her and the baby, but soon it was just for her. The baby did not die. He had acted. She had died for nothing.

No human will ever know why the saved child was beyond help. They can't have known what horror they were unleashing on themselves. The child grew into an adult, only this adult was like no other. Something broke the night of its birth, something there was no turning back from. Imagine a foetus growing inside a corpse, and burrowing out of an unresponsive stomach with no one to act as a guide.

Imagine being born into a cage of wicker and dirt, the only escape being a seemingly impossible one. And to live without food or care for over two years, growing physically weak but somehow finding the strength to at last do what was needed. Not even Finlay can say how it made an escape that night. A vampire born in such a manner is never right. Never sane. There are only few, and none made it out without help. The most haunted graveyards in the world stemmed from incidents just like this, where vampire children were born into a prison of earth. Those vampires are deranged. The town it grew up in was put to rest along with the child's mother. They sleep now, killed by the beast. One day Finlay's offspring will be a powerful vampire, and will undoubtedly hunt the man who had never sought to help. Finlay wishes he could die, like his partner and the rest of the town, and hide from the monster in death.

And how do I know all this? How do I know what Finlay thinks and feels? I am Finlay. I am the monster that spawned a monster. This story is from the Collision Of Worlds series by Sandra Giles. To learn more about this world, visit www.sandragiles.wordpress.com .

HARUMI HAMASAKI:

GREG ALLEN (CEO SONIXPHERE, CHICAGO):

So my wife was hired by a friend of hers to style a video shoot he was working on. The artist was 16 year old Celine Marie. Seeing as you could throw a dart into the suburbs and hit a kid that can sing her ass off, it didn't really get my attention initially. The dime a dozen American Idol hopefuls tend to bore me to death these days, only adding hay to a seemingly needless stack. Anowhow, so Jenna took Celine shopping and pimped her out in 3 fabulous looks and was off to the shoot. It was raining that night and since I already don't like to be alone, when the thunder came, I headed for the studio to climb into the protective arms of my braver wife. When I got there, I heard a killer voice with a razor sharp edge. Proceeding around the corner to the live room, I saw a charisma I rarely see these days. I've been to too many video shoots in my day to know that by the 11th hour, energy is contrived at best. Not in this case. Take after take of her new single "This is Your Day" was more energetic than the previous. Celine had an uncanny ability to make you feel like one of her bffs as she simultaneously projects the rock start archetype. The difference in this case, from

Celine, it's all real. I was intrigued and decided to dig a little deeper.

Jenna introduced me to her dad, Greg Allen. Coolest dude I've met in a while and it didn't take long for us to forge a friendship. Turns out Greg is creator, founder and owner of a custom music shop, Sonixphere. Not the indie GC or Sam Ash but instead a musicians dream. Sonixphere is a company whose clients solicit music beds for every media platform imaginable. Once they've got their marching orders, Greg gets together with his stable of writers to create the perfect sonic accompaniment for TV commercials, film, webisodes, etc. From All-State Insurance to MacDonald's, Greg's company has formed a brilliant business for musicians (such as himself, btw) in an ever-deteriorating industry. Maintaining the critical creative aspect that we all crave while providing career opportunities for gifted musicians is something we all need to appreciate and admire. I've already worked with Greg in a few capacities and can only hope to continue to do so.

In short, Celine Marie is a talent that has what it takes these days and will breakthrough in only a matter of time. Her dad is an amazing asset to the industry that could use as many assets as it can find. They're both forward thinkers with artistic gifts, charisma and fantastic entrepuneurial expertise..

FISAL AHAMED:
My
Journey

I find this pretty weird feel like some kind of Freudian 'tell me about your life' kind of thing. There's not much to tell about myself, but considering a load of Madina Lake fans will be reading this I'll have to make it interesting so you don't fall asleep. For those that don't know me I get to work events of all kinds all over the country acting as security, it's kind of funny as I've been going to gigs for six years and now I get to work on the other side of the barrier. I guess I'm still with it so I can become a cop somewhere down the road. I even want to write movie's considering I have a college degree in that. On top of that I'm training in Mixed Martial Arts, I think I wanted a career in that, some other days I thought getting hit for a living is not the place to be, I feel like I'm still a kid listing of all the things he wants to be when he grows up. So who knows where I'll end up, I'm still young maybe I'll be able to do all of those things since life's too short just focusing on one dream.

I'm also quite the geek into the whole comic books and comic con adventures. Been going to them since I was 17 in England and in the USA and still go to them now. So many good memories experienced there, probably the only fun fact about me (laugh out loud).

July 2007 If I remember correctly.. I remember it clearly as it was the same day my back then college girlfriend had ended things with me. Ah well shit happens right, not to start things on a depressing note or anything, Ha!

As soon as I got home I switched to Kerrang straight away and what was playing introduced me to a whole new world known as Madina Lake. It was kind of ironic as the song that was playing was 'One Last Kiss', it was one hell of a sign to follow and so I ran with it. The first time I saw Madina Lake live was at the Kerrang Tour 2008 that same year at Manchester Academy and seeing them live was like something I've never experienced before and it wouldn't be the last time seeing them live. I would see Madina Lake on every UK tour they arranged, so looking at five years. It wasn't until late 2009 that I got to know Nathan & Matthew Leone, I think I connected with the Leone brothers the most as they were they first two I had met from the band from when I had first watched them live.

2009 was a great year as they had supported Papa Roach and the thing I remember the most was carrying a drunken Matthew from 'Sheffield Corporation', was funny knowing that I was holding the bassist from my favourite band, It was quite a surreal moment to be perfectly honest I guess it makes a great ice breaker at parties. The rest is quite a blur now after seeing the guys on nearly every tour, but I couldn't really thank them enough. Since they have been so connected to me, whenever I feel depressed or having an anxiety attack their music can restore the balance. Not only have they produced some beautiful music over the past seven years, but I've never met individuals that are quite like Madina Lake to pull out all the stops no matter what obstacle they have to face.

All I can say is that I've never experienced anything known as Madina Lake a band that connects so much with their fans and project so much energy whenever they play live. They have been possibly one of if not the best bands I've have ever met. First saw these in 2008, and been to every tour they have done in the UK. Knowing that 2013 will be the last UK tour breaks my heart. Madina Lake my boys from Chicago Illinois Nathan, Matthew, Dan and Mateo you will always be with me forever.

I just hope we get to meet again somewhere in another life.

CHARLOTTE RIBAR:
Bottom of the Hill

The clinking of glasses. The stamps and X's on my hands and arms. The smoke. The patio. The old stairs to the old showers. The posters and stickers. And t-shirts: one of them mine, given to me by a friend with a warm voice. The embrace of a hero with art on his body. The comparison of arms and photos. Names.All of their pride in front of them. Begging for screams. Bending down. Jumping up. Rotating. Shaking. Grinning and laughing and bleeding. Playing. Working hard. Not holding a real job. Dropping out of college. Showing the world what they are made of. Doing what they love. Drinking and spraying and dropping. Hitting and strumming. Closing eyes. Opening eyes. Doing whatever it takes.You are feeling bigger. Becoming alive. Crying. Bumping against the stage. Feeling hair slide through your fingers. And dropping the earplugs you have no use for. Then the next day wishing you hadn't dropped them because of the ringing, yet still sort of proud. Experiencing pain that does not hurt and knowing that your life has started.So many have come. All their names and marks on the wall. Each still singing and smiling. Promising to come back before they hit it big. The caress of cheers and jumping. And the smell of sweat. And the taste of blood. The love of your life. The break down. The kids. The heroes. The enemies. The traitors. The friends.

Have all been here.

Why I Write

I first wrote because it was required. I wrote because I had to have decent hand writing. I wrote to prove I could spell "remember" and "because." I wrote to show my 5th grade teacher my vast knowledge of Balto the sled dog and Comanche the war horse. And to graduate elementary school. Then middle school. Then high school. To prove myself worthy of a scholarship. To show what a good private school education could do. Now?

I write because there's no greater title than that of a story teller. Because I like the sound of keys on a computer. I write because for once I can see my thoughts organized. Because I need organization. I write because I'm not very good at speaking. Because I do too much of it. I write because the only important things I ever do come from my hands. But sometimes even those aren't all that important. I write because I'm afraid I'll forget everything. Because I need something to talk to. I write to express some sort of idea that my voice betrays or makes clumsy. I write because I can't sing for shit. I write because I like the creases and dents pens make on a page. Because I can think of about 20 other ways I could have won that argument. I write to keep myself sane and because I fancy myself a creative individual. I write because I fancy myself an individual. I write because I can't remember to use all the pretty words I know in everyday conversation. Technicolor, dilate, illustration, illumination, requiem, cavalier. I write because I have an ego that tells me my ideas, thoughts, and style, are something that are important to the world at large and need to be released. I write because I can't always draw what my head sees. Because my friend told me this really funny joke the other day, and God it's so hilarious, do you want to hear it? ....Well. I thought it was funny. I write because I there are things that are sacred. Because there are things I would want people to find out. Because I figure I should be constructive. I write because everyone I've ever loved has written and God how I want to write all those lovely little words back. I write because I've got thousands of last words that need stories. I write because I was given an education and I plan on using it. Because my friends and I consider a game of "story monsters" or "one word and move on" a wild night. I write because there's a little voice in my head that asks me to. I write because I have a large list of names that need to be used in one way or another. I write because nothing gives me more joy than personification and gratuitous amounts of onomonopia. I write because onomonopia. Because when writers talk the world starts turning a little differently and I'd like to make the world stop for a second. I write because I'd like to think I have something to say, and if I don't right now I'd like to know that when the time comes I'd be able to put it down in a proper fashion. I write I write I write. Because no one actually knows who Socrates is because he didn't bother to write anything himself. Because, like Paul Auster, I found myself with a pen in my pocket.

SARAH MCSHEFFREY:

I have been a fan of Madina Lake for over five years now and have been lucky enough to have seen them live 8 times in Australia! My yearly trip from New Zealand for Soundwave is something I look forward to for the whole year because I get to see and meet my favourite bands, it's better than Christmas.

When I found out Madina would be returning to Soundwave in 2012 I was so excited and decided to do four dates. 3wise records ran a competition where the prize was a trip to the zoo with your favourite 3Wise artists so I entered on a whim. I was ecstatic to find out I had won and would be going to Sydney's Taronga Zoo with Madina Lake and Fireworks! Three of my friends also won the competition. It was such an amazing experience, a day I will never forget.

Sarah McSheffrey

395

28996134R00223

Made in the USA
Charleston, SC
27 April 2014